Newsworkers

# Newsworkers

*Toward a History of the Rank and File*

Hanno Hardt and Bonnie Brennen, editors

 University of Minnesota Press

Minneapolis

London

Published by the University of Minnesota Press
111 Third Avenue South, Suite 290, Minneapolis, MN 55401-2520
Printed in the United States of America on acid-free paper

**Library of Congress Cataloging-in-Publication Data**

Newsworkers : toward a history of the rank and file / Hanno Hardt and
   Bonnie Brennen, editors.
      p.   cm.
   Includes index.
   ISBN 0-8166-2706-1 (hc)
   ISBN 0-8166-2707-X (pb)
      1. Press—History.   2. Mass media—History.   3. Reporters and
   reporting.   4. Press—United States—History.   5. Mass media—United
   States—History.   6. Reporters and reporting—United States—History.
   I. Hardt, Hanno.   II. Brennen, Bonnie.
PN4781.N37   1995
070.9—dc20                                                                      95-13849

The University of Minnesota is an
equal-opportunity educator and employer.

# Contents

# Introduction

## Hanno Hardt and Bonnie Brennen

The traditional construction of media history has relied on notions of democracy, progress, and community leadership to produce the image of an institution that has secured the place of journalism in the annals of the United States. Current attempts to modernize the representation of media history through widely used textbooks repeat traditional views of what constitutes a history of the press; they present ideologically predisposed accounts that fail to consider issues of work and class. The result has been a history of institutional power without any consideration of the rank and file and their contribution to the social and political empowerment of contemporary media industries.

This project is an effort to recover an alternative media history that addresses the historical place of newsworkers and the role of labor in the rise of media capitalism. It addresses primarily the period between 1890 and 1940, perhaps the most eventful and dramatic period in the rise of the American press, as it relates to the commodification of news and follows commercial interests. It was also a time in which the relationship between technology and democracy was defined by "mass" communication and used to explain progress and freedom in American society.

Thus, the rise of the mass press coincides with the industrialization of the United States and the emergence of the working class, which was strengthened by the flow of immigration and the intensity of urbanization. But because its existence and influence relied on the well-being of the urban culture, the power of the working class faltered with the advancement of capitalism and throughout periods of economic depression, which first began in the 1870s. Although the American labor movement advanced steadily throughout the last decades of the nineteenth century and into the twentieth, to protect its members it settled for class collaboration in industry and welcomed the middle-class reform movements that occupied the Roosevelt, Taft, and Wilson administrations. Yet, job security and the protection of workers against sickness or unemployment, for instance, remained an ideal, albeit a lofty one, throughout the 1920s. Newspapers embraced the push for industrialization as a path toward economic progress and expressed the sentiments of the business community. When the press emerged from the Great Depression, it also reflected the new structural patterns of industrialization in mergers and consolidations that resulted in part from dwindling circulation figures and the collapse of many newspapers. Its ownership frequently displayed a conservative, anti–New Deal attitude, particularly toward the unionization of individualistic and poorly paid newsworkers and attempts under the terms of the child labor laws to stop the hiring of underage newsboys.

Newsworkers were also caught in the rise of journalism as mass entertainment. They served the increasing demands for sensationalism, which created conformity, diffused partisan interests, and produced the realities by which society followed the visions of corporate America in the name of freedom of the press. Their middle-class backgrounds or ambitions were deflected, despite promises of professionalism, and squashed by the social and economic realities of newswork within a social and political climate that fostered industrial growth and led to the triumph of business interests. Their own voices were rarely heard and their story remains to be told.

This book includes a collection of eight original essays by authors who share an interest in the need for a critical media history and a different vision of the press as a place of employment, an environment of work, and a site of struggle over conditions of labor and ideas of freedom.

A history of newsworkers not only explains the nature and extent of industrial growth in the newspaper industry, but also defines progress in terms of human capital, that is, the investment of labor, knowledge, and experience in the service of media ownership. In fact, most of the contributions to this book share an understanding of the centrality of newsworkers and class consciousness for the making of a history of newswork. A comprehensive approach to the history of newswork would include those taking part in all the activities—ranging from typographical workers and printers and their unions to clerical workers and others—involved in the production of newspapers. However, the concept of newsworkers, as it emerges in this book, recognizes primarily individual and collective actors in the editorial process whose work is based on professional practices that are largely defined and enforced by press ownership. However, the contributors also acknowledge the importance of those whose primary responsibility has been the actual distribution of newspapers under the rules and regulations of press management. Both newsworkers and newsboys are part of a working-class history; they share the experience of work under the institutional constraints of a newspaper industry and the process of absorbing such experiences in cultural terms under the specific conditions of their social and economic existence. In this sense, the essays in this book incorporate a notion of class consciousness based on E. P. Thompson's definition of class as a historical phenomenon that occurs in human relationships over periods of time, through which patterns develop in ideas, relationships, and institutions. Thompson, whose contributions to a cultural approach to labor history are widely recognized, guides this alternative history of the American press.

The volume suggests that the fundamental nature of a history of class consciousness in the development of the American press is an essential chapter in the development of public communication. By doing so, it creates a visibility for those whose work has shaped contemporary media and addresses the continuing need for an understanding of their history among others who will contribute to the economic and political growth of the press with their own labor.

Traditional press historians have concentrated primarily on the structure of the institution and its major forces as well as on the importance of protecting content, instead of addressing the issue of production in terms of labor and newsworkers. They have done so under ideological conditions that have generated a top-down history of the press that privileged property and ownership at the expense of an understanding of newswork.

This book addresses the need for a history of newsworkers by focusing on a wide range of issues that relate to the conditions of journalism history as well as to the professional practices of newsroom workers and others in their specific historical situation. The result is a series of essays that provide individual visions of newsworkers and collectively offer possibilities for a reconceptualization of press history as a history of work.

The introductory essay, by Hanno Hardt, explores the conditions of media history in the context of intellectual and theoretical developments in American historiography, its marginal existence, despite the recognized importance of communication in the development of the United States, and the challenges of theories of culture and society that have affected considerations of media and communication across a number of disciplines. Hardt concludes that the blind spot of American media historians remains their inability to react ideologically and politically against a persisting and overwhelming feeling of homogeneity, wholeness, and a sense of singular purpose that permeates the general histories of American journalism at the expense of recognizing diversity, conflict, and contradictory goals among newsworkers and their contributions to the making of media history.

Elizabeth (Elli) Lester observes how journalism history textbooks preclude a working-class analysis of journalism history and alienate prospective journalists from their real conditions of experience in the workplace. The employment of discursive strategies to structure and present history becomes the location for the construction of preferred readings and preferred readers. But textbooks also reflect the general problem of journalism education, which remains defined by skills training and service to the communication industry and readily adopts the ideological perspective of textbook presentations of the profession and the industry.

Marianne Salcetti describes how technological and commercial influences of the late nineteenth and early twentieth centuries shaped the working conditions of reporters as well as the work itself. This era of economic growth was characterized by specialization and compartmentalization of labor, but also by low wages and lack of job security. It was a time when reporters discovered that the division of labor and the subsequent standardization of occupational practices did not result in a better work life, but in a struggle for economic and professional survival. Because they had neither the financial resources nor the political control to become owners of the press or to participate decisively in the process of newsroom decision making, they did not define the role of the press in the twentieth century, although their labor shaped the face of American journalism.

Bonnie Brennen uncovers the existence of a cultural discourse on newsroom labor in fictional accounts of the 1920s and 1930s and draws on the richness of these sources for a description of reporters and their working lives. These objective conditions of professional practices and existential problems among journalists are corroborated in the popular literature of reviews and are reflected in autobiographical statements. Together, these explanations not only provide insight into newsroom practices in the United States during the interwar years, they also demonstrate the creative use of an alternative method of retrieving the memory of the time to reconstruct a history of reporters and their struggle in the workplace.

William S. Solomon describes the emergence of a professional hierarchy within American newsrooms, beginning during the latter part of the nineteenth century, when economic growth and technological advancements shaped work routines and conditions. The simple editor-reporter relationship was replaced by a system of editors, whose responsibilities ranged from the supervisory tasks of city editors, for instance, to copy preparation by copy editors. The latter formed a newsroom labor force that operated between reporters and managing editors. The division of labor also meant a division of power, with the result that publishers and their managers could manipulate their workers without serious consequences, because individual copy editors were easily replaced.

Barbie Zelizer observes the adaptation of photography in the newsroom by considering the dynamics of internal discussions and positions of authority surrounding the rise of photojournalism. The recognition of photography as a powerful professional practice helped demonstrate editorial commitment to immediacy, facts, and objectivity. It also helped shape its initial role within the news-gathering community and resulted in the emergence of the "disembodied photographer" whose presence defined professional discourse related to images. When the shift to an acknowledgment of the photographer as photojournalist occurred at the time of World War II, the legitimacy of the image prevailed among journalists who had undertaken a considerable struggle against a visual extension of their work and the outright adaptation of a new technology.

David R. Spencer offers a comparative perspective of the consequences of intellectual and ideological conflict in newswork that helps locate the American experience within a larger cultural context and suggests the potential of optional strategies of dissident journalism in the United States. His essay presents the social, political, and intellectual richness of such journalistic efforts by individuals in Canada who were dedicated to notions of education and communication that resulted in the sharing of an understanding of the world through journalism. Spencer describes the potential of a dissident culture whose journalistic production could flourish within a tradition of journalism as intellectual labor that reflected its European (British and French) roots rather than the example of American journalism. He also demonstrates how a form of dissident journalism that exposes the state and supports the efforts of members of the working class to understand their own conditions by learning about the privilege of bourgeois life in society was largely absent from American journalism of the early twentieth century.

In the final chapter, Jon Bekken discusses the emergence of newsboys (a term that refers to both boys and girls) in the development of the newspaper industry and their central role in the process of distribution. Celebrated in popular culture and valorized by publishers as symbols of capitalism at work, newsboys have assumed a major position in the social history of the press. Their own history, however, is more a reflection of the labor history of the times. They depended financially on the goodwill of publishers and suffered under poor working conditions. The failure of newspaper organizations to respond to their demands resulted in unrest, culminated in strike activities, and reflected their abilities to organize unions and seek affiliation with the American Federation of Labor. Although the press has moved away from child newsboys to adult carriers, newspapers still rely on this workforce to distribute their products and have adopted a variety of schemes to hold down labor costs.

The essays in this collection constitute a fragmentary and incomplete project, but they are joined in their ultimate goal, that is, in their affirmation of a press history whose central concern is the notion of work. They also suggest the potential of alternative sources of historical inquiry beyond institutional self-references, including official documents, government studies, and the diverse products of a culture, ranging from autobiographical writings to creative expressions at a specific historical moment. In this effort, these essays move beyond the traditional use of sources, but they rely on the richness and diversity of cultural resources available to the social and cultural historian. Collectively, these writings produce a climate of scholarly curiosity and professional interest in the stories of individuals whose lives have been dedicated to the practice of journalism, and whose efforts have become synonymous with the idea of the press as a public institution, largely without an understanding of their personal and professional struggles to survive in an atmosphere of commercial pressures and political considerations. In a yet larger social and economic context, this collection of essays advocates the development of a media history that privileges work and the place of workers in the making of the world through words and images.

Book projects are always collaborative efforts; this book is no exception. Beyond acknowledging an intellectual debt to the contributions of Critical Theory and Cultural Studies to our own work and way of thinking about media and communication in society, we would like to thank the contributors for their willingness to prepare essays for this book and for their patience throughout the editorial process. Also, comments by John Nerone and a second, anonymous, reader during the review process provided welcome and constructive criticism and guided us toward clarity and a more pronounced focus on the topic. Whatever shortcomings of this collection remain, they are our responsibility. In addition, we would like to thank our respective academic units, the School of Journalism and Mass Communication at the University of Iowa and the Department of Communication at SUNY Geneseo, for the material support of this project, and the Qualitative Studies Division of the Association for Education in Journalism and Mass

Communication for the opportunity to present the need for a history of newswork and the topics of some of these essays during the association's annual meeting in 1994. There are also a number of individuals who deserve credit for the completion of this project. They include Robert McChesney (Wisconsin) for his early support, Jeffrey Smith (Iowa) for comments on Hanno Hardt's essay, Sue Lafky (Iowa) for suggestions on Bonnie Brennen's chapter, Maynard Cuppy (Iowa) for his unfailing technical assistance, Steve Konick (Geneseo) for his computer wizardry, and, finally, Janaki Bakhle and Robert Mosimann of the University of Minnesota Press for their assistance and encouragement throughout this process.

# 1 / Without the Rank and File

## Journalism History, Media Workers, and Problems of Representation

### Hanno Hardt

The history of media workers remains obscured by its precarious location among intellectual traditions and academic disciplines. Neither journalism nor mass communication studies in the United States has fully explored the notion of media work and the process of labor, and both have remained on the margins of intellectual developments in historiography that have profoundly affected the thrust and direction of historical explanation for many years. Thus, despite major shifts toward a social or cultural perspective of history that address the links and interactions among structural conditions in contemporary societies, and despite modest reforms in journalism education and the rise of media criticism in these fields, mainstream media history continues its preoccupation with constructing and reconfirming the ideal relationship between media and democracy in American society. This essay traces the dilemma of media history by focusing on the need for a labor perspective that concentrates on both media workers as producers and the circumstances of production.

Especially since the late 1960s, contemporary media history has operated in the margins of a considerably larger field of social history. Although the social significance of communication as a fundamental social process and the cultural and political impact of the media structure on the development of society have been widely recognized and operationalized in the theorizing of modern society, media history has yet to realize the potential for a social and cultural history of communication to become a major contributor in an emerging theory of society. By focusing on work and on the performance of labor as structural elements in an explanation of professional practice, media history would shift from being a history of power to being a resource for alternative representations of the relationship between exploitation, socialization, and communication within the institutional boundaries of American journalism. Such a shift meets not only the demands for a history of media work, but also the desire to address related issues of class, race, and gender in traditional journalism or media history. This is an important project, particularly when one agrees with John Nerone (1990) that history as discourse confers power, because whatever "has a history...acquires acknowledged legitimacy; therefore the way to acquire legitimacy is to invent or discover history" (18).

Modern journalism is a result of the Industrial Revolution; it is also an active component in the process of modernization. George Gerbner's (1972) observation that media "are the cultural arms of the industrial order from which they spring" (51) remains a succinct and powerful assessment. In a society where media are the manufacturing plants of cultural goods, the idea of work remains central to an understanding of the commitment of journalists. It is fundamental to view them as producers of information and opinion, locate them in their relationship to others in the workplace and in society, and, last but not least, provide them with a strong sense of their own history and their own place in the making of American culture. Such efforts may ultimately serve the interests of labor and the needs of the working class to rediscover its own history and understand its current situation.

Media work focuses on the construction of realities and helps maintain the institutional power of the media; it involves the labor of journalists, among others, who are hired to perform to the expectations of their bosses and in the name of freedom of the press. The subsequent confrontation between lofty ideals and the need to make a living becomes an existential question, and the results reflect the pressures of industrial demands and the ability of individual journalists to compromise. To paraphrase E. P. Thompson's (1978) classic conclusion about class, the wrong assumption is that media workers exist and that they struggle because they exist; instead, their professional accomplishments are shaped by a permanent struggle involving societal inequities, institutional barriers, and personal commitments. Because the process of work is typically anonymous and disappears in the product, a history of media work discloses the relationship between specific representations of reality and the particular professional practices of distinct media workers at a specific historical moment in society, revealing a new perception of newsworkers and the American media. Likewise, it exposes the values and beliefs of media historians and their participation in the reconstruction of such struggles.

About ten years ago, Eric Hobsbawm (1984) observed the flourishing practice of labor history in many countries; it was an observation, however, that did not characterize the efforts of journalism historians in the United States, whose work remained uncommitted to creating an understanding of the central nature of labor in the history of the American media, and who failed to provide a social and economic awareness of the collective profes-sional life of newsworkers during any particular phase of institutional media development. But even labor historians have paid little attention to media workers. For instance, most of a dozen or so pertinent articles published in *Labor History* over the past thirty years have dealt primarily with labor jour-nalism, and even fewer have been case studies of unionization or strikes.

Yet the conditions of media work and the plight of journalists had be-come legitimate concerns, especially since the end of World War I, when newswork encountered industrialization and became identified with urban-ization, making the modern press into an important political and cultural in-stitution in Western societies. At the same time, newspapers were organized like factories, operated in the spirit of capitalism, and were politically empow-ered to shape, reflect, and represent public opinion. Those who were em-ployed by the media to produce suitable realities for mass consumption, how-ever, were not protected from the power of media ownership and faced the social and economic consequences of an increasingly complex world of labor.

Media historians responded to the agonies of modernization by translat-ing their obsession with power into a fascination with technology as a social and economic determinant of society. They concentrated their efforts on describing the quick succession of media technologies since the mid-nineteenth century, while ignoring their profound effects upon the nature and quality of professional journalism. Their work reflected the influence of their times and the writings of Marshall McLuhan and Harold Innis, in par-ticular, whose technological determinism provided intriguing answers to the problems of communication in modern society. It was also an ideologically fitting contribution to the literature of mass communication, which, since the Second World War, had begun to accommodate industrial concerns by con-centrating on issues of media technologies and their effects on audiences as consumers. Such efforts have tended to reflect and reinforce preconceived notions about the beneficial nature of technology in the course of producing effective and financially successful media systems; but because they focused on the production and consequences of messages rather than on the processes of industrial production and the problem of labor, McLuhan and Innis neglected or ignored the different social perspective of media workers/producers who were participants and potential casualties of industrialization and technological change.

However, the need to explore the conditions of the working press was articulated as early as 1925 by the International Association of Journalists, which requested a study of its professional and economic situation to help aid journalists in their self-understanding. Thus, when the International Labor Office (1928) in Geneva issued a report about the state of journalists in thirty-three countries, including the United States, it was based on the observation that journalists found themselves in a difficult and serious situation, particularly because of "the consequences of the vast economic upheaval which followed the war and which, while it affected all workers, was particularly disastrous to brain workers, including those who live by journalism" (1). The report called attention to "an evil from which journalism has suffered since its beginnings, but which was becoming more and more threatening as the profession developed—incoherence, arbitrariness, the absence of a code which would define rights and duties, and would introduce a little order, and at the same time a little justice, in the conditions in which this great modern profession is unfolding" (7–8).

By doing so, the report also described, albeit by chance, the situation in the United States during a period when newswork was significantly affected by the combination of an adverse economy and a lack of organized resistance to the commercial goals of publishers. For instance, George Seldes (1938) remarked in *Lords of the Press:* "The reporter throughout our history has been the lowliest of animals. Believing himself to be too good to join in any organization or movement, he has found himself exploited by everyone, and he has been so blinded by his egotism that he has refused to look out for his own material interests" (370). In addition, there were technological achievements that offered new perspectives on editorial practices, such as the utilization of telephones, photography, and even the increasing importance of radio as a competitive technology. Thus, media workers faced economic and professional hardship under a general predicament of change. Their fate and the development of the profession in the face of subsequent technological advancements has remained essentially undisclosed by media history. Ted Smythe (1980/1992) has noted the virtual absence of historical consideration of reporters as they emerged at the turn of the century. His essay dealing with the status of reporters at that time remains a rare contribution to a history of "working conditions and their influences on the news."

It is also important to remember that the first journalism historians had their roots in the profession. They were trained in neither history nor the social sciences; rather, they had often left careers in journalism without ever telling their own stories and, therefore, without contributing to the professional biography of newsworkers. This lack of historical consciousness may have been the result of their short-term commitment to journalistic work, which was considered primarily a temporary stage or a passage into other writing or editing jobs and thus hardly suited for creating any allegiance to the idea of the profession and its practitioners as a historical condition. In fact, journalists never acquired a collective sense of themselves, except perhaps through the sporadic fictional treatment of reporters and editorial work (Brennen 1993) and, more recently, through the publication of survey data, when journalists emerged from individualized biographical references of the past to be reproduced in contemporary social-scientific representations of the profession (Johnstone, Slawski, and Bowman 1976; Weaver and Wilhoit 1986, 1991).

Although sociological contributions to media studies have occurred for a long time, starting with the work of the Chicago sociologists and moving into the current environment of effects and audience studies (Hardt 1992), the sociological imagination did not conquer the minds of media historians until the past decade. Nord and Nelson (1981) observed that until the 1980s at least, the "impact of social science on journalism history has been slight," noting a certain methodological know-how, but a general lack of theory among journalism historians. These authors encouraged journalism historians to appreciate scientific knowledge and ask communication scientists for an understanding of the "value of history" to make a qualitative difference in the future (300-304). Similarly, Yodelis Smith (1981) argued for "an integrated discipline of empirical history" in light of the fact that impressionistic history has ill served any development of mass communication history (319).

Yet not much is known about the history of media workers since the accessibility of empirical methods to history. In fact, the introduction of a sociological perspective seems to have been restricted to considerations of appropriate methodologies, rather than to any systematic treatment of journalists as a social group or journalism as a cultural phenomenon. Therefore, the failure of media history to expand its notion of what may constitute a new or relevant topical perspective and, more specifically, to respond to the need for a labor perspective, continues to be a major concern and invites explanations, at least for those who seek to understand the traditions of the field in order to develop alternative practices. At stake is the neglected cultural history of intentions, negotiations, and compromises to secure the production of texts and the construction of social, political, and economic realities under historical conditions of media work.

There are several distinctive, yet related, possible ways to account for the circumstances under which media history has operated without recognizing the importance of work and the consequences of employment for the definition of professional practices. Most important among these are a traditional commitment to an early version of social history; resistance to radicalization during the 1960s; blindness toward the journalism of class, race, and gender; and an institutionalized ideological proximity to commercial interests.

The rise of social history coincides with the beginnings of media history in the United States. It reaches from the Lamprecht *Streit* among German historians in the 1890s and the demands for a cultural history articulated by Charles A. Beard, Carlton J. H. Hayes, and Carl Becker, and James Harvey Robinson in his 1912 book *The New History* to the challenge of historical positivism in the United States by Frederick J. Turner and the proposed need for an expanded vision of history within the social sciences. Its contemporary development embraces the more recent emergence of a comprehensive social history in France, under the prewar influence of Marc Bloch and Lucien Febvre and the postwar leadership of Fernand Braudel, and the intellectual challenge of the political conditions during the 1960s in the United States, culminating in the claims of the New Historicism to have discovered a different way of negotiating a sense of history.

These developments reflected an academic tradition that has been carried forward by arguing for a broad, multidisciplinary approach to the study of history and, implicitly at least, for the convergence of history and social theory. The result was a practice of history that relied on the totality of human experiences, rather than exclusively on the activities and conditions of the ruling class. Turner (1939), for instance, suggested as early as 1904 that "behind institutions, behind constitutional forms, lie the vital forces that call these organs into life and shape them to meet changing conditions," and he advocated the study of the social and economic life of society with the help of other fields of social-scientific inquiry (73-74). Thus, the subsequent replacement of political history by social history also reflected a belief in the potential of common knowledge as a source of historical insights that privileged the social sciences as informant and collaborator in the creation of extended historical realities. In addition, the linking of science and reform to history, particularly in response to Pragmatism, provided status and credibility to history, which rose quickly to become a major power in the struggle for control over explanations or definitions of contemporary conditions in society and therefore over shaping images and influencing the aspirations of a nation.

Media history emerged with the rise of the modern press as a formidable political institution and was subsequently reified in professional curricula of journalism education at American universities. Not unlike journalism itself, media historians at that time found themselves consistently drawn to the study of communities of decision makers, concentrating their gaze on media ownership and management. They produced a historical narrative that resembled the type of political history that sought to explain situations, practices, and events of the powerful by investigating and analyzing the activities of a media elite of owners, editors, and star reporters of media enterprises. Consequently, media historians provided an example of history as a cultural construct, based on an ideological vision of communication, media, and democracy that privileged the bourgeois definition of socially relevant and politically decisive groups in society. But perhaps more important, by equating, at least implicitly, the labor of journalists and other media workers with the media, they treated media institutions as representations of media workers and supported the efforts of media ownership to emphasize the organization. As a result, biographies of famous journalists become welcome celebrations of media institutions rather than reflections on the process of editorial labor.

In this context it made sense to produce an ambitious biographical series on American newspaper (1690-1950) and magazine (1741-1900) journalists that included biographical backgrounds and bibliographical sources of America's well-known journalists during specific periods of journalism history (Ashley 1983, 1984a, 1984b, 1985; Riley 1988, 1989). These efforts served to legitimate and ground a new professional culture of journalism in society by identifying the process of media work with the purposes of media institutions rather than with the collective practice of newsworkers. Thus, when media history engaged in description attending to the surveillance of the immediate social and political environment—such as describing the forms of rural and urban journalism, journalistic genres, and professional practices—it produced a variety of monographs dealing with the histories of state or local newspapers, journalistic writing, and related experiences that were embodied in biography. In fact, institutional and personal biographies constituted the most significant category of historical research in journalism at least until the early 1980s. Various guides to journalism literature attest to the popularity of biographical and autobiographical writings featuring, almost exclusively, highly respected and well-known journalists, with dozens of entries under the respective categories (Price 1959; Price and Pickett 1970; Taft 1986; Wolseley and Wolseley 1961, 1986). The latest compilation of reference works by Cates (1990), with more than a hundred entries under bibliographies and bibliographical guides, suggested the considerable growth of media studies in this particular category.

These prevailing compilations of biographical records, which confirmed the power of individuals or institutions, also marked the ideological boundaries of mainstream media history. They offered an essential perspective on journalism historiography and have been useful as part of the cultural context, suggesting the social or political process in society and signifying power relationships and the presence of hegemonic struggles over issues of class, gender, and race, for instance.

In addition, the recurring interest among authors of aggregate media histories (Bleyer 1927; Emery 1962, 1978; Emery and Emery 1992; Folkerts and Teeter 1994; Hudson 1873; Jones 1947; A. Lee 1937; J. Lee 1923; Mott 1962; Payne 1920; Sloan, Stovall, and Startt 1989; Tebbel 1969) in covering specific periods, from colonial beginnings and the American Revolution to the Civil War, industrialization, and modernity, has led to a standardized vision of the media within a larger social and political context. The result has been a linear notion of development that Bonnie Brennen (1995) addressed in her critique of media historians, who "often combine a linear understanding of history directed toward progress with a belief in time-bounded and unchanging historical truth" (200).

In fact, when these histories functioned as public resources and standard college texts, they related a story of the American media that is incomplete at best and perpetuated a specific myth of communication, media, and democracy that reinforced the perception of the entrepreneurial character of newspapers, or their political mission, and ultimately "legitimates the teaching of journalism as a form of industrial production" (Hardt 1989, 129). On the other hand, a critical cultural history of journalism may expose the reigning ideology of society and test the validity of freedom of the press as a celebrated principle of society.

The bourgeois version of media history as a structural representation of communication and power (influence) in society also relied on a particular reception of science and scientific truths. Its ideological framework rested on accepting that the beneficial relationship between science, technology, and democracy that had marked the era of urbanization and industrialization and that were inspired by the positivism of the last century also guided the search for validity and stability in the American media system in the latter part of this century. For instance, since notions of media, freedom, and democracy became synonymous features in an ensuing historical narrative, observations and descriptions of media institutions and practices have always been supportive. Even in their criticism, they reinforced a belief in the centrality of media as democratic institutions, and strengthened it with cumulative evidence of industrial and political power in media organizations. Thus, in his review of Edwin Diamond's 1993 book on the *New York Times,* James Boylan (1994) recounted how Diamond "retells the stories of individual rebels against the Times system" and documents a media bureaucracy at work, but he also noted the absence of any accounts of "organized dissidence" expressed through lawsuits by women or minorities, or through union activities, and came to the conclusion that for Diamond "such matters are no more than gnats on the hide of the elephant" (51).

There was an awareness, especially in later historical accounts, of the role of the media at every stage of the development of American society, and of the need for media historians to address issues such as those concerning the relation between media and politics or the relations among media, commerce, and popular culture. But most efforts have simply turned into series of duly recorded social or political phenomena or technological stages in the development of the American media. None adequately addressed the cultural contexts and the social processes of change that were to affect and characterize new professional practices among media workers. Throughout the past hundred years, the subordinate class of newsworkers has not only lived with its exploitation, it has also created forms of resistance through individual or collective opposition, the organization of labor unions, the negotiation of professional practices with media institutions, and personal compromise. However, these efforts have remained largely undiscovered by media history, even after social historians and sociologists began to offer assessments of the importance of communication and journalism in American society.

Instead, the overall quality of journalism history remained lacking, as was any sustained interest in historiographical issues. When Alan Nevins reviewed the state of journalism history in 1959, his criticism was devastating; however, it seemed to have had no effect on the subsequent development of the field. He spoke of the "thin" and "uneven" quality of historical research and suggested that although it is "marred by...[an] overemphasis on editorial personalities and opinions as distinguished from reporters and news, it has one still more glaring fault. Taken as a whole, it is deplorably uncritical and some of it is dishonest." Acting on his observation that institutional biographies, for instance, were frequently produced by insiders, Nevins traced the reasons for "silences" and "misrepresentations" among journalism historians to their role as "a *laudator tempus acti* who hangs nothing but spotless linen on the line" (418-19). His observations were not new. In fact, when Sidney Kobre advocated a "sociological approach" to the writing of journalism history in 1945, he also found a trail of older, outmoded historical methods that treated "the newspaper as an isolated institution, failing to relate the newspaper to the 'society' or the social environment of which it is an indisseverable part," and by doing so failing "to comprehend the true or actual character of this highly integrated-with-society institution and its past" (13-14).

Kobre's comments were particularly relevant because early social historians in the United States had attempted to broaden the familiar narratives of individual and institutional power by embracing sociological perspectives on rural and urban existence, ethnic minorities, and women, for instance. However, the resulting representations served to illustrate rather than to support any theoretical claims. They were less analytic and more descriptive in their study of everyday life, and they were based on a notion of social history as nonpolitical by nature and subordinated to other views of history, with the result that social history failed to realize its potential of becoming a major source of understanding the past. Some exceptions, however, that served as potential examples for press historians, include the work of Charles A. Beard and Mary R. Beard in *The Rise of American Civilization,* published in 1927; the influence of Arthur M. Schlesinger in *The Rise of the City, 1878-1898* and *Prelude to Independence,* published in 1933 and 1958, respectively; the contribution of Henry Steele Commager in his 1950 book, *The American Mind;* and the scholarship of Richard Hofstadter in *The Age of Reform,* published in 1955. These works, among others, arose from the interests of American social and intellectual historians in the role of the American press during the formative years of U.S. society.

Media histories during the same period, such as Thomas D. Clark's (1948) work on the southern press, still provided descriptive studies of journalism in the United States, although they moved beyond pure chronology or biography into considerations of the social environment and related the position of the press to the community or the region. There was still no serious attempt to engage the material in efforts to understand the relationship between media and change in American society and to analyze the role of individual actors, such as reporters, in this cultural and political process.

Instead, media histories produced abstractions such as "the American press" or "American journalism" that celebrated the institution and implied a concept of work that emphasized outcomes and measured success or failure of the media in terms of public appeal or level of consumption. Nerone (1990) provided a relevant comment on such concepts located in the titles of journalism history texts. He suggested that these titles "implicitly dismiss the notion that today's 'American journalism' is not the mature version of yesteryear's child, but the dominant segment of many heterogeneous, indeed competing, presses, and that yesteryear's American journalism was even less homogeneous" (20). Indeed, Nerone introduced the possibility that because American journalism is fictitious, it cannot have a history in and of itself (23).

Consequently, the idea of work remains implied in descriptions of the product and the collective effect of a particular medium as a credible or famous source of information. It did not involve identifying and describing the actual process of work or a notion of labor, which would reflect the historical conditions of individuals in their news or reportorial work environment, such as the concrete conditions of labor and the undeniable reactions of reporters to their professional experiences with editors and publishers. On the other hand, there have been numerous and diverse historical explanations of communication in society, including contributions by newsworkers, often in autobiographical accounts, sometimes in oral history projects, and often reinforced by the production of fictional narratives of newsroom conditions and the lives of reporters. For instance, in 1922 Theodore Dreiser recalled that "in the city newsroom the mask was off and life was handled in a rough-and-ready manner, without gloves and in a catch-as-catch-can fashion. Pretense did not go here. Innate honesty on the part of any one was not probable. Charity was a business with something in it for somebody. Morality was in the main for public consumption only" (152). Almost forty years later, Charles Lindstrom (1960) described the newsman, "caught by the cutting edge of creeping deadlines and lashed to the newsroom clock in the pit of circulation unlimited, a cavernous maw nearly filled with ads, gewgaws, divertissement, and fiction. The pit must be further filled with the issue of reporters' typewriters, with 'news of the moment,' or store-bought features" (22-23). There are also the memories of individual reporters, whose recollections of work practices are vivid reminders of their predicament vis-à-vis management demands. For instance, the UCLA Oral History Project (1970) includes the voice of a reporter who remarked:

> I was canned because they issued an order that each of the reporters had to carry a common folding Kodak and take his own photographs. They were so hard up they couldn't afford photographers.

They were missing a lot of pictures of divorcees and others. You had to get "leg art," as it was called and if you covered the courts you had a lot of women you could use for this purpose. But finally I was fed up; I refused to do it; so they said they were going to can me. (45-46)

Although newsworkers' voices were not heard in the sweeping accounts of the advancement of the media through the past century, it is possible that a collective history of newsworkers existed in the biographical and autobiographical writings of former journalists or in the novels of their times. Brennen's project (1993) on journalism and cultural history offered insights into the detailed accounts of newswork found in fictional works and demonstrated their significance in the contemporary setting of 1920s and 1930s America. In addition, there is a growing literature of film analysis dealing with images of media workers as they have been produced by Hollywood over the past seventy years or so (e.g., Barris 1976; Ghiglione 1990; Good 1989). Such portrayals are expressions of specific historical periods; they are representations of a profession by Hollywood filmmakers that reflected public interest in newsroom practices and constituted valuable sources of information concerning the construction of newswork as fiction and its reception among media professionals, film critics, and the general public. They have often been critical of the American press and its practitioners and have questioned the self-defined role of the media in society. But because these treatments have also negotiated the boundaries between fact and fiction in their attempts to grasp a sense of reality among competing interests in society, there has been a reluctance to consider them as evidence. Few researchers have recognized such texts as the manifestations of historical realities because distinctions between fact and fiction and measures of validity traditionally have relied on social-scientific expertise rather than on theories of culture as a "whole way of life" (Williams 1989, 4).

The growth of media history, beginning with the efforts of journalism historians during the past seventy-five years, has been significant in terms of the sheer quantity of studies that may reflect a belief in the relevance and importance of such contributions. At the same time, journalism historians succeeded in perpetuating a specific theoretical position that favored the political or ideological safety of the "great-man history" and its perspective from the top at the expense of visions of history that acknowledged the whole process of social existence. This position relied on the availability of facts and documents from traditional business and government sources at the same time it rejected accessible cultural or social expressions of existence and participation in the world of journalism and communication. The resulting historical narrative focused on the editorial role of journalism and constructed the press as a moral leader in society, disregarding a different, less uplifting or restorative, function of reporting. The desire to identify with the glorious potential of a working relationship between media and the idea of democracy is reflected in the subsequent representations of media and their development in the United States. The actual process of newswork, however, remained a peripheral concern, particularly as its practices are often uncontrolled, dubious, at variance with notions of ethical conduct, and not necessarily utilized in service of the image of communal or national leadership. Again, Dreiser (1922) offered a pertinent example in his description of his attraction to the "pagan and un-moral character" of reporting "as contrasted with the heavy religionistic and moralistic point of view seemingly prevailing in the editorial office proper (the editorial page, of course), as well as in the world outside" (151).

In an exhaustive and continuing search for answers to a myriad of social problems that continue to plague American society, however, the media, as symbols of freedom and democracy, have encountered mistrust and disbelief. Their institutional power and effectiveness has been challenged by public opinion, which charges that the media have helped create and reinforce problems such as pornography and violence, and by the rise of cultural criticism and cultural studies, with its reconsideration of media influences and the study of audiences, in particular. Thus, more recently historians began to act on the potential strength of a cultural history, encouraged, in part, by the acknowledgment that culture is a significant arena for historical inquiry and that history is an appropriate method of locating the development of social institutions, such as media, and social practices, such as media work, within a particular culture. The result may be new meanings and new understandings of media practices for alternative visions of progress and human emancipation (Hardt and Brennen 1993).

The success of social history in the United States as a significant force in the explanation of contemporary conditions began in the 1960s, when the notion of "we, the people," and its institutional manifestations of the media as the "voice of the people," was replaced by inquiries into the life and work experiences of individuals, whose social and cultural practices shaped the world around them (see, for instance, Howard Zinn's *A People's History of the United States,* 1980). The interest in the working class and its collective practices as well as the exploration of material culture were inspired partly by the considerable contributions of French *Annales* historians and Fernand Braudel's (1980) call for rethinking history and a "whole new way of conceiving of social affairs" (33) and partly by the work of British historians, in particular E. P. Thompson's (1963) study of English working-class existence. These perspectives were also joined by those of American social historians in their attempts to respond to the specific demands of their own times. Such viewpoints constituted a political answer to social historians' need to identify and locate new social movements, ranging from civil rights to women's liberation and gay rights, whose collective biographies provided different and alternative insights into American society. These developments also included the rise of the study of labor history, which was stimulated by the original contributions of sociologists and social workers to an understanding of the effects of industrialization, urbanization, and immigration and which provided yet another perspective on social history through analyses of workers and their role in the social and economic process of society. Its time had come in an era when political causes helped shape research agendas and provoked alternative and more inclusive explanations of society. Hobsbawm's (1984) observation that "labor history is by tradition a highly political subject, and one which was for long practiced largely outside the universities" (1) acknowledged the problematic and helped explain its intellectual appeal at this particular time. A few years later, Mari Jo Buhle and Paul Buhle (1988) traced the cultural approach to a working-class history in the United States, as inspired by Thompson's work, and the appropriation of culture by American social historians. They also observed the subsequent shift from Thompson's understanding of culture—under the assault of structuralism and poststructuralism—to new possibilities for the study of individuals or groups and their involvement in the making of meaning and, therefore, history.

Social history had become the new frontier of a struggle between alternative understandings of history, including Marxist perspectives, and the existing representations of the past. It promised to reveal the failures of earlier interpretations and raised the possibility of social and political change through the refiguring of the idea of history. The new accounts of social historians privileged a "bottom-up" perspective, emphasizing the role of human agency and centering on notions of cultural, political, or economic power, while reaching across disciplinary boundaries for sociological theories and methods in efforts to analyze and explain contemporary phenomena through historical insights. What emerged from developments within the field of social history was an agreement "that social conditions and social changes underlay and interacted with other historical processes, as opposed to the conventional historical assumption of the independent operation of formal ideas or political actions" (Stearns 1993, 244).

There is very little evidence to suggest that the radicalization of the 1960s, which produced a new appreciation of social history as an empowering explanation of the present, also produced a radical approach to media history as a form of social knowledge. Media historians operated under specific social and political conditions that shaped their experience of reality and affected their recollections of the past, including the ways in which they asked questions and conducted their investigations. Major events, such as revolutions or periods of social and political unrest, and public responses, including the practices of press and broadcasting, are necessary contexts; they also provide opportunities for raising new questions, suggesting directions, and thereby offering insights into the meaning of the present. Yet media histories continued to reproduce compilations of facts, sometimes assisted by a trend toward quantitative history, but always relying on traditional, ideological constructs of media history.

Thus, the field not only remained isolated from new developments in social history, but was further confined to the margins of professional journalism programs when social or cultural historians began to discover the importance of media and communication for their own work. For instance, organized journalism historians pleaded as late as 1970 for the centrality of journalism/mass media history, and when they did, their rationale reflected traditional concerns over knowing the stories of "great" men or events, and, given the political circumstances of 1970s America, understanding the importance of recognizing minority media. There were no references to the roles of men and women in the media workplace, which seemed to apply directly to the career goals of most journalism students, or to larger questions about media and change in American society, including the relationship between exploitation and communication in late industrial capitalism. Instead, the plea was for recognizing yet another institutional perspective that privileged the media and media ownership (Morrison 1970), reinforcing the idea that journalism history was meant to instruct about the institutional power of the press, rather than about its record of individual participation in the making of media realities and in securing professional status in society. The traditional preference for simple explanations, however desirable for the construction of media realities, was no longer a sufficient solution but collapsed under the weight of questions related to the social and political problems in society. While supporting dominant commercial and political interests, the media had helped dehumanize social relationships and alienate individuals, and new historical inquiries promised to shed light on the problematic relationship between media and society, the viability of the public sphere, and the potential for change.

Indeed, Zinn (1970) approached the issue of radical history with questions related to the need to redirect the practice of history when he asked, "What kind of awareness moves people in humanistic directions, and how can historical writing create such awareness, such movement?" (36). He suggested that radical history not only can expose social and political power but can help demystify everyday life; it is not the privilege of a dominant class, which uses history to maintain and reinforce its own standing in society, but a process that can liberate and provide answers to contemporary issues by privileging historical explanation and making it a necessary condition for a critical discourse in society.

The arrival of the New Historicism privileged the realm of culture and relied on the relationship between culture and history to focus on the significance of discourse, text, and material practice in the renegotiation of historical representations. Its resulting appeal to cultural studies or media studies, including media history, rested on its challenge of conventions and insistence on the cultural sphere as a central arena of interpretation. In fact, a reconceptualization of media history as a history of the media as texts promised to uncover a new awareness of communication in society. The identification and description of interpretive communities and their appropriation of competence, emanating from the study of the actual process of work and its reception by audiences, emerge and constitute the basis for relocating the sense of media power, including the power to define journalism, for instance. Such a task would concentrate on notions of accessibility and use, and on how processes of social communication forge definitions of media and society.

The resulting shift in power relations, however, was never realized, as media history continued unscathed to perpetuate its own ideological position based on the enduring strength of the turn-of-the-century idea of Progressivism, an idea that is central to an understanding of the rise of American journalism to power and influence. As Richard Hofstadter (1955) noted, it is "hardly an exaggeration to say that the Progressive mind was characteristically a journalistic mind, and that its characteristic contribution was that of the socially responsible reporter–reformer" (186). Newsworkers rose in prominence, upholding values that were determined by their personal backgrounds and the conditions of their work and that they ultimately passed on to contemporary generations of journalists (Gans 1980, 206-12). In the 1990s, Progressivism continues to provide a convenient mind-set as well as a predictable historical narrative for media historians, who may see themselves as the defenders of enduring values and media as the epitome of responsible entrepreneurship.

In fact, when James Carey (1974) in the inaugural issue of *Journalism History* launched a major attack on the established practices of journalism historians in his essay titled "The Problem of Journalism History," he flatly stated that the "study of journalism history remains something of an embarrassment" (3). Carey observed that the interpretation of journalism history as a "slow steady expansion of freedom and knowledge, from the political press to the commercial press, the setbacks into sensationalism and yellow journalism, the forward thrust into muckraking and social responsibility," had finally exhausted itself. Instead, he pleaded for a cultural history to recover "past forms of imagination," particularly the history of reporting (4). Because "journalism is a cultural act," he suggested that historians trace the emergence of the report "as a desirable form of rendering reality" until "its disappearance or radical reduction as an aspect of human consciousness" (5). His insistence on the importance of a cultural history, reminiscent of Raymond Williams, however, concentrated on the historical potential of the text as product. It fell short of engaging in an examination of Williams's idea of culture as a "whole way of life"; instead, Carey proceeded without further references to institutional power, the importance of the process of work, and the impact of being in the world of journalism on the construction of texts. Nevertheless, his essay offered a first theoretical break by an informed and sympathetic critic of journalism history and suggested opportunities for reconstructing journalism history comprehensively and much closer to contemporary debates of the uses of history in the context of cultural studies.

There were others who pleaded a similar case for a cultural history of the media following Carey's initial critique. A special issue of *Journalism History*, "Seeking New Paths in Research," appeared in 1975, and featured attempts to "operationalize," or modify, Carey's suggestions. An emphasis on texts and alternative methodologies rather than a shift of perspectives to labor issues and the role and function of newsworkers prevailed. However, in her outline of a cultural history of journalism, Marion Marzolf (1975) included "the people in the profession—the printers, editors, journalists," as well as their outputs and "the culture in which the profession develops" (42). A few years later, Jean Ward (1978) and Marzolf (1978) explored the potential of interdisciplinary approaches, particularly American Studies, to provide models and guidance for journalism history. Again, Marzolf addressed the need to know about the identities of reporters and editors, their genders and ethnicities, the process of socialization, and how their individuality added "to newsroom judgments about news" in the past (15).

Over the next twenty years, after the arrival of British Cultural Studies and the acknowledgment of historical explanation in the context of Marxist visions of media history, criticism of journalism history became more self-conscious, with an increasing recognition of the theoretical and political significance of the media and the potential for a cultural history of communication. There have also been attempts to modify the practices of traditional journalism history through a rededication to a history of the structural elements of media institutions, their economic and political power, however, without considerations of media workers (Nord 1988).

But radicalization did not mean simply the adoption and celebration of socialist theories of society, or an adherence to the litany of utopian visions of the world. It also meant a redefinition of intellectual boundaries and the application of theories and methodological practices that seemed to fit the scholarly task, rather than sticking with the orthodoxy of disciplinary maps. Indeed, many academic fields began to expand into interdisciplinary activities, only to discover the centrality of communication and media in the debates over issues of participation and human agency. In due course, the field of (mass) communication research was discovered, interrogated, and used as a methodological resource, while its theoretical claims, if they had ever been a major concern, were simply ignored. In fact, (mass) communication research had produced a number of observations concerning structures and functions of communication and media related to the production and consumption of culture and the adoption of attitudes and ideas related to social and political behavior that suggested the usefulness of inquiring about the roots of these sociological phenomena. Consequently, sociology crossed into the domain of traditional media history, where it was reproduced for the purposes of understanding change and development. Michael Schudson's work supplied an appropriate example of this approach, combining the predilections of a historian with a sociological perspective on society. Schudson (1978) offered a "social history of American newspapers" that extended an account of the rise of "objectivity" in American journalism and therefore an understanding of the embeddedness of journalism in the culture of science and technology. In this context, his work supplied a glimpse of the role of reporters in the institutionalization of the factual as a representation of reality and their relationship with editors (61-87). Dan Schiller (1981) also offered a most interesting argument concerning "the subordination of journalists to an explicit objectivity" (194) in an atmosphere of scientific expertise, which legitimated news-gathering practices and changed the profession again. An equally thought-provoking insight was provided by Hazel Dickens-Garcia (1989), whose sociological understanding of change focuses on the interaction between journalism and society, and on the ways in which the press adapted to a changing cultural environment. Here, too, explanations of journalistic conduct gave at least a sense of the working conditions at that time.

Another break with traditional versions of historical narratives has occurred in the contributions of a number of younger historians whose understanding of history provides potential for new insights into the relations among communication, media, and American society. For example, William S. Solomon (1993) recognized that "accounting for a culture industry requires different histories than would account for a pluralistic and democratic media system" and attempt to "redress the imbalance in journalism and mass communication historiography" (2). Although Solomon and McChesney's (1993) text demonstrated the power of a social and cultural analysis of concrete historical conditions, the value of contextualization, and the way in which each wave of new media technologies has affected the life of society, broadened the power base of the media industry, and allowed the state to help define the relationship between public and private interests, they did not consider issues of media work and the organization of professional practice. Nevertheless, the work of these authors suggested that a critical perspective on media history is emerging; whether it will help raise the historical consciousness of the field by addressing a wide range of social and economic issues and reconstituting a cultural history of media practices and public interests, however, remains to be seen.

The experience of the 1960s challenged the imagination and provided opportunities for a break with the traditional representation of the past. Most obviously, there was a new focus, particularly on issues of class, race, and gender, that inspired and also was inspired by feminist theories. Simultaneously, a forum for Marxist thought was provided in debates over power, equality, and definitions of democracy that had direct impact on explanations of the rise of media institutions and their effects on social formations and individual struggles.

Akin to practices of traditional social history, media histories had long determined that the rise of American journalism, for instance, was effectively told by offering biographies of individuals and institutions whose activities reflected the ideas of progress and private enterprise and who were appropriate examples of journalism as successful entrepreneurship. These people and institutions also represented power, and descriptions of their national or regional influence helped maintain and reinforce a vision of the press that served the larger social and political context of definitions of freedom and democracy. By providing historical evidence of continuity and righteousness and thereby protecting the image of the media business, media history became a reliable source of institutional strength and individual satisfaction, particularly for those who felt that the United States had a special destiny and that the press played a major role in extending past accomplishments into the future. Such views relied on the continuity of values and beliefs as a determinant of historical experience and catered to expectations that social and political structures, including the structure of communication and the media in American society, were fixed and thus immovable. They reflected a strong faith in the pertinence and permanence of social institutions (including the media) and their original missions, and found it difficult under these circumstances to comprehend or, worse, tolerate cultural or political breaks that could threaten the notion of America as a (God-)given idea. It has been equally problematic for alternative social theories to offer different understandings of the power and influence of media in American society that succeed in overcoming the liberal-pluralist representations of the past.

Consequently, the journalism of gender, race, and ethnicity that has been a significant contributor to the growth of culture and communication in American society, and that provides an alternative representation of the past, threatens the ideological basis of traditional media history. By acknowledging the diversity of media production, the participation of women, African Americans, and immigrants in the production of culture, and the reality of prevailing social, cultural, and political differences, the white, male, bourgeois privilege of communication and media use becomes a class-specific phenomenon whose history propagandizes domination and reveals the ideological practice of media history.

The work of women journalists, like that of African American and other ethnic minority journalists, has typically been captured by media historians with the help of familiar sources and traditional ideological perspectives that privileged stardom or popularity as cultural values. For instance, the cultural approach utilized by Marion Marzolf (1977) in her treatment of women journalists, and the reliance of Kay Mills (1988) in her history of female reporters on Bleyer and on the pioneering work of Ishbell Ross in 1936, as well as work by Jean E. Collins (1981) may be seen to return to traditional visions of journalism history as a biography of power. Brennen (1995) wrote about the "reification" of sources in some recent studies of women journalists, that is, their use of standard media texts to provide a sense of history without a critical assessment of their limitations. On the other hand, the contemporary literature on women, work, and media is growing steadily (e.g., Lafky 1991; Sanders and Rock 1988). It promises to become a rich source for media historians who realize the problem of representation by traditional, standard media histories and their biases concerning gender and institutional power.

Similarly, considerations of the African American press since Frederick Detweiler's (1922) account of "the Negro press in the United States," which examined newspapers as cultural texts, have remained taxonomic rather than interpretive (Wolseley 1990), and the first account of the journalism of American Indians was not reconstructed until the late 1970s (Murphy and Murphy 1981). And finally, histories of immigrant groups and their presses have typically been conceptualized around the conflicts between their root-edness in culture, language, and tradition and the pressures of the American environment, as their authors have managed to provide informative narratives of conflict and tension in the formation of American society. Catherine Cassara (1991) suggested that "there may be strong parallels between the treatment of immigrants in American history generally and the historical treatment of their presses" (3). She found that studies of immigrant media exist, but do not find their way easily into the mainstream accounts of American journalism.

Other recent analyses of the ethnic press not only offer different perspectives from outside traditional media history, but also suggest that other fields of social and cultural inquiry have recognized the relevance of minority concerns to a study of American society (Harzig and Hoerder 1985; Miller 1987). The three-volume annotated bibliography of the immigrant labor press in the United States edited by Hoerder and Harzig (1987) provided a sense of the labor struggle in the realm of communication, and Herbert Gutman's (1976) work revealed the diversity and oppositional character of the labor press. Much earlier, Robert Park's (1922) sociological study of the foreign-language press was fueled by history and offered equally provocative insights into the ideological power of the immigrant culture and the rationale for its diverse press. But these contributions to an understanding of media practices failed to arouse much interest among media historians to analyze the journalism of class and minorities as part of the developing media culture in the United States. In fact, in the standard histories of journalism there remains no appropriate acknowledgment of the role of the foreign-language press as a constituent form of cultural diversity; instead, they remain "predictable, standardized, and encyclopedic treatments of the growth of English-language newspapers in the United States" (Hardt 1989, 115).

The lack of a labor perspective of media history is also related to a more general neglect of media and communication histories of marginal groups (Hardt 1989; McIntyre 1981) whose experiences never acquired social or political weight, and whose significance in terms of serving the need for institutional biographies of power could therefore be considered minimal at best. If they appeared as descriptive context, they remained marginal topics, even after major works on working-class culture, including immigrant cultures, had become accessible sources of social and economic insights. In general, considerations of minority media followed traditional methods of producing series of institutional biographies; they became social or racial phenomena in a prominantly white media culture, suggesting that media history is a product of the cultural consciousness of its time. Considerations of minority media have also been driven by economic determinants, which help reinforce prevailing notions of media as viable economic enterprises rather than as cultural institutions. Yet the historical bias of cultural studies toward the conditions of society promises new opportunities for understanding the issues of class, race, and gender within media history.

A cultural media history requires a different look at the contemporary conditions of journalism and demands a new sensitivity to expressions of cultural identity while it examines various media and their social uses; the writing of a cultural media history as a critical history, however, exposes and reassesses the ruling assumptions of liberal pluralism and analyzes the relationship between state, journalism, and society (Hardt 1989, 127). Such a research agenda is not only ambitious, but difficult to "operationalize" in an increasingly conformist educational and academic environment, because it questions theoretical assumptions about freedom and democracy and emphasizes the process of work and the place of labor. For instance, the proximity of journalism education to media industries, coupled of late with a new sensitivity toward the demands of commerce and industry to implement practical courses and address professional concerns in university curricula, may have created a real or imagined political climate that affects the practical commitment to any sustained and substantive discourse on labor and media ownership.

In fact, the strained relationship between the press and organized labor is a congenital condition that emerged in the antilabor attitudes of media ownership and is reinforced by a general lack of labor and union reporting, except in the sensational context of strikes. This antagonism is neither new nor surprising, as it reflects the position of American business, which has always resisted the notions of labor unions and collective bargaining concerning the specifics of hiring and firing, working conditions, and social benefits. When Joseph McKerns (1977) suggested almost two decades ago that "there is much that can be learned about the capitalistic character of the American press by studying its role vis-à-vis labor, both as a commentator on daily events and as an employer" (91–92), he invited a close analysis of the relationship between media and labor that is yet to be realized by his colleagues as a topic of research or instruction in journalism departments. Media organizations represent a significant faction of the American business establishment. When they faced the demands of organized labor, particularly in the period between the two world wars, they responded by pressing for a differentiation between the blue-collar workforce of printers and pressmen and the white-collar contingent of newsworkers, identifying the latter as professionals and successfully splitting the interests of media workers by reference to class (Leab 1970; Salcetti 1992).

Although university journalism programs have been staffed by media professionals with their own definitive roots in media work, they were established with the political and financial commitments of publishers. Again, media professionals were hired, this time to help train journalism practitioners within university settings. Subsequently, journalism programs turned into mass communication departments, with academic staffs and social-scientific research agendas that offered additional support to the media industry. As a result, financial assistance for research and training from media organizations has helped sustain and develop the idea of journalism education. There has never been a major ideological break with a tradition of service to the industry; therefore, any critique of media practices is offered in the spirit of collaboration and typically lacks a critical edge. Instead, it is remedial and fits well into the framework of a liberal-pluralist theory of media and society. On the other hand, media studies programs may be in a slightly better position to address independently the intellectual dilemma of an "administrative" perspective on the social and political problems of the current media system, although university ties to industries, including the media, and pressure to place students in industry jobs may well affect teaching and research everywhere.

Thus, at this time any disengagement of journalism programs from media influences seems highly unlikely. When state universities began to face financial problems during the late 1970s, fund-raising became a necessity that was often written into the job descriptions of deans and department chairs. In fact, universities have been assimilated by their socioeconomic environment, and they engage in commercial promotion and marketing practices (Wernick 1991). Encouraged by a receptive academy, media organizations began to invest in journalism education, and journalism educators and media researchers proved willing, if not eager, to provide a home, not for the interests of professional media workers, but for the agendas of the media industry. It has proved difficult, if not impossible, to follow a path of critical journalism and media studies, when significant annual subsidies are at stake. Work that is dedicated to discovering, defining, and assessing the contribution of media workers and the role of labor in the development of journalism and mass communication in the United States remains a marginal concern in the current environment. In view of this context, desirable first agendas may include closer contacts with labor unions, professional service organizations, and individual media workers, and cooperation on a variety of contemporary issues as well as on history projects, such as oral histories, and the establishment of document centers to collect private and official papers. More than fifty years ago, George Seldes (1938) suggested that it was time to "invite newspapermen to run the newspapers" and to prove that freedom of the press means "letting the editorial staff run the newspaper" (381-82). Although that invitation was never extended, Seldes raised important issues of professionalism and codetermination that remain significant contemporary topics in a media environment that is determined more by commercial interests than by the professional judgments of newsworkers.

There has been no major theoretical break and therefore no new historical narrative concerning the development of the American media. Instead, their history has followed and clung to a traditional pattern of nineteenth-century American historiography, while the dominant paradigm of media history continues to reproduce itself in biography and periodization and reinforces the currency of standard media histories. Nerone (1993) has recently addressed the continuation of the tradition of "grand narratives" in communication history; he observed that its practitioners operate "within a relatively insulated institutional framework," and noted that the resulting work rarely meets or engages cultural studies in historical analysis (154-55). In fact, the traditional approach to media history is now becoming marginalized by a series of theoretical developments, including the work of culturalists. Media history has been rediscovered through these Marxist and non-Marxist traditions of cultural studies and reproduced in attempts to define and understand larger social and political issues in contemporary society.

Although modern concerns regarding the contribution of marginalized groups to the development of a journalism of gender, race, ethnicity, and class and its role in society have found a voice, much needs to be done to reconstruct the history of communication in these communities. The blind spot of

American media history remains its inability to react ideologically and politically against a persisting and overwhelming feeling of homogeneity, wholeness, and a sense of singular purpose that permeates the general histories of American journalism. These efforts have successfully masked the historical conditions of diversity and reinforced problems of social and racial segregation by ignoring the potential strength of a journalism of multicultural interests.

At the same time, the political nature of labor history, as suggested earlier by Hobsbawm, could lead to giving the plight of minorities, including media workers, expression, and beyond that, could encourage critical support. The differences between political advocacy and cultural history become insignificant when both express a common concern for recognizing the importance of people and groups as participants in the creation of history. Moreover, a cultural history of media workers provides the foundation for strategies of intervention in current media practices. Finally, a history of media work is crucial to an understanding of the nature of professional practices, their changes, and, therefore, their possibilities among alternative forms of communication and journalism in society.

There is yet another consideration that was prominent among earlier historians, namely, the relationship between intellectuals and workers, that is, between the presence of reformist concerns in their own work and the experience and consciousness of workers. For instance, Leon Fink (1994) talks about the "dichotomy between scholar (intellectual) and scholarly object (worker)" that has "long played a constitutive role in the writing of labor history" (224). It must be the goal of contemporary media historians to overcome such "dichotomy" not only by understanding these differences—and dealing with them in the interpretation of historical work—but by realizing that areas of anticipated concerns, such as labor policies or media reform, may reflect personal preferences or an intellectual climate of historical thought rather than the concrete experiences of the conditions of work and the fate of workers. The result is an emphasis upon contextualization within a cultural approach to concrete historical experiences.

Through such an emphasis, cultural historians of communication could help shape the agendas of change by liberating media workers from the expressed inevitability of their condition and help them to recognize and act on the structures of work and inequality with explanations that allow individuals to deal successfully with the problem of conferred histories. They could engage in the support and development of oral history projects in collaboration with newsworkers and strengthen their relationship with professional organizations in an effort to provide students of journalism and mass communication with a history of work and editorial practices that features the contributions of workers and addresses the complete range of current freedoms and limitations of media work within the industry and within the larger culture. The ultimate objective must be a working-class history that serves the interests of media workers and not the intellectual interests of middle-class academics, which are likely to perpetuate and reinforce the dominant perspectives on media history.

## References

Ashley, Perry J., ed. *American Newspaper Journalists, 1873-1900*. Detroit: Gale Research, 1983.

———. *American Newspaper Journalists, 1901-1925*. Detroit: Gale Research, 1984a.

———. *American Newspaper Journalists, 1926-1950*. Detroit: Gale Research, 1984b.

———. *American Newspaper Journalists, 1690-1872*. Detroit: Gale Research, 1985.

Barris, Alex. *Stop the Presses! The Newspaperman in American Films*. South Brunswick: Barnes, 1976.

Beard, Charles A., and Mary R. Beard. *The Rise of American Civilization*, 2 vols. New York: Macmillan, 1927.

Bleyer, Willard Grosvenor. *Main Currents in the History of American Journalism*. Boston: Houghton Mifflin, 1927.

Boylan, James. "The Unchanging of the Guard." *Columbia Journalism Review* (Jan./Feb. 1994): 50-52.

Braudel, Fernand. *On History*. Chicago: University of Chicago Press, 1980.

Brennen, Bonnie. "'Peasantry of the Press': A History of American Newsworkers from Novels, 1919-1938." Ph.D. diss., University of Iowa, 1993.

———. "Newsworkers during the Interwar Era: A Critique of Traditional Media History." *Communication Quarterly* 43 (Spring 1995): 197-209.

Buhle, Mari Jo, and Paul Buhle. "The New Labor History at the Cultural Crossroads." *Journal of American History* 75 (June 1988): 151-57.

Carey, James W. "The Problem of Journalism History." *Journalism History* 1, no. 1 (1974): 3–5, 27.

Cassara, Catherine. "The Foreign-Language Press in America: A Historiographic Analysis." Paper presented to the History Division at the annual meeting of the Association for Education in Journalism and Mass Communication, Boston, 1991.

Cates, Jo A. *Journalism: A Guide to the Reference Literature*. Englewood, Colo.: Libraries Unlimited, 1990.

Clark, Thomas D. *The Southern Country Editor*. Indianapolis: Bobbs-Merrill, 1948.

Collins, Jean E. *She Was There: Stories of Pioneering Women Journalists*. New York: Messner, 1981.

Commager, Henry Steele. *The American Mind*. New Haven, Conn.: Yale University Press, 1950.

Detweiler, Frederick G. *The Negro Press in the United States*. Chicago: University of Chicago Press, 1922.

Diamond, Edwin. *Behind the Times: Inside the* New York Times. New York: Villard, 1993.

Dickens-Garcia, Hazel. *Journalistic Standards in Nineteenth-Century America*. Madison: University of Wisconsin Press, 1989.

Dreiser, Theodore. *A Book about Myself*. New York: Boni & Liveright, 1922.

Emery, Edwin. *The Press in America: An Interpretive History of Journalism*. Englewood Cliffs, N.J.: Prentice Hall, 1962.

———. *The Press and America*. Englewood Cliffs, N.J.: Prentice Hall, 1978.

Emery, Michael, and Edwin Emery. *The Press and America: An Interpretive History of the Mass Media* (7th ed.). Englewood Cliffs, N.J.: Prentice Hall, 1992.

Fink, Leon. *In Search of the Working Class: Essays in American Labor History and Political Culture*. Urbana: University of Illinois Press, 1994.

Folkerts, Jean, and Dwight L. Teeter. *Voices of a Nation: A History of the Media in the United States* (2d ed.). New York: Macmillan, 1994.

Gans, Herbert. *Deciding What's News: A Study of CBS Evening News, NBC Nightly News, Newsweek and Time*. New York: Vintage, 1980.

Gerbner, George. "Mass Media and Human Communication Theory." In *Sociology of Mass Communications*, ed. Denis McQuail, 35-58. Harmondsworth: Penguin, 1972.

Ghiglione, Loren. *The American Journalist: Paradox of the Press*. Washington, D.C.: Library of Congress, 1990.

Good, Howard. *Outcasts: The Image of Journalists in Contemporary Film*. Metuchen, N.J.: Scarecrow, 1989.

Gordon, George N. *The Communications Revolution: A History of Mass Media in the United States*. New York: Hastings, 1977.

Gutman, Herbert. *Culture and Society in Industrializing America: Essays in American Working-Class and Social History*. New York: Knopf, 1976.

Hardt, Hanno. "The Foreign-Language Press in American Press History." *Journal of Communication* 38, no. 2 (1989): 114-31.

———. "Newsworkers, Technology, and Journalism History." *Critical Studies in Mass Communication* 7, no. 4 (1990): 346-65.

———. *Critical Communication Studies: Communication, History and Theory in America*. London: Routledge, 1992.

Hardt, Hanno, and Bonnie Brennen. "Communication and the Question of History." *Communication Theory* 3, no. 2 (1993): 130-71.

Harzig, Christiane, and Dirk Hoerder, eds. *The Press of Labor Migrants in Europe and North America, 1880s to 1930s*. Bremen: Labor Newspaper Preservation Project, 1985.

Hobsbawm, Eric. *Workers: Worlds of Labor*. New York: Pantheon, 1984.

Hoerder, Dirk, and Christiane Harzig, eds. *The Immigrant Labor Press in North America, 1840-1970s: An Annotated Bibliography* (3 vols.). Westport, Conn.: Greenwood, 1987.

Hofstadter, Richard. *The Age of Reform: From Bryan to F.D.R.* New York: Vintage, 1955.

Hudson, Frederic. *Journalism in the United States from 1690 to 1872*. New York: Harper, 1873.

International Labor Office. *Conditions of Work and Life of Journalists* (Studies and Reports, Series L, Professional Workers, No. 1). Geneva: International Labor Office, 1928.

Johnstone, John W. C., Edward J. Slawski, and William W. Bowman. *The News People: A Sociological Portrait of American Journalists and Their Work*. Urbana: University of Illinois Press, 1976.

Jones, Robert W. *Journalism in the United States*. New York: Dutton, 1947.

Kobre, Sidney. "The Sociological Approach in Research in Newspaper History." *Journalism Quarterly* 22, no. 1 (1945): 12-22.

Lafky, Sue. "Women Journalists." In *The American Journalist: A Portrait of U.S. News People and Their Work*, ed. David H. Weaver and G. Cleveland Wilhoit, 160-81, 255-57. Bloomington: Indiana University Press, 1991.

Leab, Daniel J. *A Union of Individuals: The Formation of the American Newspaper Guild, 1933-1936*. New York: Columbia University Press, 1970.

Lee, Alfred McClung. *The Daily Newspaper in America: The Evolution of a Social Instrument.* New York: Macmillan, 1937.

Lee, James L. *History of American Journalism* (rev. ed.). Boston: Houghton Mifflin, 1923.

Lindstrom, Charles E. *The Fading of the American Newspaper.* Garden City, N.Y.: Doubleday, 1960.

Marzolf, Marion. "Operationalizing Carey: An Approach to the Cultural History of Journalism." *Journalism History* 2, no. 2 (1975): 42-43.

——. *Up from the Footnote: A History of Women Journalists.* New York: Hastings, 1977.

——. "American Studies: Ideas for Media Historians." *Journalism History* 5, no. 1 (1978): cover, 13-16.

McIntyre, Jerilyn. *The "Industrial Worker" and the San Diego Free Speech Fight: A Study in Working-Class Consciousness.* Columbia, Mo.: Max Eastman Society, 1981.

McKerns, Joseph P. "The Limits of Progressive Journalism History." *Journalism History* 4, no. 3 (1977): 88-92.

Miller, Sally, ed. *The Ethnic Press in the United States: A Historical Analysis and Handbook.* Westport, Conn.: Greenwood, 1987.

Mills, Kay. *A Place in the News: From the Women's Pages to the Front Page.* New York: Dodd, Mead, 1988.

Morrison, Joseph L. "On 'Irrelevant' History." *Journalism Quarterly* 47, no. 4 (1970): 817-18.

Mott, Frank Luther. *American Journalism: A History: 1690-1960.* New York: Macmillan, 1962.

Murphy, James, and Sharon M. Murphy. *Let My People Know: American Indian Journalism.* Norman: University of Oklahoma Press, 1981.

Nerone, John. "The Problem of Teaching Journalism History." *Journalism Educator* 45 (Autumn 1990): 16-24.

——. "Theory and History." *Communication Theory* 3, no. 2 (1993): 148-57.

Nevins, Alan. "American Journalism and Its Historical Treatment." *Journalism Quarterly* 36, no. 4 (1959): 411-22, 519.

Nord, David Paul. "A Plea for Journalism History." *Journalism History* 15, no. 1 (1988): 8-15.

Nord, David Paul, and Harold L. Nelson. "The Logic of Historical Research." In *Research Methods in Mass Communication*, ed. Guido H. Stempel III and Bruce H. Westley, 278-304. Englewood Cliffs, N.J.: Prentice Hall, 1981.

Park, Robert. *The Immigrant Press and Its Control.* New York: Harper, 1922.

Payne, George Henry. *History of Journalism in the United States.* New York: Appleton, 1920.

Price, Warren C. *The Literature of Journalism: An Annotated Bibliography.* Minneapolis: University of Minnesota Press, 1959.

Price, Warren C., and Calder M. Pickett. *An Annotated Bibliography, 1958-1968.* Minneapolis: University of Minnesota Press, 1970.

Riley, Sam, ed. *American Magazine Journalists, 1741-1850.* Detroit: Gale Research, 1988.

——, ed. *American Magazine Journalists, 1850-1900.* Detroit: Gale Research, 1989.

Robinson, James Harvey. *The New History.* New York: Macmillan, 1912.

Ross, Ishbell. *Ladies of the Press: The Story of Women in Journalism by an Insider.* New York: Harper, 1936.

Salcetti, Marianne. "Competing for Control of Newsworkers: Definitional Battles between the Newspaper Guild and the American Newspaper Publishers Association, 1937-1938." Ph.D. diss., University of Iowa, 1992.

Sanders, Marlene, and Marcia Rock. *Waiting for Primetime: The Women of Television News.* Urbana: University of Illinois Press, 1988.

Schiller, Daniel. *Objectivity and the News: The Public and the Rise of Commercial Journalism.* Philadelphia: University of Pennsylvania Press, 1981.

Schlesinger, Arthur M. *The Rise of the City, 1878-1898*. New York: Macmillan, 1933.

———. *Prelude to Independence: The Newspaper War on Britain, 1764-1776*. New York: Knopf, 1958.

Schudson, Michael. *Discovering the News: A Social History of American Newspapers*. New York: Basic Books, 1978.

Seldes, George. *Lords of the Press*. New York: Julian Messner, 1938.

Sloan, William David, James G. Stovall, and James D. Startt. *The Media in America: A History*. Worthington, Oh.: Publishing Horizons, 1989.

Smythe, Ted Curtis. "The Reporter, 1890-1900: Working Conditions and Their Influence on the News." *Journalism History* 7, no. 1 (1980): 1-10. Reprinted in *Media Voices: An Historical Perspective*, ed. Jean Folkerts, 214-31. New York: Macmillan, 1992.

Solomon, William S. "The Contours of Media History." In *Ruthless Criticism: New Perspectives in U.S. Communication History,* ed. William S. Solomon and Robert W. McChesney, 1-6. Minneapolis: University of Minnesota Press, 1993.

Solomon, William S., and Robert W. McChesney, eds. *Ruthless Criticism: New Perspectives in U.S. Communication History*. Minneapolis: University of Minnesota Press, 1993.

Stearns, Peter N. "The Old Social History and the New." In *Encyclopedia of American Social History* (Vol. 1), ed. Mary Kupiec, Mary Cayton, Elliott J. Gorn, and Peter W. Williams, 237-50. New York: Scribner's, 1993.

Stevens, John, and Hazel Dickens-Garcia. *Communication History*. Beverly Hills: Sage, 1980.

Taft, William H. *Encyclopedia of Twentieth Century Journalists*. New York: Garland, 1986.

Tebbel, John. *The Compact History of the American Newspaper*. New York: Hawthorn, 1969.

Thompson, E. P. *The Making of the English Working Class*. London: Golancz, 1963.

———. "Eighteenth-Century English Society: Class Struggle without Class." *Social History* 3 (May 1978): 146-50.

Turner, Frederick Jackson. "Problems in American History," in *The Early Writings of Frederick Jackson Turner,* comp. Everett E. Edwards. Madison: University of Wisconsin Press, 1939.

UCLA Oral History Project. "Newspaper Reporting in the Twenties: Reflections." Oral history of Arnold B. Larson, interviewed in 1965 and 1966 by Elizabeth Dixon. Collection number 300/79 (1970).

Ward, Jean. "Interdisciplinary Research and Journalism Historians." *Journalism History* 5 (Spring 1978): cover, 17-19.

Weaver, David H., and G. Cleveland Wilhoit, eds. *The American Journalist: A Portrait of U.S. News People and Their Work* (2d ed.). Bloomington: Indiana University Press, 1991.

Wernick, Andrew. "The Promotional University." In *Promotional Culture: Advertising, Ideology and Symbolic Expression*, 154-80. London: Sage, 1991.

Williams, Raymond. *Resources of Hope*. London: Verso, 1989.

Wolseley, Roland E. *The Black Press, USA*. Ames: Iowa State University Press, 1990.

Wolseley, Roland E., and Isabel Wolseley. *The Journalist's Bookshelf: An Annotated and Selected Bibliography of United States Print Journalism*. Indianapolis: Berg, 1986.

Yodelis Smith, MaryAnn. "The Method of History." In *Research Methods in Mass Communication,* ed. Guido H. Stempel III and Bruce H. Westley, 305-19. Englewood Cliffs, N.J.: Prentice Hall, 1981.

Zinn, Howard. *The Politics of History*. Boston: Beacon, 1970.

———. *A People's History of the United States*. New York: Harper & Row, 1980.

Zynda, Thomas H. "The Hollywood Version: Movie Portrayals of the Press." *Journalism History* 6, no. 1 (1979): 16-25, 32.

# 2 / Discursive Strategies of Exclusion

## *The Ideological Construction of Newsworkers*

Elizabeth (Elli) Lester

Undergraduate journalism education prepares and socializes prospective journalists to enter the workplace in highly specific ways. Through classroom instruction, choices of textbooks, internship programs, campus newspapers, radio stations, and other outlets, students are instructed in the techniques and practices of journalism and how to think about their future as workers. There is frequently a journalism history course, among required courses in the curriculum, that purports to place journalism and journalists in a broader social, cultural, and historical context.

This essay examines journalism history textbooks from the point of view of their construction of journalistic workers within the industry. Because this is a textual analysis, a close reading of one exemplar journalism history text, with ancillary notations on others, it does not take into account the other types of instruction to which students are exposed. Although this is an omission, textbooks serve as a more permanent mode of instruction than others, remaining tangible when classroom instruction and other forms are only memories. Textbooks are (quite literally) solid reminders and touchstones that provide concrete memory, raise and answer specific questions while excluding others, and to a large extent usually direct both classroom instruction and student attention. On one level, textbooks themselves represent institutions (publishing and the academy, to name two) and thus provide an opportunity to analyze the stakes that other institutions have invested in journalism and journalism education. Furthermore, journalism history encompasses other forms of journalism instruction, providing the basis for understanding current normative practices such as the divisions between "hard" and "soft" news, between news and entertainment, and among journalism, public relations, and advertising.

The form of textual analysis incorporated in this essay follows principles articulated by Stuart Hall.[1] An exemplar text is examined for certain discursive strategies that work to construct both a specific ideology of journalists and a preferred reader of the text itself, the prospective journalist instead of a critical citizen. The findings discussed here indicate that journalism history textbooks utilize liberal journalism values of "progressivism" and "objectivity," along with strategies of omission, anthropomorphism, and romanticism, to construct workers in contradictory ways. They appear as professionals and as such have specific social obligations as well as job responsibilities; they are also invisible, the supporting cast or chorus line to the great men (and a few great women) editors, publishers, and owners, and of secondary importance to media technology. Such construction precludes a working-class interpretation that would focus on journalists' partnership with others such as printers, office workers, and technicians, and therefore alienates prospective journalists from their real class basis and interests. In other words, liberal or Progressive history is extremely problematic because it seamlessly *presents* its narrative, obfuscating its actual task of *representation* (Carey 1974; McKerns 1977).

Representation of journalism history has several consequences: it helps shape the actual content of the news, structures labor relations, and directs students' attention toward specific aspects of the industry and away from others. At a time in United States history when media ownership is becoming increasingly concentrated, workers' salaries remain low, fewer jobs are available, and labor has been attacked in the liberal press as well as in other sectors of society, this type of education has implications for the propaganda machine of the powers that be, the same institution that is normatively constructed as a watchdog over the powerful.

Previous studies indicate that Herman and Chomsky's (1988) propaganda model of the press has been ignored in journalism research, to the detriment of the advancement of that research (Lester 1992). Although their model does not specifically address journalism education, it has implications for an analysis of textbooks. Herman and Chomsky's propaganda model utilizes five specific news filters: economic situation of the media; advertising as the primary source of media income; media's reliance on government, business, and expert sources; "flak" as a means of control; and anticommunism as a dominant ideology. These filters may be seen to offer insight into the construction of textbooks in the field of journalism history as well as into the practice of journalism itself. Not surprisingly, in fact, the history of U.S. journalism is the history of how competing discourses and practices within the field emerged into today's dominant journalistic discourse and practice. The history that is told in textbooks mirrors the news that is reported in the media, inasmuch as it is the history of business and government rather than the history of working people. In addition, the history that is told is the winning version of history: dominant journalistic practices are not unrelated to those incorporated in the writing of textbooks. Both, of course, are forms of mass media and part of a broadly construed culture industry.

Textbooks often remain taken-for-granted purveyors of normative principles and values in any particular field. Most often used in large or introductory courses, they are standard bearers, providing guides or touchstones for more in-depth study. Thus, in one sense, they almost by definition present the conventional views of any particular discipline.

In her study of the construction of gender in news reporting textbooks from 1890 to 1990, Linda Steiner (1992) offers insights into previous journalism textbook research and appropriate methods for such study, as well as into the construction of gender. She explains:

> Textbooks socialize students by articulating and re-producing disciplinary paradigms. They emphasize rather than challenge prevailing definitions; they dramatize, not undermine, conventional practices and relations of power. Conversely, the issues they do not engage do not exist as issues. . . . Textbooks' role in the academic training of reporters has always been significant, if understudied. This is no less true now, when over 80 percent of the college graduates being hired by newspapers are journalism majors. (1)

Steiner's study is one of very few that treats journalism textbooks seriously, according them their full weight as part of the ideological and pedagogical apparatus that socializes as well as instructs. She points out:

> Taken collectively, journalism textbooks document what has been described and prescribed to students not only about what is newsworthy and how to report news, but also who can or should report the news and what personal attributes reporters need for success. (1)

Steiner focuses on issues of gender and how or if women are written into newswork through textbooks. She offers a chronological analysis of journalism textbooks, thus suggesting at first implicitly and finally explicitly that she is looking for "improvement" in the treatment of women:

> The history of newswriting and reporting textbooks shows consid-
> erable progress, given the initial and long-continuing overt hostility
> to women. Textbooks' presentation of the connections between so-
> cial identity and professional behavior are being pushed by feminists
> toward further changes. (32)

Her interpretation "emerges from dense readings grounded in extensive quo-
tations" (3), but she does not offer a systematic textual understanding. Despite
the lack of quantitative analysis, Steiner's is a content analysis that considers
the surface, manifest meanings of textbook copy.

Steiner's notion of improvement over time also suggests support for a
liberal or Progressive model of history that always presupposes that "good"
will eventually triumph, good in this case being recognition of women's roles
in journalism. Furthermore, when such progress does not occur, it is incum-
bent upon the marginalized group to insist on change. Progressivism tends to
inhibit a more structural account of the ideological.

In contrast, this study offers a textual analysis that identifies discursive
strategies that structure the text. These strategies are used tactically to present
a highly constructed vision as an obvious or natural one. Thus, rather than
consider many textbooks, one exemplar text has been chosen to analyze in
depth. *The Press and America: An Interpretive History of the Mass Media,* by
Michael Emery and Edwin Emery was chosen as exemplar because of its
coverage of journalism history and its extensive and persistent use in classrooms over time. The seventh edition of this popular textbook, which is
known as *PAA,* was published in 1992 by Prentice Hall, a major college
textbook publishing company.

Once *PAA* was chosen as the exemplar, another reading of the text, a
"long, preliminary soak," suggested specific discursive strategies for more in-
tensive analysis. Analyzing such strategies can reveal how a text makes meaning and how meaning is structured to both privilege a specific reading and to
actively construct a reader. Organizational aspects of the text, the use of particular illustrations and typeface as well as verbal aspects were also taken into
account, although greater weight was accorded to the verbal.

The thesis that working-class interpretations are precluded from journalism history textbooks, and that therefore prospective journalists may be
alienated from their class interests, necessitates a specific understanding of the
concepts of alienation, the working class, and false consciousness, along with

such related concepts as productive labor and intellectual work. A problem in understanding the real position of journalists under capitalism is that journalists tangentially engaged in intellectual work are also wage laborers employed by capitalists.

*Alienation* in this context means separation of the worker from the means of production on the one hand and from his or her own life activity on the other. The latter part of this definition then embraces the product of labor but also solidarity with other workers and, explicitly, healthy knowledge of oneself. *The working class* refers here equally to wage and salaried workers engaged in (re)productive labor, including labor that produces ideas, consciousness, or culture; and, although most journalists may not be intellectuals in a more general sense, they are specifically engaged in intellectual production.

*False consciousness* is central to this reading of texts even though it is in some sense an outmoded or incomplete way of dealing with the concept of ideology. The concept of false consciousness captures the meaning of ideology as it relates to alienation on the one hand and to real but often hidden material conditions on the other.

The model of journalism that is both described and promoted in *PAA* depends on the finessing of language, so that terms such as *media, press, communication, free,* and *truth* are presented opaquely, untheorized and therefore unproblematized. Liberal journalism's normative purpose, whatever small or large permutations it may encounter, is to fulfill the needs of "the people." This perspective is well illustrated in the final chapter of *PAA*:

> In this age of power and influence it was incumbent upon the men and women who worked in the rush of technological change not to forget that the freedom to speak and write the truth is never secure, never certain, always capable of being lost. (Emery and Emery 1992, 600)

The discourse of liberal journalism permeates this history of journalism; through the strategies of omission, anthropomorphism, Progressivism, objectivity, and romanticism, the text evades issues that lie outside the boundaries of dominant ideology.

The narrative structure of history is articulated in the preface to *PAA*. The use of narrative structure, with its attendant elements of voice, character, and plot development, thematic development, denouement, and resolution, helps construct a history that appears to move naturally toward a goal. The omniscient voice of the authors lulls or soothes the reader into acceptance of both the voice and the plot:

> Journalism history is the story of humanity's long struggle to com-
> municate: to discover and interpret news . . . in the marketplace of
> ideas. Part of the story has as its theme the continuing efforts by
> men and women to break down . . . barriers. . . . Another aspect of
> the story is concerned with the means . . . by which essential news,
> opinion and other desired information reached the public. . . . Just
> as important to this story are the heroes and villains, as well as the
> bit actors, who made the world of communication what it is
> today. Finally, all of this becomes truly meaningful when the de-
> velopment of America's journalism is related to the progress of its
> people. (vii)

Emery and Emery make the story of journalism history the epic tale of "humanity's long struggle," where heroes, villains, and bit actors all play their parts.
"Journalism is related to the progress of . . . people" rather than to relationships
between institutions and classes. The preface promises an exciting if wholly
predictable story that chronicles the progress toward the development of
something already understood—that is, properly liberal social relations. The
history, as it unfolds, focuses on the leaders of institutions, certainly cast as heroes and villains, but—if one wishes to extend the metaphor of the stage—the
chorus of working journalists and others engaged in manual and office labor is
absent.

This method of history and representation is synchronic: it limits timed
experience to a series of events that unfolds. A diachronic interpretation, in
contrast, might suggest a constant dialectic and the possibility of the inter-
ruption of "events," with therefore challenged and unpredictable outcomes.
Synchronicity suggests that history is "always already" told, not necessarily in
terms of concrete events but in terms of movement toward a goal. Diachrony
actually would help predict concrete events but eliminates the need for an
"always already" ideal end.

The Emerys' interpretive history of the press treats the press itself as the
subject, rather than the object, of study, equating stars with institutions; thus
the institutions are anthropomorphized, with only specific classes of workers—owners and stars—being treated as visible or significant. The "press" as
an institution is treated anthropomorphically, and real workers other than
"star" journalists are treated as objects. It is clear from the chapter titles in
*PAA* that the institution itself is endowed with agency. Titles such as "The
Surviving Newspaper Press," "Television Takes Center Stage," and "The Heritage of the American Press" suggest that the press itself (or the media more
generally) contains life and thus is susceptible to ill health and recovery, thes-

pian proclivities, and a genealogy. Again, this strategy precludes interpretive history from becoming a dynamic history of human actors.

The first sentence of Emery and Emery's preface establishes the human-like qualities of the press: "Journalism history is the story of humanity's long struggle to communicate" (vii). Although this is certainly hyperbole, it also mystifies the particular nature of the inquiry—that is, the specific history of the press and mass media in the United States—conflating it with a much broader study where journalism history is equivalent to humanity's history. The claim, made later in the preface, that "the book surveys landmark events in communications history, probing significant issues, personalities, and media organizations, all the while tracing how major events in American history were covered" raises the central question of this analysis: who and what coalition of interests define the terms *landmark, communications history*, and so forth, and how do those definers create a specific version of U.S. media history?

Linked to the agency of the press are visible heroes and stars: publishers, editors, and political columnists. Rank-and-file newsworkers are referred to anonymously, often only with passing references to the numbers of reporters represented on particular staffs. The technology of the media, on the other hand, is discussed in great detail; apparently, the development of particular technological innovations is judged to be of greater importance than the lived experiences of working anonymous journalists (Hardt 1990).

It is common practice in media history texts to link mass media practices to communication practices of ancient times.[2] *PAA* similarly claims that American press history had its germination "at least 10,000 years ago" in the Middle East and Asia. This linkage is a textbook convention, but a questionable one, for it establishes a mythical stability to the object of study, which here has become the subject, that suggests a certain seamlessness with a distant exoticized past. The burden of proof should lie with the historian to show a link with "the earliest known news writers" of 59 B.C. to A.D. 222, rather than glossing the supposed connection. Thus, the press—and, even more, the journalistic work of representing such information—is turned into a timeless activity of human nature rather than discussed as a historically specific one embedded in social relations. What has changed most substantively, then, is simply available technology. This is but one example of how the discourse of progressivism alienates the reader from an understanding of the effects of reality, that is, through the practice of exoticizing unfamiliar activities, objects, or people.

The final chapter of *PAA*, "Media Technology: The Challenge of the

1990s," captures most of the key themes of the textbook: new technology, big business, and simple dichotomies of socioeconomic status (rather than a dialectical analysis of class). In this chapter journalists are briefly held accountable for "their faults" (601), but twenty-nine pages of the thirty-four-page chapter are devoted to descriptions of new technology and corporate involvement:

> From the first thoughts of Gutenberg to the computerized newsroom, the implications of printing technology had enormous impact. By the 1990s those involved with the distribution of printed information had quickly integrated themselves with the emerging broadcast technology....newspaper publishers moved into ownership positions. (572)

> Another improvement in communications came with the gradual installation of optical fiber systems. (577)

Here the text again demonstrates the seamless, even inevitable connection between present-day technology and the "thoughts" of Gutenberg, along with the notion that technology necessarily "improves" communication. Communication is reduced to its technological component, a component the ownership of which requires significant capital. The stars of present-day media are described, like those in the past, in ironic tones that are ultimately admiring:

> Murdoch, Ted Turner, and Allen Neuharth were the three most controversial media owners, because of their enormous personal wealth, their unsatiated appetites for purchases, and their peculiar personalities. Murdoch, ruthless to the core if he had to be when dealing with employees, also could be the charming Australian. Turner, the sailboating playboy, was the unpredictable daredevil who took risks with his holdings. Neuharth was the flamboyant chairman of Gannett's board. (579-80)

The individuals discussed in the final chapter, the history of the present and the recent past, are presented as exemplars of the human face of the press. However, the presentation of stars is highly individualistic, focusing, for example, on personality quirks as a way of analyzing journalism history. Descriptions of journalists' current working conditions, employment expectations, or any other evidence that would suggest the activities of the women and men who actually gather and write the news, or any analysis of their relationships with the stars, institutions, or technology, are entirely absent.

In what follows, each discursive strategy with the exception of "omission" is noted in turn, although the separation is for analytic purposes only.

Omissions are pointed out throughout the following discussion, and linked to the other three discursive strategies.

Anthropomorphism as a discursive strategy accomplishes more than simply linking inanimate objects with human beings; it tends also to link human beings with objects in an indirect, particularly pernicious way. Even the expression of the principal journalistic ideal, a "free press," suggests that the institution possesses an ability that is extrasocial. Other, less dramatic, examples of anthropomorphizing the press are illustrated in chapter subtitles such as the "Growth of the Press," "The Press Moves Westward," "Genesis of the Associated Press," and "The Black Press Survives." In each of these a metaphor of life or growth confers a status on an institution that suggests the institution itself possesses animation. When an inanimate object apparently possesses the characteristics of a living creature, the status of the creature is removed.

This textual process occurs after the anthropomorphizing subtitle. For instance, in the case of "The Black Press Grows," the description of the black press that follows defines black newspapers as those "owned and edited by blacks for black readers" (228). A list of such papers, each identified with a title, city of origin, owner's name, and editorial stance, is then featured. The working conditions of the reporters for these newspapers are not mentioned at all; in fact, a reading of this section does not make it clear that these newspapers had staff other than ownership. But Emery and Emery write about the institutions themselves as if they were human: "Criticizing the more affluent blacks for not doing enough to help the poor, the *Tribune* organized charities and scholarship programs as a part of its community responsibility" (228). The process of anthropomorphizing institutions obscures the real social, cultural, political, and economic actions that accompany what appear in the text to be responses of institutions. The gloss of "community responsibility" neglects the legitimate questions of which community and to whom and by whom responsibility is owed.

Another example of anthropomorphism is found in the chapter "Television Takes Center Stage," with its subheading "Television Shapes the 1952 Campaign." The use of commonplace metaphors and clichés (e.g., "shapes" and "takes center stage") again accomplishes a specific task: that of obscuring processes that were initiated by people and omitting any discussion of workers. This chapter presents evidence that television was becoming a dominant journalistic force in the early 1950s, calling the time "TV's Golden Age" (367). And, following the established textbook format, the chapter highlights stars such as Edward R. Murrow and Huntley and Brinkley, portraying the former as a lone activist against the forces of reaction. It is the stars and the technology that occupy the text's space and the reader's attention. Missing is any discussion of the impact of changing technology on the workplace, on workers and prospective workers, or on accessibility of information to audiences. The impact of changing technology on business interests is discussed in detail. Again, in a section that begins, "Television had written radio's obituary" (372), technology is endowed with human qualities.

Anthropomorphism includes the discursive endowment of objects with the ability to give birth; for example, "United Press spawned some legendary newspeople" (376). Such metaphors detract from an appreciation of the working conditions, struggles, and practices of people, eliminating the possibility of personal rejuvenation or class warfare. When objects or institutions are endowed with animation, certain questions go unasked: Who created the legends around specific newspeople? What constitutes legendary status? What institutional biases either constrained or encouraged "excellence" in news reporting?

The strategy of progressivism is linked with the news value of objectivity and a philosophical orientation toward empiricism. Presenting history as "progressive" compels the history to be read as a step-by-step journey in a generally positive direction, with the specific implication that through linear time, the subject of study improves. Raymond Williams (1983) describes the genealogy of the concept of progressivism in a way that is suggestive for its usage here, and furthermore shows how it has come to be held as a positive value by conservatives, liberals, and (some) leftists. Thus, its power as a strategy is enhanced by its overwhelmingly positive connotations.

In *PAA,* the story of "great men" is counterposed with the story of enumeration: how many newspapers, how large their staffs, how many women, how many African American-owned papers. The *one* is opposed to the *many* in such a way as to suggest that in terms of the working journalist, access to greatness is simply a matter of individual ability.

Early in the text, in their description of the period of American colonialism, Emery and Emery link the press specifically with commerce; indeed, they call commerce the "forerunner of the press" (18). They treat the notion that there is a causal link between commerce and the development of a "popular press" as fait accompli, rather than as a research question or hypothesis. In other words, they appear to make an assumption that a popular press in fact is the predestined outcome and that commerce is a necessary stimulant. Furthermore, they introduce the assumption that a "free press" is an "objective" one without so much as a question:

> Some historians have called this period the "Dark Ages of Journal-
> ism," because of the scurrility of the press. This was a transition
> period, however, and perhaps violent partisanship, as reflected in the
> press, was a means of expending some of the venom stored up
> against the British after the war. (67)

It is an unspoken base point that a partisan press, although understandable
within specific historical conditions, is a phase in the development of a free
and objective one, a "transition." In the closing paragraphs of the same chapter, Emery and Emery assert that the role of the press is the promotion of
"every principle which leads to the achievement of our independence" (71).

According to the text, the initiation of "modern" journalism was the period of the latter part of the nineteenth century. "The editorial staff...had
taken recognizable modern form by 1890 in numbers and in departmental-
ized activities" (177). Later, the authors credit the "arrival of modern journalism" to the "expansion of the editorial staff and its news-gathering activities"
(183), but the major subjects addressed are technology and what the authors
single out as "the business side" (183).

Development is treated as a positive "good," a perspective dictated by the
epistemology of liberalism or Progressivism. Press development means
"growth"—primarily technological and economic. "Efforts to Improve," a
subtitle of chapter 19, suggests that the press is moving away from its gross partisanship toward a more neutral, professional, and businesslike establishment:

> [Those within the profession began] improving professional work-
> ing conditions, establishing effective media associations, writing vol-
> untary codes of conduct, developing professional organizations de-
> voted to the high purposes of journalism, encouraging education
> for journalism, supporting studies of the press, sponsoring press
> councils and journalism reviews, improving the status of minorities
> and women in the profession, and defending the press against legal
> and governmental pressures. (508-9)

The task of this sort of writing is to suggest continual onward movement toward an ideal; the notion of an ultimate goal is foreshadowed by words such
as "improving," "professional," "developing," and "defending." These forms of
speech connote both stasis and movement, the permanency of the established
goal and the constancy of movement toward it.

Discussion of the strategy of romanticism in *PAA* provides a way to
highlight the seamlessness of the joining of this particular text to the broader
public version of history current in society, its resistance to contrary readings.

Bommes and Wright (1982) argue that there are particular ways in which "the past" is "written into present social reality," noting especially how social relations are categorized and dichotomized as either public or private. They point out:

> The word "public" is...applied to a welter of different objects, ideas and practices: the public house, publication, the public event and image, public buildings, the public interest etc. Against this, the main events of social life are customarily understood to be private: the family, but also through the legal definition of work, the experience of production itself. (258)

The significance of this statement is that workers are constructed as private individuals rather than as cohering as a class; thus, "working-class interests...cannot appear in a qualitatively different public form [from that of the bourgeois public]....Legitimation [of interests] is structurally weighted from the start" (262-63).

Romanticism as a discursive strategy reveals that history is staged in the text, rather than analyzed as a product of real relations of experience. As mentioned previously, this text constructs its stage as world history "spanning all continents and at least 10,000 years" (Emery and Emery 1992, 1):

> A series of developments in printing and writing, beginning in the Middle East and Asia, slowly spreading to Europe and finally to America, led to today's marvelous linkage of reporting talent, computers, high-speed color presses and satellites. (1)

With such an introduction, it is difficult to conceive of any alternative; all alternative readings are closed off by this lack of interpretation. Ancient artifacts are labeled as "enlightened" (1), already suggestive of the development of "the most novel product of the printing press" (3), that is, the newspaper, dated some 1,700 years later. As described in the text:

> Telling the story of those newspapers and their printers and writers is a major theme of this book. Later the story of the print media merges with those of the visual and electronic media, equally important today. (3)

The introduction to chapter 11, "Bastions of News Enterprise" provides an example of how the story of the major theme is told: the format links "famous" newspaper with colorful personality, usually its owner or managing editor. James Gordon Bennett is described as "tall, slender, full of nervous energy, but bearing himself with a military erectness accented by steel-gray hair and moustache" (240). Carr Van Anda is represented as "not a colorful, dynamic leader; rather he was reserved and cold in appearance and his piercing gaze was called the 'Van Anda death ray'" (237). These personal details individualize and romanticize; they provide human-interest news value to a historical period, but they also orient historical attention away from other sorts of details. Fundamentally, this orientation is toward property and away from work. Even the use of the word "bastion" in the chapter title connotes a permanent stronghold from which variation is unlikely and to which others must aspire.

Emery and Emery describe the period of the early twentieth century as one that "completely altered the pattern of life that a comparatively peaceful nineteenth century had produced" (251). They describe the war of 1914–17 as a "world war... [in which] the United States [embarked] on a 'great crusade' to make the world safe for democracy" (251). What follows in the text are literary descriptions of Europe: kings mounted on horses wearing scarlet uniforms, beplumed and gold-braided riders signifying empires, and so forth. The language evokes a colorful array of images with which the press, in its role as reporter on world war events, is then inextricably linked.

High technology is also romanticized. The authors call the 1990s the "age of electronic marvels" (567), and the power of that age is enormous: "The world's largest corporations took the lead... investing uncounted billions"; "the integration... of the electronic circuit... turned the media world upside down" (567). The text presents technology as magnificent; the authors do not neglect to mention concomitant "moral and ethical problems," but they view technology as magnificent and irresistible nonetheless.

The issues at stake in the presentation of ideological material through textbooks are both intellectual and pedagogical: intellectual in the sense that a textbook may represent current mainstream thinking on a particular subject, especially, but not only, to its market of college students; pedagogical in the sense that the textbook is a tool that teaches both its subject matter and a way of approaching understandings more generally. If it takes a linear approach to its subject matter, it teaches that linearity is an appropriate mode of intellectual discourse. If it presents itself as objective, it teaches that objectivity is a desirable and perhaps necessary mode of interpreting evidence. And, although any particular reader can read the text from a position of opposition or resistance, the text itself constructs a proper (preferable) position from which to grasp its meaning. Furthermore, especially in larger undergraduate classes, the textbook is considered as authoritative, rather than simply as one piece of historical evidence to be interrogated. Thus, the notion of the "preferred reader" is of the utmost importance. The naturalizing function of the textbook discourages the preferred reader from noticing ideological discourses and the possibilities of resistance readings. In part this is also a function of other institutions, such as the semester or quarter teaching systems, in which vast amounts of material must be "covered" in relatively short amounts of time, and in the context of competing demands. The reproductive work of *PAA* serves hegemonic needs of industry, academia, and the larger social formation.

It is noted above that "textbook discourse" is operative in *PAA* along with discourses specific to journalism history textbooks. Textbook discourse includes devices and practices such as the use of subheads to guide readers to material, and perhaps away from other material, the use of an omniscient third-person voice of narration, formal illustrations, and a strong thematic presentation of material with frequent references to a mythic past. In this sense, textbook discourse and the particular romanticism of journalism history textbooks overlap.

Choosing an exemplar text does not exclude awareness of other history textbooks that instruct prospective journalists and help socialize them into their role, whether as profession or working class. For example, the textbook *Voices of a Nation: A History of Media in the United States,* by Folkerts and Teeter (1989), takes a quite different perspective toward journalism history from that of *PAA,* one that attempts a more complex, multivocal analysis of that history, although it too is a conventional textbook in the senses outlined above (as perhaps it must be to compete in the marketplace). And yet, in spite of Folkerts and Teeter's attempt, the notion of journalists as belonging to the working class, and thus of having a deep real connection to workers in other industries, is obscured in their book by the notion of journalism as a profession.

Reporting, editing, broadcast news, and advertising textbooks portray a view of journalism that is also industry and skills oriented. Thus, none of the mainstream textbooks challenges the predominant view of journalism— even the advertising textbooks, which of course take a very different approach to media.

There are, of course, books that instruct prospective journalists in alternative ways. Raymond Williams' *The Long Revolution* (1963) remains one of the best histories of the press and its relationship to changes in both the social formation and individuals. It is not, however, an undergraduate text. Further, it focuses primarily on Britain and it situates the press within the social formation rather than extracting the press from it. However, it may present a model for a potential U.S. undergraduate text. The long and continuing work of Edward Herman and Noam Chomsky, covering most of the twentieth century, represents perhaps the best effort to analyze the position of the press within the U.S. social formation. Herman and Chomsky situate journalists within their political-economic context—that is, as wage laborers—but do not develop the history of journalists' position. Thus, their work provides a direct connection to and the space for a critical history of newsworkers. However, it has been ignored by a majority of mass communication researchers and it is highly doubtful it will be adopted widely in journalism history courses.

*Understanding News,* by John Hartley (1982), is a basic teaching book and part of a series of books on studies in communication that presents oppositional journalism and journalistic practice as a way of life. This series is designed to be read by beginning students:

> If readers can write better essays, produce better projects...I shall be very satisfied; but if they gain a new insight into how communication shapes and informs our social life, how it articulates and creates our experience of industrial society, then I shall be delighted. Communication is too often taken for granted when it should be taken to pieces. (Hartley 1982, xiii)

This introduction to a basic book is quite a contrast to the stated intentions of *PAA.* However, *Understanding News* cannot be considered as carrying the weight of *PAA* or the Folkerts and Teeter text, for several reasons. First, its publisher, Methuen, does not have equivalent textbook publisher status with Prentice Hall or Macmillan, Folkerts and Teeter's publisher. Second, it is written from a British point of view, which may make some potential U.S. adopters wary. And third, it presents a challenge to the establishment, and thus in some ways contradicts the assumptions of what journalism education is about.

In *PAA* there is a description of journalism education that makes the reasons for its inception clear:

> The ties between campus and city room were strengthened greatly in the second quarter of the twentieth century.... In this first period of journalism education, emphasis was placed on establishing technical courses....During the second phase of journalism education emphasis was placed on the study of journalism history and of the press as a social institution.... Closer ties between newspaperpeople and schools were established....Journalism schools in the 1990s were thus well established....They had close ties with the profession. (516-18)

This description of journalism education emphasizes the ties between industry and academia even as it attempts to show that an academic discipline has been delineated within the university community. But unlike other social sciences, the study of journalism essentially emphasizes skills and professional preparation, with critical perspectives generally reserved for marginalized attention. The analogous field of education, which, like journalism, is often taught separate from the arts and sciences curriculum, fosters a lively critical pedagogy with contributors from both academic departments and the "field." Furthermore, there is dynamic interaction between First and Third World educators that fosters the development of truly critical approaches. This stands in stark contrast to journalistic education and practice, in which the standards of a U.S. style "free" press exercise hegemony in spite of the existence of other models of journalism.

The discursive strategies described above construct a preferred reading of journalism history, a liberal view that holds that the real purpose of the press is to be a political watchdog. These strategies close the text in a way that overwhelms. By taking a perspective that favors industry, management, and technology over the lived experiences of working journalists and others, the text pushes a hegemonic reading. Furthermore, textbooks are themselves commodities, and there is fierce competition for their large but limited markets.

More important, these strategies construct a preferred reader. The reader, in this instance most likely a college student, is instructed to regard him- or herself in specific ways equally as much as he or she is instructed about the history of journalism. In other words, the text works hard to help produce working journalists who will understand their proper role within the workplace and will distinguish first of all between stars and others and second between intellectual workers and manual or clerical workers.

The problem with journalism history textbooks reflects the larger problem of journalism education, which is often regarded as primarily a skills or training program that, although taught within institutions that provide liberal arts education, serves the communication industries by helping them to recruit at least partially socialized members. Furthermore, as Hardt (1990) points out:

> The physical and ideological separation of journalists and printers created conditions of the workplace that enhanced the mechanisms of managerial control over...labor....
>
> ...the process of professionalization also affects the media's content and goals and suggests fundamental changes in the responsibilities of newsworkers and the nature of the press, which becomes

more interested in hearing its own authoritative voice echo in the public sphere than in producing an active and critical public. (360)

This process finds support in the pedagogy of journalism history, which, guided and encouraged by an authoritative text, tells students how to grasp the relationships embedded within the dynamics of history.

The discursive strategies flatten the history and then reshape it into a form that mirrors and nurtures power structures; they provide textual tactics for presenting material. They do indeed construct "an interpretive history of the mass media"—one in which the interests of industry and ownership are paramount.

Steiner (1992) suggests in her survey of textbooks regarding their treatment of women that the construction of gender both reflects and helps create a narrow acceptable space for women in journalism. My argument is that textbooks' treatment of class has a devastatingly alienating impact on the possibilities for working journalists to do other than contribute to a propaganda machine—albeit willingly and with the best of intentions to do otherwise.

The vision of the press, and of the news media more generally, that is constructed and then presented in journalism history textbooks belongs to an "invented tradition" where that phrase suggests a "set of practices...governed by overtly or tacitly accepted rules...which seek to inculcate certain values and norms of behaviour" (Hobsbawm 1983, 1). This set of journalistic practices is linked by the textbooks so that there is an established continuity with a suitable historic past. An examination of discursive strategies within the text can help readers, including students, understand the constructed nature of the text and the history of journalism history.

## Notes

1. In particular, see his analysis of mugging in *Policing the Crisis* (Hall et al. 1978) and his earlier methodological introduction to *Paper Voices* (1975).

2. See *Kleppner's Advertising Procedure* for an example outside of journalism in which the authors state that advertising is as old as civilization. As *PAA* describes these daily gazettes, they contained all the essentials of current daily newspapers and television magazines, such as "government decrees, legal notices, and...gladiatorial results" (Russell and Lane 1990, 3).

## References

Bommes, Michale, and Patrick Wright. "'Charms of Residence': The Public and the Past." In *Making Histories: Studies in History Writing and Politics,* ed. Richard Johnson et al. London: Hutchinson, 1982.

Carey, James W. "The Problem of Journalism History." *Journalism History* 1, no. 1 (1974): 3–5, 27.

Chomsky, Noam, and Edward S. Herman. *After the Cataclysm: Postwar Indochina and the Recon-struction of Imperial Ideology.* Boston: South End, 1979.

Emery, Michael, and Edwin Emery. *The Press and America: An Interpretive History of the Mass Media* (7th ed.). Englewood Cliffs, N.J.: Prentice Hall, 1992.

Folkerts, Jean, and Dwight L. Teeter. *Voices of a Nation: A History of Media in the United States.* New York: Macmillan, 1989.

Hall, Stuart. "Introduction." In *Paper Voices: the Popular Press and Social Change, 1935-1965,* ed. Anthony Charles H. Smith with Elizabeth Imirzi and Trevor Blackwell, 11-24. London: Chatto & Windus, 1975.

Hall, Stuart, Chas Critcher, Tony Jefferson, John Clarke, and Brian Roberts. *Policing the Crisis: Mugging, the State, and Law and Order.* New York: Holmes & Meier, 1978.

Hardt, Hanno. "Newsworkers, Technology, and Journalism History." *Critical Studies in Mass Communication* 7 (1990): 346-65.

Hartley, John. *Understanding News.* London: Methuen, 1982.

Herman, Edward S. *Beyond Hypocrisy: Decoding the News in an Age of Propaganda.* Boston: South End, 1992.

Herman, Edward S., and Noam Chomsky. *Manufacturing Consent: the Political Economy of the Mass Media.* New York: Pantheon, 1988.

Hobsbawm, Eric. "Introduction: Inventing Tradition." In *The Invention of Tradition,* ed. Eric Hobsbawm and Terence Ranger. Cambridge: Cambridge University Press, 1983.

Lester, Elli. "Manufactured Silence and the Politics of Media Research: A Consideration of the 'Propaganda Model.'" *Journal of Communication Inquiry* 16, no. 1 (1992): 45-55.

McKerns, Joseph P. "The Limits of Progressive Journalism History." *Journalism History* 4, no. 3 (1977): 88-92.

Russell, J. Thomas, and Ronald Lane. *Kleppner's Advertising Procedure* (11th ed.). Englewood Cliffs, N.J.: Prentice Hall, 1990.

Steiner, Linda. "Construction of Gender in Newsreporting Textbooks, 1890-1990." *Journalism Monographs* 135 (1992).

Williams, Raymond. *The Long Revolution: An Analysis of the Democratic, Industrial, and Cultural Changes Transforming Our Society.* New York: Columbia University Press, 1963.

———. *Keywords: A Vocabulary of Culture and Society.* New York: Oxford University Press, 1983.

# 3 / The Emergence of the Reporter

## Mechanization and the Devaluation of Editorial Workers

Marianne Salcetti

In his utopian dream of *Looking Backward,* Edward Bellamy (1887) character-ized the late nineteenth century as one of "profound pessimism as to the future of humanity," in which people were bound "from mental and physical absorption in working and scheming for mere bodily necessities" (238). Bellamy and others bemoaned the human cost of the mechanized changes occurring at that time in how work was accomplished, how and where peo-ple lived, and, ultimately, how American society was reshaped in the late nineteenth and early twentieth centuries.

Others embraced this era of inventiveness, as ever-increasing types and sizes of machines replaced forms of work previously done by hand. Machines served many purposes for their proponents: as economic and productivity predictors for work performed; as a glorification and celebration of social progress; and in cases like the following, as the cultural and artistic embodi-ment of the age itself.

> The mills of Minneapolis are as impressive as the cathedrals of France. There are places on the river where they group themselves into the same compositions, with the bridges below them, that I found years ago at Abli—only the color is different; the rosy red of the French brick is changed to dull concrete gray. (Center 1920, preface)

As machines entered most arenas of human activity, the mechanization factor, as Jacques Ellul (1964) has described it, became the standard by which most work was conducted, judged, and controlled: "The machine is solely, exclusively technique; it is pure technique one might say. For wherever a technical factor exists, it results, almost inevitably, in mechanization; technique transforms everything it touches into a machine" (4). This technological imperative by which work was defined and divided indelibly influenced the newspaper industry in the late nineteenth century, given the inventive prodigiousness of the time along with commercial and capital opportunities. This chapter takes a slightly different stance in its discussion of newswork, developing the notion that changes in how newswork was performed in the late nineteenth century reflect Ellul's notion that technique "constructs the kind of world the machine needs and induces order" (5). Newsworkers' labors were increasingly bordered, and in turn valued, by their technological place in the production process of gathering, writing, and producing news.

Also, the product of this industry—newspapers—were themselves democratic embodiments of what Daniel Boorstin (1973) characterized as "the newer forms of leveling in America." This "mass-producing the moment" offered access to more and different types of information, as presented in newspapers, with such a leveling impact that "none was more remarkable than the changed meaning of the moment" (359). Newspapers, and the mechanical advancements made during this time in their production and distribution, significantly altered the work of newspaper reporters and the public's expectations of that work. Machinery as an encroaching technique in the work of journalists also meant increased capital investments and eventual profits for newspaper publishers because: "The technology of the repeatable experience was self-propagating. Each step taken toward capturing, recording, and making replayable another aspect of experience opened the way and created a demand for still another improvement and still newer techniques" (379).

Numerous journalism historians (e.g., Emery, Lee, Bleyer, Mott) have characterized the late nineteenth century in American journalism as a time that still included the great editor-publisher, the rise of popular journalism, and increases in the literacy rate. They have also noted such factors as the completed western expansion, the rise of cities, and immigration, all of which contributed to increased numbers of newspapers and readers. Often their discussions have noted the technological advancements that occurred during this time in the newspaper industry.

What has come to be viewed as the modern newspaper reached its mechanical stride in the late 1880s: "The present-day newspaper is a machine-made product to a greater extent than ever before" (Bleyer 1927, 389). As Willard G. Bleyer observed in 1927, "The year 1890 marked a turning point in the evolution of the American newspaper" (392). By 1890, numerous technological changes within and outside the newspaper industry had influenced the content, production, distribution, and marketing of the newspaper product.

The preceding twenty-five years saw the refinement and increased use of the telegraph (1850s), the telephone (1880s), and the typewriter (1880s). All of these devices affected the work of newspaper reporters by changing the amount of time it took to gather the news and, in turn, produce a news story. The deadline of time was forever altered as reporters could obtain news faster and relay it more quickly to the newsroom, where a typed story was produced faster than a handwritten one, along with a reduction in composition costs (Mott 1962a, 499). In fact, the first news story phoned in to a newsroom concerned a lecture held in Alexander Graham Bell's laboratory in Salem. The story was published February 13, 1877, in the *Boston Globe,* with the byline, "Sent by telephone" (Jones 1947, 386).

Continued improvement in R. Hoe's printing press increased the ability to produce, by 1882, 24,000 twelve-page newspapers in one hour. In the mid-1880s, folders were developed to attach to presses to "cut, paste, fold, count, and deliver 24 pages at press speed" (Mott 1962a, 497). By the 1880s, stereotype plates enabled duplicate plates to be made for simultaneous printing on different presses and by 1900, the invention of the autoplate enabled stereotype plates to be cast and trimmed by machine (394, 396). By 1890, Otto Mergenthaler's linotype machine, which set news type mechanically, rather than by hand, was in newsrooms around the country. The linotype significantly reduced the cost of human labor in the printing part of the newspaper, as it increased the mechanical capabilities to produce the news once it was written.

Harold Adams Innis (1949) has noted that use of the linotype "was followed by a reduction in the cost of composition by one-half" (6). By 1896, the Bureau of Labor Statistics reported it cost $33.64 to set four newspaper pages by machine and $72.16 for the same task by hand (A. M. Lee 1937, 151). During this time the making of paper also changed, due to increased use of wood pulp over rag pulp in production of newsprint along with advances in both "size and speed" of the Fourdrinier papermaking machine (Mott 1962a, 498). Newsprint prices declined in the 1880s and 1890s to the point where a pound of newsprint cost 1.5 cents in 1897 (Innis 1949, 6).

Technology had reshaped so many phases of the newspaper industry that by 1893 Murat Halstead wrote:

> Thus the inventors realized their share of the profits of the news-papers, and it has for several years been the general hope of news-paper proprietors that improvements of presses should be arrested, and as they do all now except editing, making up and reading of the journals, there does not appear to be room for additional mechanical facilities. (207)

While indeed most of these inventions continued for decades and, in some cases, still define the production of newspapers, their influence was significant in two other areas—the role and work duties of newspaper reporters and increasing capitalization-commercialization of the newspaper industry.

Machines provided the means to produce large quantities of newspapers quickly, and "all great publishing concerns are taking advantage of the new discoveries, devices and inventions for reducing costs and increasing production" (Hungerford 1931, 136). In order to participate in the mechanized business of newspapers, capital on a large order was a prerequisite. The late 1880s saw another modernization influence on the newspaper industry. In order to run a newspaper, more than a set of type in a wagon or a desire to influence people was needed. Financial capabilities were required to afford the technology, because "these big publishing companies are the outcome of the modern tendency towards combinations and mergers" (136).

This shift from editor-publisher to publisher-financier was explained by Frances Leupp in 1910:

> Of course, the transfer of our newspapers from personal to corporate ownership and control was not a matter of preference, but a practical necessity. The expense of modernizing the mechanical equipment alone imposed a burden which few newspaper proprietors were able to carry unaided. . . . Partnership relations involve so many risks, and are so hard to shift in an emergency, that resort was had to the form of a corporation, which afforded the advantage of a limited liability, and enabled the share-holder to dispose of his interest if he tired of the game. (1910/1918, 34)

Four years earlier, Rollo Ogden (1906/1918) noted that this change in the financial essence of the newspaper had other consequences: "The immensely large capital now required for the conduct of a daily paper in a great city has had important consequences. It has made the paper more of an institution, less of a personal organ" (3).

Not only did newspapers lose the distinctive persona of their editor-publisher as they became institutionalized products within corporations, but reporters experienced changes as a result of technology and commercialization. Bleyer, Lord, and Halstead, among others, observed how the various machines shifted reporters' work in the late 1880s. Halstead (1893) noted that the advent of the telegraph provided the means to send and receive news, but that "men who knew news at a glance were scarce. The faculty of understanding, gathering and presenting intelligence in good form for publication was rare" (204). Use of the telephone had consequences for both the reporters' role and the division of labor within newsrooms. "By telephoning the bare facts of the news to rewrite men in the newspaper office, reporters and correspondents tended to become news gatherers rather than news writers" (Bleyer 1927, 397). The introduction of faster machines to gather and produce the news resulted in a work environment where "the new order of 'speed before everything' . . . brought about its changes at both ends of the newspaper staff" (Leupp 1910/1918, 41). As James E. Rogers observed in 1909, "The word RUSH is written all over the average paper" (161).

Time and speed became interwoven within a commercial imperative that machines could deliver news faster to readers, thereby outpacing the commercial competition. The time period is fittingly described by James M. Lee (1923) as one of "Financial Readjustment," in which technology "made news a most perishable commodity" (353). The typewriter hastened work deadlines within newsrooms. As Chester Lord, former managing editor of the *New York Sun,* described in 1922:

> The invention of the typewriter has helped vastly to speed up newspaper composition. The reporter may dictate his narrative. In the old days frequently he had to make a long journey to the newspaper office before beginning to work with pen or pencil. Nowadays, if need be, he dictates his report through the telephone to a typewriter in the office. (43)

This mechanized division of labor between the gathering of news by the reporter and the processing of news by rewrite workers in the newsroom is a rather telling one. Technological advancement enabled the division between the two parts of producing the editorial news product—the gathering from the writing-editing of it. This division was such that by 1930, Nancy Mavity stated, "Getting a story and writing it are in reality two different activities" (95).

Reporters in the late nineteenth century were not so special or different from other work groups whose labors have been characterized as merging with and becoming one with the machines of their trade or industry. Halstead (1893) observed during this time:

> The editorial "we" is not somebody with convictions, purposes, principles, ardor, ceaseless energies, writing the lessons of experience with resolution and devotion, with some sense of manly responsibility to mankind. . . . the "we" is an association that invests a machine that grinds jobs. (207)

The association of "we" in the newspaper business during this time was increasingly a financial consortium of bankers, stockholders, and venture capitalists. From the late nineteenth and into the early twentieth century, the financial ability to publish newspapers required more funds because of mechanization costs. As Bleyer wrote in 1913:

> Expensive additions to the mechanical equipment and other exigencies often make it necessary for the newspaper company, like other business enterprises, to secure financial assistance by borrowing considerable sums from banks. Such has become the magnitude of the business side of the newspaper, that ownership by stock companies is the rule today instead of the exception as it was in 1845. (333)

Hamilton Holt (1909) cited government figures from 1900 to 1905 that indicate the printing industry was one of the fastest-growing corporate sectors of the time:

> Since 1850 the whole industry has increased over thirty-fold, while all other industries have increased only fifteen-fold. . . . The latest available figures, published in 1905 by the Government, show that capital invested in the publishing business has doubled in the preceding half decade. (5-6)

Financial investments increased during this time, as the number of publications expanded within an economic framework of increased mergers and consolidations. The business facet of newspapering had become a commercial enterprise in the hands of those who could afford the initial technological costs or investors interested in short-term risk for long-term gain. As Bleyer, Lee, Emery, and others have noted, the operation of chain newspapers started in the 1870s and 1880s with Frank Munsey, Randolph Hearst, and the Scripps brothers. Yet it was during the late 1880s to around 1910 that the business practice of running newspaper chains as a commercial endeavor became the economic norm. By 1909, James Edward Rogers observed, "Since newspaper business demands a large investment, we naturally find that most of our newspapers have become huge corporations owned by a few individuals . . . The trust tendency among our newspapers is marked" (199).

Various writers have reported the increase in newspapers (daily, weekly, semiweekly, and monthly) as exploding during this time from 9,810 in 1880 to 16,948 in 1890; 21,272 in 1900; and 21,394 in 1905 (Holt 1909, 6-7; Jones 1947, 387). Following World War I and the decline of the foreign-language press, by 1919 the number of publications had dropped to 15,799 (Flint 1925, 261). Nonetheless, the newspaper business remained a profitable one for those who could afford it. Receipts for 1905 were reported at $256.8 million (Holt 1909, 6); for 1919, they were $566.3 million (Flint 1925, 261).

As profits and ledgers continued to spiral upward, the role of the reporter during this economic growth became a compartmentalized one within the total corporate workings of the newspaper. After all, "the newspaper business is essentially a moneymaking scheme, dependent on one hand upon its popularity with the public, on the other hand, upon the money market. It takes money to run it and it is run to make money" (Rogers 1909, 197). The running of a newspaper enterprise was characterized by Edward Alsworth Ross in 1910: "More and more the owner of the big daily is a businessman who finds it hard to see why he should run his property on different lines from the hotel proprietor, the vaudeville manager, or the owner of an amusement park" (1910/1918, 81).

Several press observers during this time expressed concerns about these trends. In 1909, Holt noted that "commercialism is at present the greatest menace to the freedom of the press" (98). Herbert Hungerford (1931) distinguished between "car-lot" publishing that was possible because of mechanical mass-production capabilities and explained that "success in publishing is merely a matter of making the proper mixture of brains, ink and paper" (135-36). The valuing of reporters in this mixture is questionable beyond reporters providing information for the news product to offset the paper's other, but profit-producing, information—advertising. "The business manager has more power in newspaperdom than has the circulation editors," complained Rogers (1909, 202), among others, during the early twentieth century.

In his newspaper career memoirs, Samuel Blythe (1912) recognized the low economic value ascribed to reporting work: "On the larger papers all the big salaries, or most of them, are paid to the men who direct the papers. The chaps with the executive brains draw down the money"(229). After his thirty-three years at the *New York Sun,* Chester Lord (1922) was one of several writers who noted that a common aspiration among reporters was to own a newspaper. Yet he cautioned:

> Since then the savings from the salary of even a successful newspaper writer are insufficient for the accumulation of property or the establishment of any considerable prosperity, and since newspaper ownership involves the investment of capital and small business ability as well, it follows that our young man must look beyond mere pecuniary gains for the rewards of journalism. (152)

Newspapering for profit belonged to the owners of newspapers, not the reporters. The era's technological advancements enabled owners to produce their products more quickly and at increased volume. Further commercialization of the press came about as increased capitalization costs, spurred by these mechanical changes, required a fiscal commitment that most struggling reporters could not afford. As commercialization in the newspaper industry provided heftier margins for the owners, the working conditions of most reporters remained one in that, "after a certain stage, experience in newspaper work counts for nothing. The great assets are youth and legs" (Blythe 1912, 217).

Long hours, mercurial editors, low wages, and lack of job security characterized the lives of reporters in the late nineteenth and early twentieth centuries. And while many writers of the era noted these job factors, there is nonetheless an energy about the doing of newswork, driven perhaps by the new machines available to do the news and the fact that many facets of American life were new and changing in its cities, its factories, and its population. In 1911 Will Irwin called the times "the age of the reporter. In even its simplest form news is the nerves of the modern world" (1).

At the heart of social, economic, and political changes were reporters—the modern-day transmitters of a city's—and now the world's—events in a matter of minutes. Part of this reportorial ethos and what have come to be viewed as the service ideals of reporters—the values, goals, and inspirations of one's chosen life task—was the notion of sacrifice on behalf of the story, or the public interest as a valued quality:

> A good newspaper man, especially one serving for a salary, whether it is large or small, who reaches out for the fullest experience which his occupation can bring to him, is ready to endure and does endure hunger, cold, heat, prolonged toil, physical danger at times, and every discomfort in order that he may carry a hazardous or otherwise difficult assignment to a successful conclusion. He is animated

by the desire to do good work in a big way, even if he must fail in many cases. (Will 1931, 277-78)

This sacrificial endurance was rarely rewarded in a tangible fashion. Talcott Williams (1925), former dean of the Columbia School of Journalism, called reporters' salaries "deplorably small" (161). And unlike other occupational pursuits, having superior intellectual faculties was no guarantee that those brains would translate to capital gains:

> In other callings the capital of brains commands success, notably in the law, in medicine, in engineering, in architecture, but in the newspaper business, while brains are absolutely essential they advance the young man only so far, give but feeble reward. (Lord 1922, 151)

Not only was newswork itself low-paying, but the means to perform the work were often hampered by the business ledger. About his first newspaper job in the 1890s, Samuel Blythe (1912) said, "Expense bills were carefully scrutinized. No reporter was to take a street car if his assignment was within a mile of the office unless there was a great rush, and all the street cars stopped at midnight" (29).

From the readings of this era, it appears two notions about reporters emerge: the actual working conditions and work performed, and the spirit and ethos surrounding reporting and the life of a reporter. Both of these elements were influenced by the technological and commercial changes and increasing professionalization of the times. Although reporters' salaries remained miserly and meager during this era, Williams, among others, noted in 1925: "The American newspaper was never able to pay living salaries to its staff until advertising began on a large scale, half a century ago" (157). Expanding commercialism meant more newspapers and, therefore, increased job positions available on newspaper staffs. Technological changes not only increased the division of labor within newsrooms, they provided a means by which to place a monetary value on the different types of newswork now required to produce a newspaper.

As characterized by Blythe in 1912, "Newspaper work is divided into two parts: the writing end and the executive end—that is, of course, on the editorial side" (227). Even within the "writing end," increased technological speed in gathering news had produced differentiated work between reporters and, as they were popularly called at the time, rewrite men. Several writers of the time discussed this distinction as one resulting from the work speedups of delivering news brought on by mechanical changes in the industry:

This is so far recognized that the last differentiation in newspaper work in large cities is the division of the staff between the reporter who goes out, gets the facts, and telephones his summary to the "write-up" man, who proceeds to clothe the bare bones of the searcher with the garniture of style, sentiment, and "human interest." (Williams 1925, 8)

The work of the rewrite man was conducted within the confines of the newsroom, and the job, as noted by several writers (Blythe, Mavity, Williams, Flint), received more economic reward than that of the reporter who phoned in the news item from which a news story would be produced. Yet, caution was expressed by several that, as Mavity (1930) observed, "a complete differentiation between the news gatherer and the news writer is not desirable; for one writes most vividly and interestingly of what one has seen or known at first hand" (96). Concerns about the manner of prose included not only its presentation but the veracity of the report. A constant reliance upon rewrite personnel "decreases accuracy and, ordinarily, increases the interest of the reader" (Williams 1925, 8):

The usefulness of the rewrite man in the modern newspaper office, where speed demands that much important news be received in more or less fragmentary form over the telephone, is sufficiently vouched for by the size of his salary. Unless abuses of the system are studiously excluded, its hazards become a serious menace to newspaper credibility. (Flint 1925, 45)

Reporters emerged as the entry-line level of work production in the increasingly modernized and mechanized newspaper. The differentiation of work placed reporters in the position of providing information they wrote themselves as news stories or information that was rewritten by someone else as news. For example, Mott (1962a) has observed, "The modern summary lead for news stories developed during the latter nineties" (603). News elements within a news story could be standardized through an emphasis on the 5Ws and H, resulting in a news production time made more predictable under deadline imperatives.

Although their work was now more standardized, reporters' lives were still economically precarious, but embodied a spirit and lifestyle somewhere between utter dissoluteness and personal sacrifice on behalf of the American reading public. Noted Will (1931), "The usual characteristics of a superior reporter or editor these days include unselfishness, modesty, a self-sacrificing disposition and intense loyalty" (279). Newswork also offered, according to

Charles Harger (1911/1918): "The fascination of doing things, of being in the forefront of the world's activities, appeals to young men and women of spirit" (265). In fact, Maurice deBlowitz wrote in 1893, "Let me affirm, immediately, that I believe in the absolute incorruptibility of any journalist whatever . . . for the special mark of the journalistic temperament is a horror of dependence" (40).

This "horror of dependence" also reinforced the spirit of individualism that has characterized reporters and their work. In fact, as deBlowitz explained it, newswork provided a sort of legitimate career for persons who perceived themselves as renegades of sorts having difficulty conforming to most occupational structures and strictures:

> For the most part they are men who have a feeling they are superior to a very normal or established disciplinary system, whom, in fact, discipline chafes, to whom the hierarchic or bureaucratic idea is an intolerable bugbear, who cannot make up their minds to follow an other's lead along a path to be traced slowly step-by-step. They leave the slower and more regular professions to enter journalism. (38)

And the nature of reporting, with its access to events and people and its inherent immediacy of the product of one's labors, was, even in the early twentieth century, providing the fodder for future stereotypes of reporters as individualistic, aggressive, and needing instant gratification from their work, the published story. "There is no denying the fascination of power and of influence, the satisfaction of persuasion and of direction" (Lord 1922, 158).

News reporting provided "the desire for an immediate result" (deBlowitz 1893, 40) that the era's mechanical capabilities and commercial opportunities helped to both foster and satisfy. The early twentieth century was also a period in which journalistic characteristics of individualism, the "quick fix," and maverick attitudes led to the image of boisterous reporters enjoying a hedonistic lifestyle:

> Many stories are told of the conviviality of the Chicago "press gang" of the nineties, and from the legends which grew up about this and similar groups sprang the concept of the romantic sot of the newspaper office which was later to add a touch of comedy to so many stories, plays and movies. That there was much drinking, with considerable drunkenness, among reporters of this period cannot be disputed; but in the second decade of the new century, the tolerance of inebriety which some publishers had shown had largely disap-

peared, and the hard drinkers were displaced by men who could be depended upon. (Mott 1962a, 603-4)

What later became enshrined as the "Front Page" heyday of journalism found its roots in early-twentieth-century newsrooms. While these social pursuits of reporters may have blunted their work-life realities, they also perpetuated the journalistic notion, as Hungerford (1931) explained, that "the author, like other men, likes to be prosperous, but he also wishes to be immortal" (311).

In doing so, the image of reporting was often a time-driven one with a consuming intensity. It was, as Albert Shaw characterized it in 1903, "an exacting kind of calling, and it offers little leisure. But if it allows scant freedom *from* work, it gives more freedom *in* work than the average pursuit" (160). Yet writers of the time period were questioning how much freedom existed in reporters' work when the economic valuing of that work was such that "in a number of newspaper offices in this country the average salary of the composing room and the pressroom is larger than the average in the writing force" (Williams 1925, 162). Mechanization of labor produced a division of labor in which reporters' work was often the least valued economically, even though it produced commercial credibility as part of a newspaper's selling point. The freedom to decide work for reporters was, as Bleyer wrote in 1913, a relative one: "A vital question for everyone engaged in newspaper writing or editing is whether or not he will obey the order of his superiors when these orders do not square with his own standards of truth and right. . . . Then it is that every newspaper worker is brought face-to-face with the problems of present-day newspaper making" (357).

The freedom to make those ethical and work decisions as they affected reporters' work products was a limited one. Henry Watterson, editor of the *Louisville Courier-Journal,* provided a routinized and mechanized description of an editor in 1910, in which both the editor and his minions assumed mechanized positions in the routine of news production:

> The editor must never lose his head. Sure, no less than prompt judgment is required at every turning. It is his business to think for everybody. Each subordinate must be so drilled and fitted to his place as to become in a sense the replica of his chief. (1910/1918, 98)

Increased speed in newspaper production produced both a division of labor and specialization of labor in newspapers. Reporters were but one widget in this mechanized process, and in spite of the stereotypes of spirited individualism and work freedom, their work life, as characterized by Francis Leupp in 1910, was not so different from that of a railroad worker or iron puddler—workers in other industries whose work was also increasingly driven by machines and speed:

> For what, pray, is the newspaper paying him, if not for tracing rumors to their original source; and further still, if so instructed? He is there to be, not a thinker, but a worker; a human machine like a steam potato-digger, which, supplied with the necessary energizing force from behind, drives its prods under nature's mantle, and grubs out the succulent treasures she is trying to conceal. (1910/1918, 41)

As labor became more specialized, the reporter's work, and the training for this work, also emerged as specialized needs and activities. The training of reporters for newsroom work was increasingly viewed as occurring within university classrooms. Journalism joined other occupations in the early twentieth century in affixing a college degree as the requirement for entry into the occupation. Joseph Pulitzer announced in 1904 that journalism was an investment and that "the spirit of specialization is everywhere" (11):

> It is true that many of the subjects needed for the general education of a journalist are already covered in college. . . . Modern industry looks sharply after its by-products. In silver-mining, gold is sometimes found as a by-product exceeding the value of the silver. So in general university courses we may find by-products that would meet the needs of the journalist. Why not divert, deflect, extract, concentrate, specialize them for the journalist as a specialist? (10)

Pulitzer's $2 million endowment of the Columbia School of Journalism was part of a trend in the early twentieth century. A college education became both a reflection of and a determinant for occupations in which increasingly differentiated work tasks resulted in differentiated status within the occupational group. Newspaper work was no exception, and although efforts to educate journalists date back to Robert E. Lee's training program for printers at Washington College in 1869 (Emery and McKerns 1987, 2), newspaper work was still seen as one in which "no single function was seen as superior to the others; all was of a piece" (Sobel 1976, 3). By 1900, however, the number of identified editors and journalists had increased three times over the preceding thirty years (Bledstein 1976, 39).

The opportunities to learn newspaper work in college classrooms expanded between 1870 and 1900 with inclusion of journalism courses and curricula at various colleges and universities, primarily located in the Midwest (Emery and McKerns, 1987, 2-3). Reactions to newspaper reporters acquiring their skills in a classroom prior to entering a newsroom were mixed. In his autobiography, Frank Luther Mott (1962b) noted:

> Journalistic ability was a "gift," argued the erudite Edwin Lawrence Godkin (Belfast '51), first in *The Nation* and later when he became editor of the *New York Evening Post*: therefore education for journalism was absurd. A large part of the "working press" agreed with him. After all, these editors had themselves received no special academic training, and see what they had done! The very suggestion of schools of journalism seems to be (and doubtless in some degree was) a criticism of them and their achievements. (149)

Many editors reflected Frederic Hudson of the *New York Herald*'s view that "the only place where one can learn to be a journalist is in a great newspaper office" (Jones 1947, 505). It was not only the existence of journalism education but the nature of that training for newspaper reporters that provoked debate as the occupation itself was experiencing increasing specialization.

Talcott Williams (1925) tied the rise of journalism education in the early twentieth century to corresponding increases in newspaper circulation and literacy: "As a population increases in intelligence and its horizon becomes more extended, the more it thinks for itself and needs for those who influence it through the newspaper a more efficient training" (121-22). Efficiency, specialization, and technology were influencing all spheres of modern life and forever changing the type of information people received, how they received it, and who produced it. Previous training for newspaper work was described by Williams and Charles Moreau Harger as acquired in a series of steps from "printer's devil," to writing-editing, and possibly owning one's own newspaper. Increased specialization in the newspaper business was influenced by technological advancement that eliminated the need to experience all facets of the business in order to do newspaper work. Instead, "the newspaper business has as distinct departments as a department store" (Harger 1911/1918, 264). "While a full knowledge of every part of the workings of the office is unquestionably valuable, the eager aspirant finds time too limited to serve a long apprenticeship at the mechanical end in order to prepare himself for the writing-room" (266).

Preparation for the "writing-room" had shifted to the classroom for reporters, whose job qualifications increasingly mirrored the editorial division of labor. The nature of that classroom training provoked, as several observers noted, an efficient and standardized method of molding reporters. "This sort of schooling does not make newspaper men of the unfit, but to the fit it gives a preparation that saves them much time in attaining positions of value," wrote Harger (267). Williams (1925) noted that "the training for a bachelor of science is, in its nature, definite, precise and capable of being reduced to rule and expressed with accuracy in terms of study hours and the laboratory" (119). Yet this standardization also produced concerns that have since been framed as the "trade school versus professionalism" debate in journalism education. Nelson Crawford (1924) explained the divisiveness of the trade side as "the function of the school of journalism is to produce reporters who can write good stories. . . . newspapers want only reporters and . . . if the school can produce reporters they can learn in the newspaper office all else that they need to know about the game" (169). He also noted, this type of training "is run frankly to furnish reporters for American newspapers" (170).

The production process of training reporters whose work skills could be both predicted and controlled by publishers differed from the professional approach in educating reporters. Crawford noted that the professional schools fostered specialization in "specific phases of modern life—in order that in their newspaper work they may be prepared the better to serve civilization" (172). The service ideal of a trade school approach was to serve the publisher, whereas the professional approach emphasized another ideal:

> Specifically with reference to journalism, it holds that the young man or woman going out to work on a newspaper is not primarily a servant for that paper, but rather a servant to humanity. . . . The professional school of journalism wants the suggestions and advice of newspaper men, but it wants them with the understanding that interests of humanity and not the preservation of the status quo in journalism are paramount. (173)

Professional training was to emphasize intellectual and ethical training as the priority over the more mechanical skills of writing news copy. Colleges of journalism, said Pulitzer (1904), "will impart knowledge—not for its own sake, but to be used for public service" (46). In 1893, deBlowitz outlined an extensive education for newspaper reporters. He viewed journalism as a profession of the highest calling, and one in which aspirants should be at least twenty-three years old, speak two languages other than English, receive tutoring in history and literature, and pass a final examination (43).

These divergent views were such that opponents of journalism education "had great influence in forestalling a rapid spread of the movement after it once had started" (Sutton 1968, 10). Newspaper work was becoming more specialized and required more systematic training because the world and its events were ones in which "social forces and society itself, political processes and events had no systematic record" (Williams 1925, 118). As technology provided publishers with the mechanical means to access society's increasing amounts of information, several writers noted it was anticipated that the gatherers and writers of that information could be so trained that publishers "would like to be able to employ graduates from such schools with the assurances they were making no mistakes" (Will 1931, 39).

Journalism education became an enduring arena in which the predictability and control of the newsroom workforce was contested around the notion of trade school versus professional training. The readings of the era indicate that participants in the debate were more often publishers, educators, and some high-profile editors, but rarely the people producing the actual work—reporters.

Schools that emphasized a liberal arts approach in introducing ways of looking at the world beyond a technical skills viewpoint met with, as described by Albert Sutton (1968), "sharp criticism—a characteristic which they of necessity were to instill in their graduates if they hoped to serve one of the primary missions of education for the profession of journalism" (10). That mission was one of public service in which the reporter's work and the training to do that work was not just for an individual's own sake. Rather, as Pulitzer (1904) outlined:

> It will be the object of the college to make better journalists, who will make better newspapers, which will better serve the public. It will impart knowledge—not for its own sake, but to be used for public service. It will try to develop character, but even that will be only a means to the one supreme end—the public good. (46)

The role of the reporter in serving several masters—editors, publishers, and the public good—was increasingly viewed as integral to the functioning of society, so that by 1930, Nancy Mavity observed:

> The responsibility of the press to the public, therefore, cannot be exaggerated. As the chief source of our immediate information about all that goes on in the world beyond our direct observation, the press is rightly held accountable to society for a high standard of truthfulness and reliability. (13)

The notion of public service was now part of a newspaper reporter's individualism—a spirit and outlook now fostered as part of a reporter's professional training in the classroom. Increased interest and demand in a reporting life indicated that by 1926, the American Association of Teachers of Journalism reported that 10,000 college graduates were doing newspaper work (Sutton 1968, 29). The number of universities meeting this need for specialized training and student demand increased correspondingly. Sutton (1968, 110) reported the following start-up figures for colleges' and universities' journalism programs showed an increase of 15 in 1869-1908, 58 in 1909-19, 166 in 1920-29, and 176 in 1930-40.

The introduction in the early twentieth century of journalism education as a prerequisite for the training of reporters provided another division of workers within newsrooms—those with college degrees and those without. This difference led to tensions characterized by Pulitzer (1904) as "class distinctions in the profession—an invidious distinction of the few who had received the benefits of collegiate training against the many who had not enjoyed this advantage" (11). For Pulitzer and other supporters of journalism education, a college degree elevated the occupation of newspaper reporting to the professional domain that included law, medicine, and engineering. Sutton (1968, 106) reported in 1940 a total of 542 colleges offered journalism training, whereas 180 schools provided legal preparation and 155 provided training for engineering.

The issue of professionalism among reporters became more complex in the early twentieth century, as the control and value of journalistic work became increasingly economically determined. Pulitzer (1904) separated the economic aspects of newspaper work in the following way:

> There is an obvious difference between a business and a profession. An editor, an editorial writer or a correspondent is not in business. Nor is even a capable reporter. These men are already in a profession, though they may not admit it or even realize it. . . . Ill or well, they represent authorship, and authorship is a profession. The man in the counting-room of a newspaper is in the Newspaper business. He concentrates his brain (quite legitimately) upon the commercial aspects of things, upon the margin of profit, upon the reduction of expenses, upon buying white paper and selling it printed—that is business. But a man who has the advantage, honor and pleasure of addressing the public every day as a writer or thinker is a professional man. (19-20)

There is an implied intellectual creativity and superiority in this distinction between business and profession, the notion of which often framed the debate of conferring professional status on newspaper reporters. It also raises one of the argument's paradoxes—if indeed journalism education was to professionalize newspaper work by making its workers more efficient and the work more standardized, then where was the time and space left for individualistic, creative endeavors by reporters? Part of this confusion arises from the fact that, as Bleyer noted in 1913, "journalism, among the last of the callings to be generally recognized as a profession, has established neither standards of admission nor a formulated code of ethics" (358).

Given the division between the counting room and the newsroom operations of a newspaper, the issue of professionalism also influenced each side's perception of the role of newspapers. In 1924, Nelson Crawford called owners of small newspapers and reporters/editors at large dailies "professional newspaper men" because "there is a tradition of public accountability and public service" in which a newspaper is viewed as a "quasi-public institution" (26). The viewing of a reporter's work as professional enhanced the service ideal of newspaper reporting, that a reporter's work is not for his or her own benefit, but for others. Noted George Payne (1941), "There is no profession, unless it is medicine, that calls for a higher regard for the simple truth than does journalism" (378). In fact, Flint (1925) referred to newspapers as serving a "public utility" function (260), and Pulitzer (1904) called journalism the "most fascinating of all professions":

> The soldier may wait 40 years for his opportunity. Most lawyers, most physicians, most clergymen die in obscurity, but every single day opens new doors for the journalist who holds the confidence of the community and has the capacity to address it. (12)

The ability to inform became as much a professional imperative for reporters as the ability to heal, to litigate, to design, or to console is in other occupations. And although a college education was the way to professionalize the training within the occupations, professional attributes endemic to other work lives did not apply for newspaper reporters. As Lord (1922) observed, "Physicians and lawyers frequently make comparatively nothing for a year or so after they begin" (147). However, the ability to determine and control the economic value of one's work is part of the professional imperatives of law and medicine, and a factor that allows persons in these occupations to enjoy a progressive incline of income during their careers. Such is not the case with reporters. An ongoing dilemma within the occupation in the early twentieth century was that reporters had increasing power to inform and influence large groups of people but lacked the economic benefits afforded professionals in other fields. Lord noted, "Many newspaper men seem satisfied to work along through life on what they can get. In all offices may be seen the pathetic spectacle of men with silvered locks who have sat at the same desk for more than a third of a century" (147).

Like the professions of medicine and law, newspaper reporting carried its own criteria of individualism—of the sort developed from the rigors and advantages befitting a college education. Yet, for newspaper reporters individualism could not be confused with independence. Doctors and lawyers enjoyed an independence in their work lives in terms of setting fees or salaries, setting work hours, and mobility of where to practice their profession. Reporters did not enjoy such professional flexibility, because although their work may have belonged to the public, it was owned by the newspaper publisher:

> For it is obvious that in journalism we find a different situation from that in medicine or law or teaching or the ministry. None of these professions is sustained by a manufacturing industry engaged in producing a commodity and selling it to the public, as the publishing industry is engaged in manufacturing and selling newspapers. (Flint 1925, 260)

Newspapers reporters may have been viewed as better educated and more professional in their approach to newswork, but the increased commercialism of the press had not made their work lives more independent. Instead, by 1925, Flint noted:

> Perhaps never in the history of the periodical press was the character of newspapermen so high as it is today. The trouble lies with bondage of many newspapermen to the advertising end of business and to the businessmen who own the capital invested in the paper. Lawyers and doctors have not become annexes of a plant, and hence lawyers and doctors are not falling down on their jobs. (260)

Several writers of the time opined that the increased commercialism made possible by advertising was the end of professionalism for reporters, not the beginning. "If journalism is no longer a profession, but a commercial enterprise, it is due to the growth of advertising and nothing else," observed Hamilton Holt in 1909 (34). In that same year, James Rogers tied the modernization of newspapers to a corresponding loss of professionalism:

> The present organization of the modern newspaper calls less for individual leadership than it does for organization and system. Journalism under the old system of individualism was a profession, but today it is nothing more than a trade. (93)

If indeed "journalism has to do with the business of writing, editing and publishing journals," as Albert Shaw (1903, 156) wrote, then the newspaper's expanding commercialized environment was part of the reporter's increasing professional role in the twentieth century, but not the sole determinant.

Reporters could not be economically independent because they had to rely on others for their salaries. Often, their work could be somewhat independent of a publisher's view, but not, as many historians note, at constant cross-purposes, or they would soon be unemployed. Technology produced divisions of labor within the newsroom, giving news stories a more standardized, summary approach. This left a reporter's individualistic style in presenting the news as provided as one level of personal professionalism.

Reporting did differ from other professions in the early twentieth century, particularly as the reporter's ability to influence public opinion emerged as a powerful force. Individualism was an accepted occupational trait for reporters within commercial enterprises, but independence exhibited through confrontation with structures in and outside the newsroom was not tolerated. As Williams observed in 1925, the professions of law, medicine, and the ministry had for generations had "the prescriptive position and conventional respect" that created "their training, their traditions and their position in society" (41). The difference between these three professions and newspaper reporting was a critical one:

> More serious still, the three callings cited are not only drawn, as to much of their membership from the advantaged; these professions are approved by the advantaged. Journalism is not so approved. Its chief achievement in the past and its chief task in the future is to reduce the advantages of the advantaged. For this it came into the world. It is the chief weapon created by many to this end. (41)

The late nineteenth and early twentieth centuries were time periods in which the accumulation of capital and resulting industrial expansion was enjoyed in most of America's corporate sectors. However, that growth and profit was enjoyed by a small group of the advantaged at the expense of and labor of less advantaged workers. Given the role of newspapers in forming public opinion, it behooved publishers as part of that corporate echelon to have a news product that reflected an antilabor bias and was produced by workers who themselves were not members of a union, particularly as the word *union* signified worker confrontation of industry through organization of a work group. Because they represented a challenge to a business owner's total control over a labor force, unions were feared and despised. The situation between labor and industry had become such that by 1914 Louis Brandeis was cautioning against "industrial despotism, even though it be benevolent despotism" (17).

Yet, as Ross observed in 1910, newspaper coverage of worker issues was such that "during labor disputes the facts are usually distorted to the injury of labor" (86):

> The alacrity with which many dailies serve as mouthpieces of financial powers came out very clearly during the recent industrial depression. The owner of one leading newspaper called his reporters together and said in effect, "Boys, the first of you who turns in a story of a layoff or a shut-down gets the sack." (89)

Newspaper publishers could not afford the wrath of advertisers, industrialists, bankers, and politicians if their own commercial success was to continue. It was more profitable to present information on labor issues that supported management's side. By 1925 the situation was such that Leon Flint wrote: "Perhaps in no field is the charge of news distortion so often made as in that of industrial controversy. The advocates of the interests of labor express entire lack of confidence in the variety of the news in which they denominate as the 'capitalistic press'" (61).

Reasons for distorting and suppressing news of labor issues and strife included economic safeguards for newspaper owners, but it was also a recognition of the role of the press in forming public opinion on labor and capital issues. The power that came from providing select information to create particular opinions on these matters was recognized as early as 1909 by James Rogers:

> Most newspapers publish daily accounts of the money and labor markets. Their influence in this regard must not be too lightly judged. Too much stress cannot be laid upon the influence of the papers on industrial problems, for the citizen's opinions as to whether a strike or boycott is justifiable or not depends largely upon what he reads in the newspapers about the dispute. The average man's knowledge of the trusts, the money markets, the economic movements and policies of different states can only be formed by what the newspapers give in the way of reliable facts. (142–43)

Newspaper reporters were the critical link between producing news on economic issues and maintaining a particular perception by the public on labor-capital issues. In their own work lives, reporters continued to be "notoriously underpaid" (Jones 1947, 573), with no job security and arduous working hours. The modern newspaper did indeed have increased technology and a division of labor that allowed more opportunities in reporting and editing, but none of these changes was of any economic benefit to newsworkers. As Bleyer observed in 1918:

> Effective organization of newspaper writers and editors has been urged as a means of establishing definite standards for the profession. It seems remarkable that in this age of organization newspaper workers are the only members of a great profession who have no national association. (xxi)

By 1918, the mechanical divisions within the organization of the modern newspaper, such as the printers, engravers, and stereotypers, had been organized into unions. Increased commercialization of newspapers had also led to the formation of associations by those in other divisions within newspapers such as newspaper publishers, circulation managers, and advertising personnel (xxi).

In a history for and about the American Newspaper Publishers Association (ANPA), Edwin Emery (1970) reported that the founding of the ANPA on February 16, 1887, occurred during a time when the "great corporations and industrial concentrations were maturing" (6). A total of forty-six publishers, business managers, and advertising managers met to form the ANPA (15). Although much of the group's business dealt with commercial concerns of advertising, labor relations with newspaper employees were included as part of a clause dealing with advertising policy "and the rendering to each other of such assistances as may be within our power" (24). This mutual assistance during instances of labor strife was necessary, said its proponent Joseph Dear of the *Jersey Journal,* because "this is a time of great agitation, of great confusion in the labor world" (24). Emery quotes Dear:

> Our employees, he said, are more or less organized, and their conduct in many cases has "placed newspapers in peculiarly unpleasant situations." Printers with a typographical union "who think they can move the world" should be met by an organization of American newspaper publishers. (24)

Thirteen years later, in 1900, labor relations so preoccupied ANPA members that a labor committee was formed, with the understanding that it would negotiate "national arbitration agreements with labor unions" (64). It was purposefully decided by ANPA members to call this body the "Special Standing Committee":

It should be noted that the enabling resolution which put the ANPA into the labor relations field was worded in terms which would permit the association to adopt a belligerent policy toward the printing unions if attempts at securing arbitration contracts failed. For this reason, perhaps, the membership shied away from the name "labor committee." (65)

By 1922, the ANPA had established an Open Shop Department to provide mutual aid and assistance with strikebreakers to publishers resisting organization:

Even the Special Standing Committee, its negotiatory agency, has taken on a more contentious viewpoint. The increasing number of local monopolies, the speed with which a group of strike-breakers may be installed, the ability of newspapers to create public opinion unfavorable to a printers' strike and the press's alliance with businessmen and politicians have contributed heavily to this significant change. (A. M. Lee 1937, 156)

Much of the ANPA's energy and policies on labor relations addressed the mechanical departments within newspaper operations. Workers in these sections were the lifeblood of a newspaper; their specific skills were required for the actual printing and distribution of the newspaper, a product that had to publish regularly to keep advertisers, subscribers, and profits at a consistent level. Reporters were expendable and replaceable, and their lack of a bargaining position for better working conditions was both self-inflicted and self-perpetuating:

About the turn of the century the highest salaries of New York reporters ranged from $40 to $60 a week; but many were paid only $20-$30, and beginners had to be satisfied with less than that. In other large cities the scale was somewhat lower and in many cities under 100,000 population reporters received only $5 to $20 a week. Moreover, tenure was insecure. (Mott 1962a, 603)

By 1925, Williams observed that reporters' salaries had increased somewhat in New York City but not elsewhere: "In Chicago, Boston and Philadelphia reporters are still beginning at $12, $15 and $20 a week. . . . Editorial writers have not gone much above $100, which were paid in these cities 20 years ago. . . . The salaries in lesser cities are small. They are not much above the salaries of 30 years ago in New York" (161).

As several writers of the time and historians have noted, reporters themselves did not see newspaper work as a lifelong job investment. The notion of individualism and personal career mobility precluded the activity of sustained organization among reporters in the late nineteenth and early twentieth centuries. As Nelson Crawford observed in 1924, "Too many newspaper men, however, still regard their work not as a profession, but merely as a job—and frequently as a steppingstone to something else" (145). The issue was also one of alliance for newspaper reporters:

> Despite meager pay, they disdain joining in a movement that would tend to affiliate them permanently with mechanical workers. They, like most "white collar" workers, intended to find financial relief through individual advancement, through taking a place among the executives, the employers in the newspaper industry or elsewhere. Reporting was merely a means to an end; typesetting and press operation was, for many, an end in itself. (A. M. Lee 1937, 667)

During this time, professionalism had become part of the occupational milieu for reporters in job perception, training, and attitude toward the credibility of one's work. Professionalism allowed reporters to hamper improvements in their own work lives much more effectively than could publisher threats or policies:

> The trade union plan of organization is looked upon with some disfavor by most of them—and perhaps with some justice, since it suggests that journalism is a trade rather than a profession. On the other hand, there is nothing in the trade union idea that should essentially bar professional workers. The argument that the newspaper man should not affiliate with a labor organization because it will impair his impartiality overlooks the fact that newspaper men as such join Chamber of Commerces, Rotary Clubs and similar organizations, without any protest on the part of those who look with horror on a trade union connection. (Crawford 1924, 152-53)

Although the majority of reporters disdained organizing as a group to secure better working conditions, there were several sporadic efforts between 1890 and 1920 to unionize reporters. The impetus for this came not from the newsroom, but from the printers. In 1891, the International Typographer's Union (ITU), long the bane of publishers and, by that time, the ANPA, amended its constitution "to authorize the issuance of charters to unions of editors and reporters" (Leab 1970, 13). As several historians have noted, this act was less one of goodwill than one of self-preservation, because reporters in the 1890s often acted as strikebreakers in the back shop during labor disputes between printers and publishers. Also, by 1891 the ANPA's Standing

Committee had accelerated its hostilities toward the ITU, and an organized newsroom within the auspices of the ITU would further blunt publishers' power within newspapers' organizations.

In October 1891, the first ITU newswriters' charter was issued to fifteen newspaper reporters in Pittsburgh, who, after witnessing the bloody labor strife in Homestead, Pennsylvania, "decided it was time for them to follow the example of the better paid mechanical workers and form a union" (A. M. Lee 1937, 669).

This formal organization of newspaper reporters had been preceded by various short-lived social clubs and press societies since the mid-nineteenth century. Their affiliation with the ITU was significant because it was the first union effort on the part of newspaper reporters. It was not to be an enduring one, however, as were most of the ITU newswriters' unions:

> Between 1891 and 1923 when the union in a referendum decided to relinquish jurisdiction over editorial employees, the ITU chartered 59 locals in over 40 cities in the U.S. and Canada. Of these only six endured for more than five years. And the great majority folded within 18 months. In general, the locals were very small, sometimes beginning with eight or nine members. (Leab 1970, 13)

Many reporters found during this time that the threat of a newswriters' union was enough to secure a paltry, but tangible, salary increase. Also, the division of labor within newspaper organizations had become more specialized, so that by 1906, ITU interest had waned because "rarely now did newspapermen come from the ranks of the printers, and thus the principal reason for interest in editorial workers was removed" (16).

There were other efforts during the late teens and 1920s to organize reporters, such as the American Journalists' Association and various press societies. It would not be until the early 1930s and the advent of collective bargaining legislation offering guarantees and protection that reporters would view unionizing as a viable approach to improving their working conditions.

Reporters emerged as a distinct work group during the late nineteenth and early twentieth centuries. Technological changes in the production of newspapers resulted in the division of labor within the newsroom, a division in which reporters became the singular workforce in the gathering and writing of news. Commercial expansion of newspapers provided more job opportunities for reporters, with increased numbers and types of positions.

As reporting became a specialized task within newspapers, so did the training of reporters. During that time, the process of training reporters became a relatively standardized and institutionalized one within college curricula. A college degree conferred a status and professionalization of reporters that gave newspaper reporting an occupational identity and rank within society.

What did not change during this time was that the work lives of newspaper reporters were still ones in which a living salary, reasonable work hours and conditions, job security, and control over one's work remained elusive work factors. Reporters continued to be a replaceable cog in the machinery of the modern newspaper.

## References

Bellamy, Edward. *Looking Backward*. New York: Modern Library, 1887.

Bledstein, Burton J. *The Culture of Professionalism: The Middle Class and the Development of Higher Education in America*. New York: Norton, 1976.

Bleyer, Willard Grosvenor. *Newspaper Writing and Editing*. Boston: Houghton Mifflin, 1913.

———. "Introduction." In *The Profession of Journalism,* ed. Willard Grosvenor Bleyer, ix–xxiii. Boston: Atlantic Monthly, 1918.

———. *Main Currents in the History of American Journalism*. Boston: Houghton Mifflin, 1927.

Blythe, Samuel. *The Making of a Newspaper Man*. Philadelphia: Altemus, 1912.

Boorstin, Daniel. *The Americans: The Democratic Experience*. New York: Random House, 1973.

Brandeis, Louis. *Business: A Profession*. Boston: Hale, Cushman & Flint, 1914.

Center, Stella. *The Worker and His Work*. Philadelphia: Lippincott, 1920.

Crawford, Nelson Antrim. *The Ethics of Journalism*. New York: Knopf, 1924.

deBlowitz, Maurice. "Journalism as a Profession." *Contemporary Review* 63 (Jan. 23, 1893): 37–46.

Ellul, Jacques. *The Technological Society*. New York: Vintage, 1964.

Emery, Edwin. *History of the American Newspaper Publishers Association*. Westport, Conn.: Greenwood, 1970.

Emery, Edwin, and Joseph McKerns. "AEJMC: 75 Years in the Making—A History of Organizing for Journalism and Mass Communication Education in the United States." *Journalism Monographs* 104 (Nov. 1987).

Flint, Leon Nelson. *The Conscience of the Newspaper*. New York: Appleton, 1925.

Halstead, Murat. "The Varieties of Journalism." *Cosmopolitan*, Jan. 1893, 202-7.

Harger, Charles Moreau. "Journalism as a Career." *Atlantic,* Feb. 1911. Reprinted in *The Profession of Journalism,* ed. Willard Grosvenor Bleyer, 264-77. Boston: Atlantic Monthly, 1918.

Holt, Hamilton. *Commercialism and Journalism*. Boston: Houghton Mifflin, 1909.

Hungerford, Herbert. *How Publishers Win*. Washington, D.C.: Ransdell, 1931.

Innis, Harold Adams. *The Press: A Neglected Factor in the Economic History of the Twentieth Century*. London: Oxford University Press, 1949.

Irwin, Will. "The American Newspaper—Part I: The Power of the Press." *Collier's,* Jan. 21, 1911, 15-18.

Jones, Robert W. *Journalism in the United States*. New York: Dutton, 1947.

Leab, Daniel. *A Union of Individuals: The Formation of the American Newspaper Guild*. New York: Columbia University Press, 1970.

Lee, Alfred McClung. *The Daily Newspaper in America: The Evolution of a Social Instrument.* New York: Macmillan, 1937.

Lee, James M. *History of American Journalism.* Boston: Houghton Mifflin, 1923.

Leupp, Frances. "The Waning Power of the Press." *Atlantic,* Feb. 1910. Reprinted in *The Profession of Journalism,* ed. Willard Grosvenor Bleyer, 30-51. Boston: Atlantic Monthly, 1918.

Lord, Chester S. *The Young Man and Journalism.* New York: Macmillan, 1922.

Mavity, Nancy Barr. *The Modern Newspaper.* New York: Holt, 1930.

Mott, Frank Luther. *American Journalism* (3rd ed.). New York: Macmillan, 1962a.

———. Time Enough: *Essays in Autobiography.* Westport, Conn.: Greenwood, 1962b.

Ogden, Rollo. "Some Aspects of Journalism." *Atlantic,* Feb. 1906. Reprinted in *The Profession of Journalism,* ed. Willard Grosvenor Bleyer, 1-19. Boston: Atlantic Monthly, 1918.

Payne, George Henry. *History of Journalism in the U.S.* New York: Appleton-Century, 1941.

Pulitzer, Joseph. "The School of Journalism in Columbia University: The Power of Public Opinion." *North American Review* (May 1904): 641-80.

Rogers, James Edward. *The American Newspaper.* Chicago: University of Chicago Press, 1909.

Ross, Edward Alsworth. "The Suppression of Important News." *Atlantic,* Mar. 1910. Reprinted in *The Profession of Journalism,* ed. Willard Grosvenor Bleyer, 79-96. Boston: Atlantic Monthly, 1918.

Shaw, Albert. "Making a Choice of a Profession." *Cosmopolitan,* June 1903, 155-60.

Sobel, Robert. *The Manipulators: America in the Media Age.* Garden City, N.Y.: Anchor, 1976.

Sutton, Albert Alton. *Education for Journalism in the United States from Its Beginning to 1940.* New York: AMS, 1968.

Watterson, Henry. "The Personal Equation in Journalism." *Atlantic,* July 1910. Reprinted in *The Profession of Journalism,* ed. Willard Grosvenor Bleyer, 97-111. Boston: Atlantic Monthly, 1918.

Will, Allen Sinclair. *Education for Newspaper Life.* Newark, N.J.: Essex, 1931.

Williams, Talcott. *The Newspaperman.* New York: Scribner's, 1925.

# 4 / Cultural Discourse of Journalists

## *The Material Conditions of Newsroom Labor*

Bonnie Brennen

*History is the recital of facts represented as true. Fable, on the other hand, is the recital of facts represented as fiction.* —Voltaire, 1764

This essay attempts to reclaim a portion of the cultural history of media workers and maintains that although a discussion of newsworkers is central to an understanding of the political and economic development of American media, to date, the history of the rank and file has not been written. Specifically, it considers the conditions of labor for American journalists during the interwar years of 1919-38, drawing on novels about newsworkers as primary source material. Incorporating cultural materialism, Raymond Williams's (1988) theory of the "specificities of material cultural and literary production within historical materialism" (5), this study maintains that newspaper novels contain insights into aspects of media history that have not been explored previously. Novels are seen to locate their plots within a specific social environment; fundamentally, this essay considers novels written about American journalists to be part of the rich disorder of the actual lived experience of interwar American society.[1]

Standard American media histories that described the 1920s and 1930s only superficially addressed the lives of often exploited and fundamentally powerless newsworkers; instead, they focused on decontextualized administrative history, exploring "significant" events, activities of major newspapers, and careers of powerful editors and publishers. Traditional media histories remain preoccupied with the collection and presentation of facts, often to the exclusion of any historical contextualization or deeper understanding. These facts have been arranged in a linear fashion and presented as "overwhelming evidence" to support the continued growth of newspapers, as well as a particular conception of freedom of the press, within the American capitalist system (Hardt 1989, 119-20). Even contemporary cultural historians who generally focused on previously underrepresented aspects of communication history have failed to address the presence and significance of rank-and-file journalists and their influence on U.S. media history.[2] In "Pages Concerning the Years of Independence," Czeslaw Milosz (1988, 371) wondered if silences, absences, and omissions could ever be justified, and suggested that individuals still exist even if their plight is no longer deemed worthy of consideration. Although the unmentioned aspects of discourse perpetuate the misnomers and constructed truths of a ruling ideology, elements that are not articulated may also clarify what is hidden, missing, or obscured. Therefore, in order to understand the history of a culture it is necessary to question the absences and to address that which has previously been left unsaid.

In their evaluations of evidence, the majority of communication historians have focused on issues of authenticity, reliability, and credibility; their event-oriented discourse has rarely addressed the conditions of production of historical artifacts and has failed to problematize the actual writing process. Adhering to traditional distinctions between fiction and nonfiction, media historians generally have rejected novels and other fictional texts as sources of historical evidence. They have tended to consider nontraditional material such as fiction, song, and poetry unreliable sources of documentation that should not be utilized as primary historical evidence. Instead, they viewed it as questionable secondary material, and only included it when it could be thoroughly corroborated by other, more "reliable," primary sources.[3]

During the past 150 years, more than a thousand novels have been written about journalists; however, until now novels have not been used as historical evidence to advance the history of media workers. Although novels have been rejected as primary sources of evidence by traditional media historians, there are scholars on the fringes of the discipline who understand the relation between cultural products and communication and who conceive of historical evidence far more broadly. Conceptualizing history as a living dialectical process of continuity and discontinuity, of evolution and revolution, cultural materialists, for example, consider novels, like all written notations, to be creative cultural practices that are produced under specific historical, political, and economic circumstances. As tangible embodiments of culture, novels are thought to produce meaning and value, and are evaluated as inherently neither superior nor inferior to any other type of writing. Novels, like all signification, are socially determined and involve interaction between the writing process and conditions of production. They are considered documentary evidence that is particularly useful when actual living participants are no longer available (R. Williams 1981, 329). Novels allow a synthesis between the personal and social that creates and judges a whole way of life in terms of individual qualities and offers a deeper understanding of culturally and historically specific experiences. In these texts it is possible to speak of a unique life, in a specific place and time, that exists as both individual and common experience. Although the majority of experience directly represents and reflects the dominant ideology, there is an area of social experience, often neglected, ignored, or repressed, that is considered resistant to the official consciousness. It is in this area of lived experience, from its structure of feelings, that art and literature are made (R. Williams 1987, 192). Although cultural materialists do not advocate the uncritical appropriation of cultural products, they do insist that novels, as well as other written notations, offer representations and misrepresentations of actual lived experience. Yet, because all texts are socially produced, it is necessary to address the specific cultural, economic, and political conditions of production, along with authors' intent, as well as critical responses to and public reception of the work.

The authors of the novels utilized in this study were newsworkers themselves; all wrote from firsthand experience as journalists. Some of the writers, such as Ernest Hemingway, John Dos Passos, Meyer Levin, and Katharine Brush, worked only briefly as newspaper reporters, correspondents, or columnists. Others, including Emma Bugbee, who spent fifty-six years as a reporter on the *New York Herald Tribune,* and Henry Justin Smith, news editor of the *Chicago Daily News* for decades, remained media workers throughout their careers. In their attempts to depict the work environment of journalists authentically, the authors frequently re-created their own experiences as newsworkers. In one sense, the novels discussed here may be seen as outlets in which the journalists articulated the fears, frustrations, dreams, and other material realities of their existence.

The writing style employed by these authors, as well as their choice of material, resonated more closely with autobiography than with fictional writing. In fact, some biographers have explicitly addressed the autobiographical nature of the novels. For example, the hero of *The Moon Calf,* by Floyd Dell, was a small-town boy who, like the book's author, left home and traveled to Chicago to pursue a literary career. In addition, Ben Hecht's experiences as a newspaper reporter at the *Chicago Daily News* from 1910 until 1924, where he specialized in crime news, were generally considered to provide the background for all of his novels, including *Erik Dorn*. Ben A. Williams's book *Splendor* was judged as a chronicle of his own experiences as a young newsworker.[4]

All of these novels were part of the genre commonly designated as *newspaper novels;* they were commercially produced and extensively distributed books that were geared toward contemporary popular audiences. Following World War I, public demand for books, particularly fiction, increased dramatically. Novels were considered "bargain" entertainment by publishers and middle-class buyers alike because they cost significantly less to produce than dramatic productions, operas, musicals, and other forms of divertissement (Tebbel 1978, 15). Book publishers responded to public sentiment, and during the 1920s the number of new fictional works released grew significantly.[5]

In general, the discourse of the 1920s and 1930s was permeated with resistance against the exploitative social relationships found in industrialized capitalist society (Rideout 1992, 115). Defining American society during the interwar years as a period of intellectual ferment and social turmoil, Daniel Aaron (1992, 173) contrasted the self-discovery and expression of the 1920s with the social discovery and expression of the 1930s. The pessimism of this period reflected the impersonal standardization of human needs and actions, as well as a fear that American society was quickly becoming economically and ethically bankrupt. Individuals exhibited a "cultural concern" for new communication technologies and their impact on American society and ruminated over the loss of community in a mechanized society (Covert and Stevens 1984, xii).

The strengths and weaknesses of this dynamic and contradictory period in U.S. history were perhaps best outlined by Joseph Freeman in his 1925 prospectus for funding the *New Masses,* a nonpartisan radical magazine that focused on literary and aesthetic dimensions of political change:

> This country is fast becoming the greatest empire in the world and with this development are appearing modes of life which have no precedent in history or art. The stockyards of Chicago, the steel mills of Pittsburgh, the mines of West Virginia, the lumber camps of Washington and California, the lynching of Negroes in the South, the clothing industries in the East, the Klan, tabloid newspapers, automobiles, and the private life of average citizens; the national political conventions, the nation-wide fetish of big business, the adven-

tures of American imperialism south of the Rio Grande, the life in skyscraper, factory and subway. (quoted in Aaron 1992, 100-101)

Interwar-era novels attempted to portray American life as it "really" was, and were therefore best categorized as examples of realist fiction, the dominant literary genre of the 1920s and 1930s. In realist fiction journalistic influences were apparent in writers' efforts to "get all the facts down." In an endeavor to capture "reality," realism attempted to reproduce in dialogue actual speech sounds and rhythms, carefully analyzed the physical appearance of characters, and offered detailed descriptions of settings and events within a specific social environment (Rideout 1992, 209). Postwar authors, "disgusted" with attempts to mollify American life, instead attempted to realistically depict contemporary material conditions and tried to offer readers the "unvarnished truth" of American society (Beach 1932, 533, 327).

In their efforts to enhance the realism of their fiction, authors often incorporated discussion of "real" people, actual events, and elements of popular culture into their novels. Labor disputes and strikes, presidential elections, the effects of prohibition, and widely reported cases of kidnapping, theft, and murder were used by authors to supply readers with a historical context for their narratives. Inventions were introduced, intriguing speeches critiqued, and qualifications of presidential candidates debated; several reporters in newspaper novels interviewed the person they regarded as the "greatest living American," William Jennings Bryan, and one newsworker, although honored to have met Bryan, expressed a profound sense of inadequacy over the assignment (Davis 1938, 19). In *Manhattan Transfer,* John Dos Passos (1925/1953) wove into the text newspaper headlines and stories from the *Wall Street Journal, Evening Graphic,* and *New York Times,* creating a montage that offered readers a critique of early-twentieth-century capitalist society. Characters actively engaged with information found in newspapers; they read and commented upon stories and occasionally acted upon material found in the daily press. An important story line in the novel began when an out-of-work attorney perused the newspaper in search of potential clients and encountered the following information: "Augustus McNiel, 253 W. 4th Street, who drives a milkwagon for the Excelsior Dairy Co. was severely injured early this morning when a freight train backing down the New York Central tracks ..." (50). In *Reporter,* actual newspaper headlines, such as "Darrow to Defend Evolution," "Loeb Not Crazy Says Savant," and "Moron Stuffs Girl, 8, in Sewer," appeared at the top of each page, offering readers background material that helped to explain the motivations and actions of the central newsworker

(Levin 1929). And in *An American Tragedy,* a local newspaper article delineating the drowning of a young couple, read by the main character, became the catalyst for his plan to kill his lover (Dreiser 1925/1981, 438-39).

Contemporary music, current motion pictures, and popular novelists were also addressed in these texts. Newsworkers in the novels evaluated the work of Sherwood Anderson, Ernest Hemingway, and Thomas Wolfe. In "*The Great American Novel,*" Theodore Dreiser was judged a "magnificent reporter" who should, however, be "required to phone all his books to a good rewrite man" (Davis 1938, 238). The interjection of news stories and elements of popular culture into the narratives may be seen not only to have helped authenticate the novels as realistic representations of the newspaper world, but also to have further blurred traditional distinctions between fact and fiction.

Representative of American popular culture during the 1920s and 1930s, these novels were generally well received by the public and critics alike. Critical responses to the novels primarily involved perceptions of reviewers regarding the authors' proximity to realistic depictions of journalists within the newsroom environment; critics also addressed the qualifications of writers to comment knowledgeably on the lives of newsworkers. Reviewers frequently commented on the "authenticity," "truthfulness," and "accuracy" of the texts; in some instances the assessment of a novel was tied entirely to its "realistic" representation of the newspaper business. For example, the treatment of the newsroom in *Erik Dorn* (Hecht 1921/1963) was described in a review as "a series of word pictures of amazing strength and realism" (*New York Times Book Review and Magazine* 1921a, 18). Another critic considered that the story of *Young Man of Manhattan* (Brush 1930) was told "with such skill and such reality" that it was "the only authentic story of a young man of the Manhattan press" (Butcher 1930, 11). One reviewer of *Sallie's Newspaper* (Lewis 1924) explained that while individuals hoped that the novel was fiction, the text, which incorporated current news and commentary, must be seen as fact (*New York Times Book Review* 1924).

Judgments of reviewers may be seen to reflect their ideological conceptions of what constituted "authentic" journalistic practices in the United States during the early twentieth century. On a fundamental level, critics considered firsthand knowledge of the newsroom essential. The *Boston Evening Transcript*'s (1923) assessment of *Deadlines* (Smith 1923), which suggested that "no one but a newspaper man could have given this graphic account of 'the Quaint, the Amusing, the Tragic Memoirs of a News-Room,'" reflected a view shared by many other critics. Reviewers frequently contrasted depictions of newsworkers with an individual author's own level of journalistic experience—and impressive credentials generally translated into positive reviews. Most notably, the journalistic achievements of Pulitzer Prize winner Royce Brier were evoked by critics to validate his first novel *Reach for the Moon.* Heralded as an example of "brilliant retrospective reporting," reviewers determined Brier's journalistic proficiency stood out "conspicuously" (*New York Times Book Review* 1934b). Critics cited Emile Gauvreau's experience as the editor of two New York tabloids to authenticate his novel about tabloid journalism, *Hot News,* and the *New York Herald Tribune Books* suggested that the realistic depiction of the journalism profession in *Trumpet in the Dust* was fundamentally the result of Gene Fowler's extensive newspaper experience (Flexner 1930). In one instance, a *New York Times* reviewer somewhat incestuously claimed that because Robert Van Gelder wrote from "first-hand experience" as one of the *Times*'s own staff reporters, there was "a real smell of printer's ink" in *Front Page Story* (*New York Times Book Review* 1937). Ethical dilemmas aside, what was fundamentally at issue here was the evaluation of fictional works based on the employment capabilities of their authors. Reviewers repeatedly emphasized journalistic experience in their appraisals of the credibility and value of newspaper novels, and consistently maintained that newsworkers were most capable of accurately portraying elements of the newspaper industry.

Realistic depictions of the newspaper environment were frequently cited by critics in support of the authenticity of these texts. In *Peggy Covers the News,* "outstanding" newspaperwoman Emma Bugbee was judged to offer young women who dreamed of newspaper careers an excellent description of the demands placed on female newsworkers. The novel, which addressed the organizational structure of a New York metropolitan newspaper, was thought to be written in "fictional terms" that were not "too rosy for reality" (*New York Times Book Review* 1936). Reviewers of *Deadlines* maintained that Henry Justin Smith accurately portrayed the "reality" of the newspaper office. One reviewer found that although its form was "fictional," Smith's work "in spirit" was the "accurate truth" (*New York Times Book Review* 1923); another suggested that "the naturalism (we should say 'accuracy' or 'realism')" of the novel made the "truth" of *Deadlines* "striking" (*Springfield Republican* 1923).

Critics also focused on the authentic representations of newsworkers in connection with larger issues of early-twentieth-century American society. The "superbly accurate" chronicle of newsworker Homer Zigler in *"The Great American Novel"* (Davis 1938) was also considered by one reviewer to be a diary of the United States from 1906 to 1937 that, in the final analysis, might have been "the only genuine novel ever written about a newspaper man" (Morley 1938). The novel was said to offer young men and women a warning to "pause before they hasten to enroll in journalism classes," along with an indictment of newspaper publishers "who have not been in forefront of providing improved working conditions" (*Christian Science Monitor* 1938). Reviewers of *Splendor* (1928) agreed that in this "story of all life" the significant changes in American society were well illustrated by Ben Ames Williams (*New York Times Book Review* 1927), and that his depiction of the life of one newsworker was also the story of millions of "plodders, inside and outside the press" (Bent 1928, 20). The *Saturday Review of Literature* (1931) found that in *Hot News* (Gauvreau 1931), the actual newspapers and newsworkers involved in tabloid journalism, along with "the wretched personalities exploited in news stories," were so thinly veiled that even tabloid readers could identify them, and the experiences of the reporter in the newsroom, and as a "victim" of the Depression, in *Two Loves* (Arnold 1934) were "uncomfortably and convincingly pictured" (*New York Times Book Review* 1934).

Only two of the novels were thought to offer unrealistic representations of the newsroom environment. The *New York Times* admonished John Mellett, a well-known journalist who had written previous novels under the pseudonym Jonathan Brooks, for his depiction of the field of journalism in *Ink,* which left "practically everything to be desired" (*New York Times Book Review* 1930, 21). The *Boston Evening Transcript* determined that "as a picture of newspaper life" *Ink* displayed "all the variety of a patent medicine endorsement" (*Boston Evening Transcript* 1930). Reviewers also considered *Success* (1921), by Samuel Hopkins Adams, distorted and misleading; it was thought to depict only the scandal and sensationalism of newspaper work, and to ignore sufficient discussion of the "honorable side of journalism" (*Outlook* 1921). The *New York Times Book Review* (1921) described the novel as a "tour de force of unreality," "painted entirely in scarlet and saffron" (30). In contrast, however, the *Literary Review* critic found that Adams had done a credible job depicting the "concessions" and "concealments and silences" that newsworkers were forced to commit in order to keep their jobs (Gavit 1921). Although reviewers generally dismissed *Success,* Adams (like other authors of newspaper novels) established himself as a popular literary figure after a lengthy journalistic career. Revered as a front-page reporter, Adams had conducted investigations of patent medicines during his time as a "muckraker" on the *New York Sun* staff that were considered to have aided in the enactment of federal pure food and drug laws (*New York Times* 1958). It is interesting to note that the labor conditions of newsworkers described in *Ink* and *Success* were actually quite consistent with those depicted in other novels. What differed was the presentation of that material. In these two texts the tone was considerably more hostile; the authors made little attempt to veil the bitterness they obviously felt toward the newspaper industry.

Critical responses to these novels may be seen as additional evidence in support of their use as evidence in reconstructing a history of newsworkers. Reviewers found newspaper novels entertaining and educational; they lauded the vast majority of them for their realistic and authentic depictions of the newsroom milieu. And they maintained that as former (or current) journalists, these writers knowledgeably addressed the working conditions of rank-and-file newsworkers. Although they may be somewhat shocking from a 1990s perspective, these depictions of the interwar-era newspaper world may have actually served to reinforce elements of the status quo. The expectations, challenges, and demands placed on newsworkers did not differ substantially from the labor conditions that many other workers endured during the early twentieth century in the United States.[6]

Often depicted as the "peasantry of the press" (Bent 1932, 144), rank-and-file newsworkers evolved as a class of workers bound not only by specific job responsibilities, but also by a sense of camaraderie, loyalty, and trust. In a diverse assortment of newspaper novels, including adventure stories such as *Scoop* (Hart and Byrnes 1930), *Contraband* (Kelland 1923), and *Ink* (Mellett 1930), romance novels such as *Two Loves* (Arnold 1934), *Private Props* (Mallette 1937), and *Round Trip* (Tracy 1934), and the psychological portraits found in *The Chicken Wagon Family* (Benefield 1925), *Trumpet in the Dust* (Fowler 1930), and *Erik Dorn* (Hecht 1921/1963), newsworkers established themselves as a unique group of workers. Reporters formed strong alliances within their group that often surpassed any specific allegiances to their individual newspapers; they worked and socialized together, and, when necessary, they protected each other. A conversation of a seasoned sob sister with her new recruit in *The Girl Reporter* pointedly addressed this relationship: "You are a reporter or you aren't! If you are, you have friends, chums, helpers, in everyone in the craft. We stick by our own!" (Claudy 1930, 48).

Unlike during the 1870s and 1880s, when overlapping story assignments by editors encouraged "turf" battles among newsworkers (Wilson 1985, 30), these novels maintained that by the early twentieth century, reporters such as those in *An Unconscious Crusader* created an "offensive and defensive alliance" among members of their class (S. Williams 1920, 121). It was a coalition that encouraged cooperation among newsworkers from rival papers, and insisted that "under ordinary conditions, all reporters assigned to a story shall work together and that if any one of their number gets into difficulties, the others shall help him out" (Van Gelder 1937/1946, 117). The novels often recounted efforts by reporters to cover for a fellow newsworker who was drunk, depressed, ill, or had a schedule conflict. This sense of class consciousness was similarly addressed by journalism historian Ted Smythe (1992, 222), who, in a study of reporters from 1880 to 1900, found that because of unreasonable work demands, reporters joined together against management, split news-gathering responsibilities, and shared information.

Fictional newsworkers shared routine information; some did it with tacit management approval, others rejected explicit demands that journalists not work together. The novels from this period maintained that although newspaper managers theoretically rejected the idea of communal news gathering, they realized that if all reporters were to gather their own information, news organizations would be forced to double or triple their staffs (Van Gelder 1937/1946, 118). Reporters did not share the exclusive angles on stories they occasionally uncovered; however, on daily news they worked to "beat" other journalists by crafting well-written stories rather than by keeping basic information from one another (Bugbee 1936/1940, 188–89). In the novels, reporters generally agreed with the newsworker's assessment in *The Moon Calf* that it did not pay to keep information from other reporters, that teamwork was the only way to succeed in the newspaper business (Dell 1921, 246).

Newsworkers in these novels also shared their plans, hopes, and dreams, as well as fantasies, fears, and nightmares, with other journalists who gave them emotional as well as physical support. They helped each other through confidence crises, writers' blocks, and depression; if their plans sometimes seemed naive utopian fantasies, other newsworkers did not seem to mind, for as one reporter in *The Chicken Wagon Family* explained, a "log house in the deep silent woods by the softly flowing stream" was a recurrent "dream home" of the majority of urban newsworkers (Benefield 1925, 152).

In *Lords of the Press,* a scathing critique of the newspaper industry, George Seldes (1938) demarcated the class of newsworker whom he termed "working newspapermen" from publishers, editors, correspondents, and columnists, the elite "trained seals" of the press. He found that reporters of the time, blinded by egotism, were usually unable to stand up for their own interests, and were therefore exploited and treated as "the lowliest of animals" (370). Novelists, for the most part, have agreed with Seldes's caustic assessment of reporters; in interwar newspaper novels, reporters perceived of themselves as outcasts, somewhat tainted by their reporting tasks. It is for this reason they preferred the "clumsy, misfit term" *newspaperman* to *journalist* or *reporter* (Adams 1921, 219). In *Peggy Covers the News* (Bugbee 1936/1940), *The Girl Reporter* (Claudy 1930), *Private Props* (Mallette 1937), and *Though Time Be Fleet* (Andrus 1937), when the newsworker was a woman, being told "you're a good newspaperman" was still considered the highest compliment a female journalist could receive. In *A Place in the News,* journalist Kay Mills (1988) maintained that during this era, when a woman was told she "did a man's job today," it meant that she was "cool, competent, professional" (47). In her history of women in journalism, *New York Herald Tribune* reporter Ishbel Ross (1936) suggested that during the 1920s and 1930s, newspaperwomen accepted a male-oriented standard of excellence because they recognized that editors rejected the "so-called woman's touch in the news" (12-13). Although novels and other historical sources written during the 1920s and 1930s, such as memoirs, autobiographies, and career books, used the term *newspaperman* almost exclusively, the majority of current media histories that discussed this time period did not address this preference.[7] However, it is also important to consider that the exclusionary use of language in these novels, which privileged a male perspective, may also be "a quiet little tip-off" to the material conditions that women confronted during this era (Mills 1988, 6).

Although women encountered experiences similar to those of their male counterparts, they also faced additional burdens, constraints, and pressures. Newspaperwomen were not seen as a separate group of workers, but as an anomaly within that class. By 1920, women represented almost 20 percent of newspaper workers, yet their work was confined primarily to women's issues and the society pages (Rogers 1931, 259). And of the nearly 12,000 female reporters and editors working in the United States during the 1930s, only a few gained access to the front pages of newspapers. Women were generally considered incapable of covering hard news (Ross 1936, 2); there were a few exceptional women, known as "front-page girls," who were "allowed the rare privilege" of covering politics, public affairs, and other front-page stories (Beasley 1992, 266). Yet, although they were tolerated, newspaperwomen were not really welcome in the city room. As one newsworker explained:

> They are there on sufferance, although the departments could scarcely get along without them. But if the front-page girls were all to disappear tomorrow no searching party would go out looking for more, since it is the fixed conviction of nearly every newspaper

executive that a man in the same spot would be exactly twice as good. (Ross 1936, 13)

During this period, newspaper novels both explicitly and implicitly addressed the restrictive treatment of female newsworkers. In many of the novels there was no discussion of women in the newsroom; in others there was an understanding of women as a "negligible factor" (Ross 1936, 600). Fearful that "crinoline and catastrophe were synonymous" (S. Williams 1920, 166), some authors believed that women were not capable of working for newspapers, and, like the city editor in *City Desk,* maintained that women could not "deliver the goods nor stand the pace" (Haddock 1937, 12). A misogynist view of women pervaded a few of the novels, with female newsworkers depicted as scheming, devious, deceitful, and untrustworthy. However, these negative depictions may also have reflected concerns regarding what one reporter referred to as the "Girl Question." During the 1920s and 1930s, many men were extremely confused regarding the entrance of women into the workplace; they often had trouble separating the physical attractiveness of women from their professional abilities, and they specifically questioned the role of women in American society (Dell 1921, 297).

For example, in *Reporter,* the cub reporter complained about what he saw as the special treatment given to one of the "prima donnas" of the newsroom. He specifically objected to one newspaperwoman using a rewrite typewriter, something the male newsworker was sure he would be excoriated for doing. Yet his obvious frustration was not based solely on an idealistic sense of fairness, but also on his unresolved and almost uncontrollable attraction to the woman. He admitted:

> It is the back of her neck that attracts the reporter. How it curves! How her throat is soft and firm and warm; how the black down of her black hair caresses her luxurious dark skin. He could fall in love with her; but he has resolved not to let himself fall in love with her. She would be too strong for him. Her will is powerful. She would dominate her lover. He feared that. What is she writing now? To whom? She is always writing long letters to someone. Endless letters. They must be love-letters. The reporter feels angry; and tries to go on reading in his book. Her complexion is warm brown, her throat is dark, but where it goes down into her breast it glides into a maddening pallor. (Levin 1929, 162)

In contrast, the few male and female novelists who discussed female reporters extensively recounted openly the prejudice against women on newspapers. Although these texts suggested that it took at least one "miracle" for a qualified newswoman to get a position on a metropolitan paper, they maintained that women had repeatedly demonstrated that they could endure both the physical and mental "strain" associated with news reporting (Bugbee 1936/1940, 247, 116). During the interwar era, daily newspapers remained content to have, at most, one token woman reporter covering news. In *Peggy Covers the News,* college-educated women seeking employment on newspapers were repeatedly told: "The policy of the paper has been to limit the number of women reporters. That is not a final or unchangeable rule, but at present we are getting along very well with only one woman" (Bugbee 1936/1940, 159). Although male journalists acknowledged the need for a woman's perspective on the news, they generally considered it less important than "straight news" (Bugbee 1936/1940, 100). In these novels, female reporters frequently addressed specific problems they encountered in the newsroom. In *Though Time Be Fleet,* one assistant city editor held a grudge against newspaperwomen; he "liked to make them work overtime and took their complaints, if they voiced them, as conclusive proof that women had no place in the newspaper business" (Andrus 1937, 142-43).

The stereotypical perceptions of "hard as nails" newswomen who no longer looked presentable because they "realize they haven't got a chance to get a man" (Tracy 1934, 52) were refuted by both male and female novelists in their depictions of competent, caring, and attractive women reporters. In novels such as *Private Props* (Mallette 1937), *The Girl Reporter* (Claudy 1930), and *Ink* (Mellett 1930), female reporters were portrayed as intelligent, competent, and creative; cognizant that they were considered "exceptions," these newspaperwomen knew that they must work twice as hard as their male counterparts to obtain and keep their jobs.

The issues surrounding female newsworkers mirrored the changing status of American women during the first half of the twentieth century. Intelligent working women challenged traditional notions regarding their role in American society; men were confused by these changes and frequently were unsure about how to treat female employees. One fictional male editor explained:

> We say we want a woman reporter to be able to cover any sort of story, and we make our women do anything the men do, yet all the time, in the back of our minds, we keep feeling that they shouldn't be doing those things and it makes us uncomfortable. . . . You women reporters make us always a trifle ashamed when we send you out on stormy days to cover East Side fires, or murders in the

Bronx. We aren't the least bit disturbed about sending the young men on those stories. (Bugbee 1936/1940, 159-60)

During the 1920s and 1930s, both male and female American news-workers encountered specific working conditions and newsroom routines that directly impacted their perceptions of themselves as well as their relations with others. Reporters worked in city rooms that were dirty, crowded, noisy, and confused. Novelists often described the "dingy and cramped" editorial rooms, with battered desks, broken chairs, and typewriters that dropped a's and e's (Brier 1934, 30-31). The heavy and stale air in city rooms, with their unwashed windows, dusty and dirty desks, and floors littered with masses of wastepaper, were compared with barns "where family cast-offs" were stored (Haddock 1937, 8) and as places where cows might very comfortably be "bedded down" (Kelland 1923, 6).

The narrator of "*The Great American Novel,*" previously used to large, neat offices filled with gentlemen working in Alpaca jackets, recounted his surprise at encountering his local city room for the first time:

> To begin with, it is a ramshackle place that quivers ominously when the presses are running. Along one side was a row of office doors for department editors, separated from the main room by a haphazard partition. There were wastebaskets, but they were little used. The floor was littered with torn newspapers and sheets of copy paper. Mr. Penny, coatless, was wearing black protectors over his striped shirt sleeves and a green eyeshade at a rakish angle on his tousled head. A little way from the city desk a man was sitting with his hat on and his feet comfortably propped on a rickety typewriter table while he smoked a corncob pipe and languidly perused an after-noon paper. Telephones were ringing, men were talking loudly and profanely. There was an air of tenseness, but also an air of immense informality and relaxation. (Davis 1938, 14-15)

In *The Young Man and Journalism* (1922), Chester Lord's description re-verberated with that of his novelist counterparts as he explained that the noise and confusion of the newsroom often distracted newer reporters and affected their ability to write. On an ordinary day, "hurry-up telephone bells are jingling and men are bawling through the transmitters. Typewriters re-sound their staccato clicking." He observed that, in the city room, people were constantly coming and going, talking and laughing; reporters often shouted for "office boys," who yelled and stumbled over each other in re-sponse. Lord, a journalist on the *New York Sun* for forty-one years, suggested that although "the old hands" might be accustomed to the noise and confusion, newer employees, more familiar with the quiet of study rooms, sometimes developed "symptoms of insanity" (26-27).

Novelists of this era speculated on the effects of the dirt, noise, and confusion on newsworkers, and suggested that although most reporters adapted to the adverse conditions, the work environment contributed to their low self-image and encouraged a sense of estrangement. In *Erik Dorn,* one editor described what he saw as a thoroughly alienated class of newsworkers:

> Oldish young men and youngish old men gravitated about him, their faces curiously identical. These were the irresponsible-eyed, casual-mannered individuals, seemingly neither at work nor at play, who were to visit the courts, the police, the wrecks, the criminals, conventions, politicians, reformers, lovers, and haters, and bring back the news of the city's day. A common almost radical sophistication stamped their expression. They pawed over telephone books, argued with indifferent, emotionless profanity among themselves on items of amazing import; pounded nonchalantly upon typewriters, lolled with their feet upon desks, their noses buried in the humorous columns of the morning newspapers. (Hecht 1921/1963, 15)

Although adverse work environments may have contributed to reporters' sense of alienation, the work routine of journalists offered additional evidence of their dehumanization and commodification. Reporters worked long hours for very low wages and endured a variety of physical and mental hardships; Lord suggested that during the 1920s and 1930s, newsworkers generally worked irregular and unlimited hours. They were required to labor as long as they were needed and often worked fifteen-hour days. Newsworkers regularly suffered from physical fatigue and lack of food and sleep, and were frequently exposed to adverse weather conditions. Their long hours tended to forestall any social life, and Lord believed that a reporter's workday tended to "end somewhat dismally by his dragging home at two o'clock in the morning, maybe through storm or sleet or tempest, to a cold, cheerless, silent, dark home" (27). Theoretically, during the 1930s reporters worked only forty hours per week; however, in practice they often covered late evening meetings and frequently labored until at least midnight. Echoing many other journalists in fiction, one newswoman in *Peggy Covers the News* insisted that "no real newspaper person ever dreamed of stopping work on a story until it was finished" (Bugbee 1936/1940, 214). During "exceptional" news days, reporters sometimes worked more than twenty-four continuous hours. For example, the journalist in the "*The Great American Novel*" told of working "steadily" during one presidential election from noon on a Tuesday until early the following Thursday morning, a total of thirty-nine hours (Davis 1938, 225).

Scholars generally agreed that during the interwar era the salaries of reporters were extremely low. In the 1920s, wages for experienced newsworkers in smaller markets ranged from less than $20 to $25 per week; in larger urban areas, salaries ranged from $25 to $50 or $60 weekly. Salaries were highest in New York, where "star" reporters could have earned close to $100 a week. The pay for cub reporters generally ranged from $5 to $15 per week, depending on the market (Bent 1927, 118; Lord 1922, 146; Rogers 1931, 322-23). In 1934, an American Newspaper Guild survey of editorial workers determined that the median weekly wage for reporters with more than nine years' experience was $30.70, and cub reporters averaged $18.63 per week; these findings reflected salaries that were considered by *Editor & Publisher* to be "scandalously out of line" with wage standards and costs (Lee 1937, 687-88).

Most novels written during the interwar years discussed the wages of reporters, and their figures were firmly in line with the salaries indicated by researchers. More important, novelists also attempted to explain the relative worth of specific wages in terms of the living expenses of journalists. The $5 to $10 that cub reporters earned each week was not considered a living wage, and these authors were quick to point out the hardships inexperienced newsworkers endured. For example, the cub reporter in *The Copy Shop*, who earned a weekly stipend of $5, paid $3.50 each week for a room in a house, and was therefore left with $1.50 a week for food, clothing, transportation, entertainment, and other expenses (Hungerford 1925, 40). Newsworkers were often depicted in these novels as merely surviving; they earned enough to take care of food and shelter, but rarely had any money for extras. Some stories, however, explicitly questioned reporters' quality of life. For instance, in *Front Page Story*, a new recruit was introduced to "leg-man's turkey," a popular dish among reporters, created by spreading a double order of butter thickly between two slices of bread and then scooping beans onto the bread to create a sandwich (Van Gelder 1937/1946, 59-60).

Even newsworkers in the novels who made fairly decent wages were concerned with the increasing costs of American life. In *Splendor*, a journalist who earned $35 a week was startled to discover that his salary, "which would ten years before have seemed to [him] like opulence," was no longer enough to support his family (B. Williams 1928, 367). This assessment was not surprising given that researchers have determined that in the 1920s, families earning less than $3,000 per year were unable to save any money (Meltzer

1969, 10). However, fictional newsworkers, like other workers, continually faced pressures of twentieth-century capitalism, which urged them to consume an ever-increasing number of products. According to historian Daniel Bell (1976), in the 1920s, technological advances, coupled with assembly-line mass production, marketing, and installment buying, produced a cultural transformation in American society. An increased availability of luxury goods, continually redefined as necessities, encouraged the rise of a consumption society that emphasized spending and material possessions and undermined "the traditional value system with its emphasis on thrift, frugality, self control and impulse renunciation" (65).

Bombarded with advertising messages, fictional newsworkers were often coaxed into buying products they could not afford. Like many other Americans, reporters in these novels replace a purchasing philosophy of only buying what could be paid for in cash with the strategy of "a dollar down and a dollar forever" (Meltzer 1969, 10), and they often borrowed money to finance their acquisitions. Yet, these reporters tended to panic when their level of debt became unmanageable; a few less stable workers had breakdowns, some took extra jobs or tried freelance writing, and others, like the newsworker in "*The Great American Novel,*" gave up reporting for the relative economic security of the copy desk (Davis 1938).

The work routine of journalists was commonly depicted as drudgery; novels from this period insisted: "The work will ask everything of you. It will suck you dry, and it will give you very little in return" (Bent 1932, 38). Although a reporter's job was sometimes exciting and adventurous, the majority of time it was routine, repetitive, monotonous, dull, and boring. Newspaperwomen were not exempt from the drudgery; they also worked extremely long hours and made "endless journeys after fruitless interviews with disagreeable people" who did not want to talk on the record (Claudy 1930, 216). In *Success,* a thirty-year-old veteran reporter explained that although it was a sense of adventure and change that kept many reporters going, an underlying sense of tedium often pervaded their lives. He suggested that "the monotony of seeing things by glimpses, of never really completing a job, of being inside important things, but never of them" was what ultimately demoralized most newsworkers (Adams 1921, 309-10).

The novels often suggested a connection between the newsroom demands, pressures, and policies encouraged by early-twentieth-century industrial capitalism and the dehumanization and commodification of newsworkers. Journalists were frequently considered expendable products, and the process of indoctrinating new reporters included lessons that instilled a sense of unimportance, worthlessness, and replaceability. When a new recruit in *The Girl Reporter* was told by a more experienced reporter, "You are not a person. . . . You have no rights, no feelings. You are a part of the job. The job is to get the news; all the news; no matter how it hurts or helps" (Claudy 1930, 45), the message reverberated warnings found in many other novels.

The positions of newsworkers in this era were rarely secure, and novelists, along with media historians, generally considered reporting a business mainly for the young. Journalism historian Gerald Baldasty's (1992, 89) assessment that gray hair was considered a "scarlet letter" in late-nineteenth-century journalism still held for newsworkers of the 1920s and 1930s. Competent reporters were displaced if they in any way became liabilities; newsworkers who could no longer endure the hectic pace, or who got "a bit rusty in their work," found they were no longer welcome in the newsroom (Hungerford 1925, 276). As one seasoned sob sister in *The Girl Reporter* insisted: "Newspaper work knows no charity! You last while you are good and you get fired if you are punk" (Claudy 1930, 53).

The cyclical nature of the commodification process was often delineated in these texts. *Splendor*, a chronicle of one journalist's entire career in the newspaper business, began when the newsworker was hired as an office boy on a daily paper. In the course of his career, he worked briefly in the reference department, then was promoted to reporter, bicycle editor, State House reporter, copyreader, makeup editor, and copy editor. Finally, he was assigned, once again, to the reference department, and the novel concluded with the newspaperman's tragic realization that he hadn't really gotten anywhere, that he worked for thirty years and merely "rounded a circle" (B. A. Williams 1928, 566).

Often the quintessential reporter who could no longer endure the demands of the newsroom was assigned to culminate his or her career in the reference department, better known as the morgue. Since many novelists envisioned the newsroom as a kind of living death, retirement in the morgue may have been seen as a fitting culmination of this process. The sense of uselessness, of utter despair, often expressed in novels during this era was fervently voiced by a newsworker in *The Chicken Wagon Family*:

> I am forty years old by the calendar and forty centuries old in spirit—and am Long Emergency sitting here at 3:30 a.m. in the "Transcript" office. When I am fifty they will probably put me in charge of the "morgue" up in the library, where I shall spend all my time clipping articles out of the papers about notable and nefarious people and events to file away in row upon row of little drawers for

barely possible future reference. When I am sixty they will assign me to the exciting job of answering letters of lunatics who would like to know the last line of the poem beginning, "The night was cold and dark and dreary," etc. And when I am seventy—well, perhaps I shall have given myself an assignment then and covered it without writing a single line about it. (Benefield 1925, 152-53)

A belief in fatalistic reservation often pervaded these texts. Reporters suffered repeated setbacks, wrote continually about shattered dreams, and frequently got to the point where each succeeding disappointment was merely "another Yesterday that Midnight will abandon and forget" (Fowler 1930, 220). All newsworkers eventually realized that even the most meaningful stories they produced quickly became little more than wastepaper.

The futility of a long-term commitment to journalism was an overarching theme found in interwar-era novels. Idealistic cubs were often warned by more experienced reporters and editors to get out of the newspaper game before it was too late, before it fastened "its writhing coils about you like the Great African Rock Python" and squeezed "the juice from you, drop by pitiful drop, the juice of youth and life" (Brier 1934, 34). Journalists frequently discussed alternative employment options with each other; they considered careers in advertising, sales, teaching, writing, or anything that might make them feel like individuals again. Demoralized newsworkers tended to equate their jobs as reporters with "being caught in a fly-wheel by the sleeve," which tossed them around "like a plaything" and then threw them aside, "limp and shattered" (Smith 1923, 32).

Not only were reporters in these novels seen by management as commodities, they also viewed themselves and responded to others as things, and found their worth almost entirely tied to their use value. For example, in *Success*, a young reporter's introspectiveness when he discovered his first published article validated a sense of self-realization that was inextricably intertwined with newspaper production. He asked:

What writer has not felt the conscious red tingle in his cheeks at first sight of himself in the magnified personification of type? Here is something, once himself, now expanded far beyond individual limits, into the proportions of publicity, for all the world to measure and estimate and criticize. (Adams 1921, 116)

Reporters envisioned themselves as newspaper clips and bylines, and judged their personal value by the number of column inches run and the frequency of their bylines. In general, bylines still did not "come easy" in the

1920s and 1930s (Berger 1938, 169), and they were considered the ultimate proof of a job well done. As the cub reporter in *Peggy Covers the News* explained, bylines were "the goal of every reporter's ambition—the greatest honor a newspaper could pay its staff" (Bugbee 1936/1940, 25). Whereas cub reporters waited eagerly for an assignment that would yield them a cherished byline, more experienced newsworkers relied on them to validate their own worth, and often became depressed and angry when they found them missing.

Although the value of newsworkers was predominantly determined by their usefulness, in novels the commodification of reporters was commonly questioned, challenged, and rejected. As authors attempted to understand the specific working conditions that newsworkers endured, they continuously called for an engagement with humanity. Their assessments of American society were rarely optimistic, and the issues at times were overstated, as if to make sure that all readers understood what was at stake. For example, in *Round Trip,* when a female reporter realized that her complete identity centered on "an eight-column streamer and a by-line," rather than on any personal attributes, she committed suicide (Tracy 1934, 37).

Central to understanding the commodification of newsworkers in the early twentieth century is the realization that the role of American reporters continued to be that of "a replaceable cog in the machinery of the modern newspaper" (Salcetti 1992, 98). Throughout these novels were references to newsworkers as machines, for, as one observer suggested, "you can't never tell where a reporter leaves off and his paper begins" (Brier 1934, 151). One journalist explained that in his pursuit of news at any cost, he quickly became a well-functioning "dehumanized piece of newspaper machinery" (Gauvreau 1931, 21). Reporters frequently found that their lack of private lives, coupled with long hours and poor working conditions, compelled them to become "automatic writing machines" (Dos Passos 1925/1953, 344), producing at breakneck speed until they eventually wore out (Adams 1921, 309).

In an effort to accentuate the dehumanization of newsworkers, some of the novelists anthropomorphized specific material elements of the industry. Newspapers were given souls to differentiate them from other inanimate objects (Adams 1921, 438-39); Douglas (1932) depicted carving tools and a walnut desk as living things that took "on a personality possessed of so many sensitive, changing moods" (103); Smith (1923) described the silence before the news day began by referring to telephones that "have not yet found their tongues" (2). One fictional newsworker suggested that if his typewriter knew he was using it as "an instrument of psychic release" it would be "outraged" and "rebellious," and would once again "refuse to write another line"

(Benefield 1925, 6). In *Scoop,* a reporter reacted to the "glaring headlines blazed across the page" that described the death of his lover by questioning the cruelty of type, which shouted out messages of death produced by newsworkers with "dead hands" (Hart and Byrnes 1930, 298). In *Contraband,* the production manager focused on the mental condition of the newspaper's press:

> Just inside the door squatted the antiquated, limping cylinder press which gave birth weekly to the Free Press, and which gave off with sullen brazenness the look of overmuch child-bearing. It knew it was going to break down in the middle of every run, and it had been cursed at so often and so fluently that it was utterly indifferent. It was a press without ambition. Of late years it had gotten into a frame of mind where it didn't care a hang whether it printed a paper or not—which is an alarming state of mind for a printing press to be in. (Kelland 1923, 4-5)

A veteran editor in one novel suggested that the dehumanization of newsworkers stemmed from their addiction to printer's ink. He explained that ink got into journalists' eyes and forced them to see only printed lines. Ink transformed all of their thoughts "into type, body type and head-lines, agate and twelve-point." Discussion in this novel resonated with the debates regarding the consequences of capitalism. Ink was considered the ultimate controlling force: it "makes you hungry, and it satisfies you. It drives you, coaxes, wheedles, bullies and begs you." In the end, "it carries you to success, or it abandons you" (Mellett 1930, 32-33).

These novels insisted that newsroom pressures and demands forced newsworkers to become prostitutes and pariahs, emotionless leeches who made their living recording the tragedies, scandals, and catastrophes of society. Reporters were expected to stay detached and feel nothing. They must "witness tears and grief, pain and agony, shame and disgrace, and remain as impersonal, as unaffected and untouched, as if they were in a play" (Claudy 1930, 185). As one journalist in *Two Loves* explained, "To a reporter people in trouble, fires, murders, suicides, court actions, rapes, all of them are just names and places furnishing the authentic base to his story" (Arnold 1934, 116). Just as the cub reporter in *Jim of the Press* who realized, when tragedy struck his hometown, that he could not waste any of his time thinking about the human lives involved, newsworkers quickly learned they must "report the news, write it, and get it in the paper," regardless of the circumstances (Dean 1933, 34).

An outsider, the reporter observed society like a "Peeping Tom looking through a window" (Berger 1938, 59), rather than as an active participant, and was often judged by members of the community as "a parasite on the drama of life" (Dos Passos 1925/1953, 320). Journalists who primarily observed only the uglier aspects of society were frequently thought to become spectators of the plagues that swept the world (B. A. Williams 1928, 521). During this era, newsworkers were depicted as alienated from their work, from others, and from themselves. Their estrangement from society was exemplified by a bizarre win-place-show office pool described in "*The Great American Novel*," in which newsworkers bet on the electrocution order of four actual New York criminals (Gyp the Blood, Lefty Louie, Dago Frank, and Whitey Lewis) who murdered a well-known gambler. Chances were sold to newsworkers for a quarter each, and the person with the correct order of death won $5.50 (Davis 1938, 176-77).

Reporters in these novels discovered that in American society, the "worst" news was actually the "best" news, and that individuals preferred to "shed their little, personal sorrows in the bigger, more devastating sorrows of others"; therefore, the larger the catastrophe, the more space it received on page 1 (Fowler 1930, 88). In *Front Page Story,* newsworkers reacted to the news value of the "mechanics" of a prominent individual's murder, rather than to the actual tragedy of his violent death; instead of focusing on the specific "facts" of the murder, they were enthusiastic about the lively effect on readers that the news would have, and the added circulation the story might bring (Van Gelder 1937/1946, 12-13).

For the most part, newsworkers in these novels distanced themselves from their work; their labor became objectified as a separate thing that existed independent from them. As Marx (1966) explained, in capitalist society, an alienated worker gave life to a product that consequently stood opposed to that person "as an alien and hostile force" (96). However, because the identity and value of newsworkers was tied directly to the production of news, not only their work but often their own understanding of themselves as individuals tended to become separated from their actual existence. In *The Moon Calf,* the objectification process was addressed explicitly when a reporter finally realized that the apprehension of society could only be achieved through an understanding of individuals. The newsworker admitted that he previously had no interest in people and explained that even during his most recent assignment he

> had forgotten the woman, forgotten those death-shadowed
> children, forgotten the innocent maniac of a husband who had led

her in that hopeless, ridiculous tragic quest across a continent, forgotten her infinite patience and absurd loyalty, except as figments of the dream which he had just recorded upon paper. They were not real to him, they never had been real—they were figures he had created, moving helplessly through a world of blind accident; they were pathetic with the lively pathos of a poem. (Dell 1921, 270–71)

The authors of newspaper novels considered the cold detachment from society—understanding people as objects, useful merely as potential circulation builders—one of the most difficult things required of newsworkers. Journalists were repeatedly portrayed as alienated from others; reporters put their work before their social lives, their families, their spouses, and even (in the case of men) the birth of their children. During the course of their careers, they were indoctrinated into believing that "an honest-to-goodness newspaper reporter" always forgot "everything in the universe except his story" (Mallette 1937, 258-59). This "absurd, grotesque, insensitive, even ludicrous" allegiance to the news was perhaps most strongly articulated in *An American Tragedy,* when the main character's mother, with paper and pencil in hand, for the first time "performed" as a reporter during her son's murder trial (Dreiser 1925/1981, 753).

Often depicted as "predatory birds, ready to swoop and bring up juicy morsels" for their readers' edification (Andrus 1937, 109), newsworkers were judged in fiction to pander to the "basest instincts of humankind" (Gauvreau 1931, 95). Writers during the interwar years repeatedly attacked the almost insatiable desire in American society for catastrophe, scandal, and pain. In *Sallie's Newspaper,* the author insisted that in the American press, the constant barrage of horrific news was destroying the memory and humanity of society. For instance, although newspapers "recorded twelve thousand suicides for the United States alone in 1923 . . . the average reader cannot recall a single name of the twelve thousand" (Lewis 1924, 283-84).

Yet newsworkers in these novels often deplored their role as servants of sensationalism, and, like one seasoned reporter in *Young Man of Manhattan,* experienced "a growing despondency" about themselves and a concern for their future (Brush 1930, 123). These journalists suffered from a profound sense of inadequacy and frequently questioned why anyone would want to give them information. As their value as individuals became increasingly intertwined with their success as reporters, a sense of self-alienation flourished. Although many newsworkers in this era eventually left the business, in novels those who endured the pressures of the newsroom faced insanity, early death from overwork, alcoholism, and drug addiction.

As workers within a capitalist media system, reporters confronted a bureaucratic chain of command and hierarchy of authority. During the interwar era, Seldes (1938) found newspaper management dictatorial in nature. He explained that when a publisher ordered a picture of a particular actress run each day, no one was harmed; however, when an order was sent "to smear a certain liberal Congressman" (as he suggested was frequently the case), that was "journalism dictatorship" (383). The dictatorship to which Seldes referred involved both the suppression of news and the subordination of newsworkers, and was a concern of both scholars and novelists during the 1920s and 1930s. In his landmark study of Washington correspondents, Leo Rosten (1937) found that efforts to keep news sources happy as well as specific newspaper policies encouraged reporters to suppress information. Newsworkers placed distinct value on their sources and omitted or played down objectionable information. In addition, correspondents who were chosen to cover Washington were those who had previously demonstrated allegiance to their publications and were familiar with newspaper policy and aware of what was expected of them. Rosten explained that because each paper embodied "an institutional atmosphere which communicated the official point of view to the personnel with precision" (231), reporters eager to "win the praise and pleasure" of their superiors were particularly adept at discerning what information was preferred and how it should be addressed (235).

In 1934, the American Newspaper Guild, maintaining that the fundamental duty of newsworkers was to give the "public accurate and unbiased news reports," condemned the "current practice of requiring the procuring or writing of stories" that newspapermen knew were false or misleading and that contributed to the oppression of persons and groups (Lee 1937, 685). The Guild felt that the "high calling" of reporting had "fallen into disrepute because news writers have been too often degraded as hirelings compelled by their employers to serve the purposes of politicians, monopolists, speculators in the necessaries of life, exploiters of labor, and fomenters of war" (684–85). Insisting that freedom of the press was a public right and responsibility rather than a privilege to be exploited by media owners, The Guild, in a "freedom of conscience" resolution, encouraged reporters to strive for journalistic integrity and editors and publishers to "curb the suppression of legitimate news concerning 'privileged' persons or groups, including advertisers, commercial powers and friends of newspapermen" (685).

Interwar-era novels frequently addressed the pressures placed upon newsworkers, by sources and management, to suppress the news. They delineated stories that were killed because they challenged an owner's ideological position or because they conflicted with other interests owned by a newspaper. In *Success,* a newsworker covered an industrial tragedy that occurred when management, in an attempt to break up a strike, employed "a small army of hired gun-men" who were responsible for the deaths of ten people, including a woman and a six-year-old child. Because of the newspaper's anti-labor policy, the strike story was rejected, and the reporter was told by his managing editor that to print such information would make the paper "a betrayer of its own cause" (Adams 1921, 286). In *Scoop,* a news story about a bus accident in which three people were killed and seven injured because of a judgment error made by an uncertified bus driver was suppressed when a major advertiser (in this case the transit company) pressured newspaper management to "ignore" particularly damaging information (Hart and Byrnes 1930, 101-2). And in *Contraband,* an extreme case illustrative of the ultimate conflict of interest: a businessman who owned the mortgage on a small-town newspaper and who maintained that the paper could not survive without his approval and support attempted to set newsroom policy and demanded to see everything controversial before it was published (Kelland 1923, 72). Newsworkers in these novels quickly learned to identify and tread lightly on the "sacred cows"—the companies, groups, individuals, charities, political parties, and public utilities who were large advertisers and wielded considerable power over newspaper management (Claudy 1930, 61-62). Eventually, like the reporter in *Manhattan Transfer,* most journalists were forced to realize that "every word, every picayune punctuation" that appeared in the press was "perused and revised and deleted in the interests of advertisers and bond-holders" (Dos Passos 1925/1953, 195).

Newsworkers were also responsible for the suppression of news; it was a generally accepted dictum that a "good reporter is the one who knows what *not* to write" (Hungerford 1925, 161). Reporters worked extremely hard to cultivate sources, and when a reputable source asked them to "forget" certain information, they often agreed. Yet, as a police reporter in *The Copy Shop* explained, although a journalist may, like himself, be a specialist in keeping questionable material out the newspaper, the suppression of news was always a "dangerous business." If another paper printed information a reporter neglected to cover, the newsworker may be fired or severely reprimanded (Hungerford 1925, 200).

Newspaper policies regarding what constituted "acceptable" news, the appropriate sources of information, the "proper" framing of journalistic reports, and the role of reporters in the production of news were repeatedly described in the novels, not as elements of a subtle observation process through which journalists slowly acquired a news sense, but rather as obvious attempts to subordinate newsworkers. Reporters were "disciplined" when they challenged management, missed an important story, or refused to cover a particularly "dirty" assignment. In *Success,* one highly valued space reporter, paid solely on the number of column inches run in the newspaper each week, delineated the treatment he received from his editors after his role in an investigation of graft in city government was discovered:

> A long succession of the pettiest kind of assignments was doled out to him by the city desk: obituary notices of insignificant people, small police items, tipsters' yarns, routine jobs such as ship news, police headquarters substitution, even the minor courts usually relegated to the fifteen or twenty-dollar-a-week men. Or, worst and most grinding ordeal of a reporter's life, he was kept idle at his desk, like a misbehaving boy after school, when all the other men had been sent out. One week his total space came to but twenty-eight dollars odd. What this meant was plain enough; he was being disciplined for his part in the investigation. (Adams 1921, 252-53)

In these novels, less experienced reporters who refused to cover a story because of personal connections, ethical conflicts, or humanitarian outrage were often fired. Newsworkers quickly understood that they must be willing to report on anything, no matter how difficult or personally distasteful. Most reporters were at least occasionally asked to do "dirty work"—assignments that affronted the privacy of individuals, made the reporters physically sick to their stomachs, or were so distasteful that the reporters must be fortified with alcohol before they could begin. In *Trumpet in the Dust,* a reporter whose editor expected him to "learn to jump" when the whip was cracked refused to construct a sensational story about his old girlfriend and was forced to spend the majority of his time at the office, doing nothing. Occasionally he was asked to do a brief rewrite but he explained that during his period of discipline he felt "like a boy with a light case of scarlet fever, quarantined and watching playmates from a window as they romped before his eyes" (Fowler 1930, 191). The disciplinary period was determined by the speed with which a reporter accepted the disputed policy and was willing to do what was expected. Newsworkers who wished to stay in the business ultimately accepted the demands of management. As an experienced reporter in *Splendor* suggested, all reporters eventually learned to compromise their ideals, or faced disgrace and tremendous disappointment. "They've all had to do rather less, or rather more than they believed they should have done; and they've all had to stifle, smother, kill off their aspiration" (B. A. Williams 1928, 521).

Although Michael Schudson (1978) found that in the 1920s and 1930s journalists began to question the "reality" of facts and establish the concept of objectivity, which rendered facts "consensually validated statements" rather than actual descriptions of the world (6-7), in novels there was less concern with the "reality" of facts than with the material conditions regarding the suppression of news. Fictional newsworkers understood that "truth" was something that could only be approximated, and believed that "no reporter, no matter how practiced," could be sure of the "final truth," or could know "how near that truth he has taken his reader" (Berger 1938, 261). And, like the newsworker in *Reach for the Moon,* most fictional journalists realized that in contemporary American society it was not possible to "write the inner truth of the people, save in paltry fragments" (Brier 1934, 233).

Yet, even though the journalists in the novels of this era understood the relativity of truth in a philosophical sense, they also confronted situations where significant actual information was suppressed, as well as occasions when incorrect news was printed. At these times, they did not console themselves with a belief in the powers of objectivity; instead, they resisted newsroom oppression by maintaining a belief in what they saw as their freedom to think what they liked, even if they were not always able to write about it (Smith 1933, 267). More than one newsworker who had confronted the "impotency to speak out openly and individually" had attempted to undermine news policy by including important economic and political information in stories. As one fictional reporter explained, "If I can sneak a tenth of the truth past the copy-desk ... I'm doing well" (Adams 1921, 214).

During the 1920s and 1930s, newsworkers were repeatedly reminded that newspapers were business properties dedicated to making a profit. And although journalists might have dreamed of newspapers as "guardians of the public welfare or organs of political enlightenment," given the private ownership of the American press, they were forced to realize that it was without justification to expect newspapers to "adhere to a different ethic or a more detached consideration of the public good than bankers, business magnates, or manufacturers of patent medicines" (Rosten 1937, 279).

Whereas press freedom claims sometimes confused newsworkers, the oppressive working conditions reinforced the economic realities of the newspaper business. The story of a wager between a young wastrel and the Devil,

recounted in *Hot News,* offered an insightful example of the capitalist ideological position that drove American newsroom demands. In this story, the
Devil challenged the man to spend the "inexhaustible funds" given to him by
the "Exchequer of Hell." The Devil maintained that without actually throw-
ing money out a window, the spendthrift could not squander all of the capital available to him. The man accepted the bet, and began by investing in the
"worst" stocks on the stock exchange; he then bought yachts, race horses, and
real estate, but everything he invested in made money, and he was unable to
spend even half of his funds. He then decided to buy a newspaper, and after
publishing it for several months he was notified by the bank that his account
was overdrawn. Repeatedly, he was forced to ask the administrator for additional funds. Finally, the Devil met with the man and asked to be released
from the wager. When the young publisher asked him why he should be released from his contract, the Devil replied, "There are not enough funds in all
of Hell to pay for a newspaper that is losing money" (Gauvreau 1931, 78-79).
The representations of the actively lived experiences of fictional newsworkers, who encountered a philosophy of profit first, no matter what the human
consequences, may be seen to illustrate a structure of feeling among American reporters during the interwar era.

Although newsworkers faced similar constraints, pressures, and demands
throughout the entire interwar period, novels of the 1920s display the most
outwardly fearful attitude toward technological encroachment. They explicitly
articulated specific aspects of alienation, dehumanization, and commodification as they affected workers, and frequently connected individual experiences
with larger issues and problems of the capitalist system. Throughout the era,
women were viewed as exceptions rather than as integral members of this
class of workers. Although work expectations remained excessive and salaries
low, and newspaper jobs were difficult to obtain, during the Depression wages
of newsworkers were cut substantially and journalists, like those in other lines
of work, were unemployed in significantly greater numbers. Writers during
the 1930s found it easier to justify the oppressive working conditions of newsworkers and tended to use the Depression as a fixed explanation for social,
economic, and political problems. An underlying sense of optimism and encouragement emerged more frequently in texts of the 1930s; writers of love
stories, psychological dramas, and adventure stories alike suggested that although American society was deeply troubled, there was hope for the future.
Throughout this era, authors resisted the exploitation endemic to industrialized capitalist society and depicted the materialization of worker alienation.
Yet, whereas novelists of the 1920s focused primarily on realistic depictions of

the social and economic realities of American society, writers of the 1930s frequently tried to interject a limited sense of hope into their narratives.

In these novels there were no calls for rebellion, revolution, or change, and no strategies to revamp the capitalist appropriation of the media. Resigned to specific working conditions, expectations, and demands, newsworkers merely fantasized about personal freedom, dreamed of escaping the bureaucratic system, and hoped for a better tomorrow. In one sense these novels may be viewed as offerings of the American culture industry; they were commercially produced, geared toward large contemporary audiences, and enjoyed considerable popularity. And although the depictions of the newspaper world informed and educated the public, the novels were also well received and critically acclaimed because they amused, diverted, and entertained.

The influence of Pragmatism, early-twentieth-century progressive American thought, may be seen in all of the novels. The achievements of democracy and the power of scientific knowledge were fundamental to the experimental philosophy of pragmatism, which emphasized "the process of gradual change, adjustment, and continuity" (Hardt 1992, 51). Tolerant of differences in human nature, progressivism emphasized the evolutionary improvement and development of American society rather than the alteration of the basic industrial capitalist system. During this era, writers who encouraged reform, not revolution, frequently incorporated realistic techniques in their effort to expose oppressive, wasteful, and obsolete social conditions.

Contemporary examinations of popular culture frequently centralize issues of audience and reception. Reacting to poststructuralist theories that "overemphasize the manipulation of audience through ideological practices" (Sholle 1990, 88), scholars such as John Fiske, Janice Radway, and Ien Ang envision elements of resistance within audience responses to cultural products. Texts are considered "polysemic," and oppositional readings by audience members are thought to "deconstruct" actively dominant ideological messages (Fiske 1987, 266). However, in practice, readings of resistance often exclude a critical assessment of the material conditions of production of specific texts.

It is tempting to read interwar-era newspaper novels as resistant texts. On one level, these books frequently described dehumanizing working conditions of laborers; the newsworkers in them resisted newsroom demands and pressures by manufacturing sources, fabricating information, and acquiring a specific group identity and class consciousness. As members of a distinct category of workers, they were bound by a sense of loyalty, camaraderie, and trust; they worked together, shared routine information, and protected each other. However, it may be an overstatement to inscribe them with solely oppositional attributes. Although the authors of these novels attempted to present a representational picture of the role of newsworkers within early-twentieth-century American society, they did not explicitly challenge existing media organizations or offer strategies for revamping the system. They questioned the treatment of newsworkers within contemporary capitalist society, but they did not advocate that the system be altered or changed in any substantive way. And there is absolutely no indication that audience members or reviewers engaged with these novels in ways that actively dismantled the prevailing ideology. Therefore, rather than considering these novels radical or oppositional, it is perhaps enough to view these novels as examples of what Leo Lowenthal (1987) has called "the great reservoir of creative protest against social misery." In their realistic depictions of the lives of American journalists, these texts addressed the debasement of individuals in early-twentieth-century American society, and yet they also allowed "the prospect of social happiness to shine dimly through" (124). A sense of class consciousness encouraged journalists to contest their oppression and challenge the dominant hegemony of the newsroom. The trust and cooperation among newsworkers, along with the sharing of information and ultimately the protection of each other's jobs, helped them to resist the excessive demands of the newsroom. Although the novels discussed in this chapter depicted demoralized, victimized, and oppressed newsworkers whose hopes and dreams were ultimately destroyed, there still remained a sense of optimism, hope, and commitment to future American society. And so, instead of the usual fantasies of economic power, control, and prestige encouraged by industrial capitalism, these newsworkers dreamed of writing stories that would be published based solely on their merit, of owning a newspaper responsive to the needs of society, and of writing the great American novel.

## Notes

1. This study addresses thirty-five American novels written during the twenty-year interwar period of 1919-38 that explicitly address the working conditions of American reporters. The novels span a variety of themes and approaches; they include adventure stories, mysteries, romances, and career books, as well as social protest fiction. Some are psychologically introspective novels, whereas others are rather straightforward journalistic accounts of life in newsrooms. In some of the novels the influences of Nietzsche, Marx, and Freud resonate; other narratives are event oriented and emphasize action over ideas. The novels are as follows: Samuel H. Adams's *Success* (1921), Phil L. Anderson's *Court House Square* (1934), Louise Andrus's *Though Time Be Fleet* (1937), Elliott Arnold's *Two Loves* (1934), Barry Benefield's *The Chicken Wagon Family* (1925), Silas Bent's *Buchanan of "The Press"* (1932), Josef Berger's *Copy Boy* (1938), Royce Brier's *Reach for the Moon* (1934), Katharine Brush's *Young Man of Manhattan* (1930), Emma Bugbee's *Peggy Covers the News* (1936/1940), Carl Claudy's *The Girl Reporter*

(1930), Clyde Brion Davis's *"The Great American Novel"* (1938), Graham Dean's *Jim of the Press* (1933), Floyd Dell's *The Moon Calf* (1921), John Dos Passos's *Manhattan Transfer* (1925/1953), Lloyd C. Douglas's *Forgive Us Our Trespasses* (1932), Theodore Dreiser's *An American Tragedy* (1925/1981), Gene Fowler's *Trumpet in the Dust* (1930), Emile Henry Gauvreau's *Hot News* (1931), Hugh V. Haddock's *City Desk* (1937), James S. Hart and Garrett D. Byrnes's *Scoop* (1930), Ben Hecht's *Erik Dorn* (1921/1963), Ernest Hemingway's *The Sun Also Rises* (1926/1954), Edward Hungerford's *The Copy Shop* (1925), Clarence Budington Kelland's *Contraband* (1923), Meyer Levin's *Reporter* (1929), Edwin Herbert Lewis's *Sallie's Newspaper* (1924), Gertrude Ethel Mallette's *Private Props* (1937), John C. Mellett's *Ink* (1930), Henry Justin Smith's *Deadlines* (1923) and *Young Phillips, Reporter* (1933), Don Tracy's *Round Trip* (1934), Robert Van Gelder's *Front Page Story* (1937/1946), Ben Ames Williams's *Splendor* (1928), and Sidney Williams's *An Unconscious Crusader* (1920).

2. This essay is based on my dissertation, "'Peasantry of the Press': A History of American Newsworkers from Novels, 1919-1938" (Brennen 1993), which includes a critique of representations of American reporters during the interwar era found in both traditional media histories (including Bleyer 1927; Emery 1962; Emery and Emery 1992; Emery and Smith 1954; Folkerts and Teeter 1989; Gordon 1979; Jones 1947; Mott 1941, 1965; Sloan, Stovall, and Startt 1989; Tebbel 1969, 1974) and "revisionist" cultural and social histories of the press (e.g., Belford 1986; Czitrom 1982; Folkerts 1992; Marzolf 1977; Mills 1988; Ross 1936; Schudson 1978).

3. For further discussion on traditional distinctions of historical evidence, see, for example, Current (1986), Gottschalk (1950), Kramer (1989), Lule (1990), Nevins (1963, chaps. 7–8), Shafer (1974, chaps. 5-6), and White (1978, 1987).

4. See biographical information on Ben Hecht (Kaul 1981) as well as obituaries of Floyd Dell (Whitman 1969) and Ben Ames Williams in the *New York Times* (1953).

5. Information compiled from *Publishers Weekly* indicates that in 1920, 1,123 new editions were printed; in 1925, 1,426 novels became available; and in 1929, 2,142 new titles were produced. Although there were fewer fictional works published during the 1930s, novels still remained popular: in 1930, 2,103 new novels were released; in 1935, 2,039 fictional works were available; and in 1939, 1,547 new titles appeared (Tebbel 1978, 683).

6. For example, see discussions of labor conditions in Dreiser's *Tragic America* (1931), Meltzer's *Brother, Can You Spare a Dime? The Great Depression 1929-1933* (1969), and Mosco and Wasko's *Labor, the Working Class, and the Media,* volume 1 of *The Critical Communications Review* (1983).

7. Although newsworkers were partial to the term *newspaperman,* this essay prefers, whenever possible, to use gender-neutral terms, such as *reporter, journalist,* and *newsworker,* to describe this specific class of workers. However, in an effort to depict the actual language of these novels, which primarily had a masculine orientation, this study leaves all gendered references in direct quotes as they originally appeared.

## References

Aaron, Daniel. *Writers on the Left.* New York: Columbia University Press, 1992.

Adams, Samuel H. *Success.* Boston: Houghton Mifflin, 1921.

Anderson, Phil L. *Court House Square.* Minneapolis: Augsburg, 1934.

Andrus, Louise. *Though Time Be Fleet.* New York: Lothrop, Lee & Shepard, 1937.

Arnold, Elliott. *Two Loves.* New York: Greenberg, 1934.

Baldasty, Gerald J. *The Commercialization of News in the Nineteenth Century.* Madison: University of Wisconsin Press, 1992.

Beach, Joseph Warren. *The Twentieth Century Novel: Studies in Technique*. New York: Appleton-Century, 1932.

Beasley, Maurine. "The Women's National Press Club: Case Study of Professional Aspirations." In *Media Voices: An Historical Perspective*, ed. Jean Folkerts, 262-73. New York: Macmillan, 1992.

Belford, Barbara. *Brilliant Bylines*. New York: Columbia University Press, 1986.

Bell, Daniel. *The Cultural Contradictions of Capitalism*. New York: Basic Books, 1976.

Benefield, Barry. *The Chicken Wagon Family*. New York: Grosset & Dunlap, 1925.

Bent, Silas. *Ballyhoo: The Voice of the Press*. New York: Boni & Liveright, 1927.

———. "A Sheltered Son of the Press." *The Nation,* Jan. 4, 1928, 20-21.

———. *Buchanan of "The Press."* New York: Vanguard, 1932.

Berger, Josef [Jeremiah Digges]. *Copy Boy*. Philadelphia: Macrae Smith, 1938.

Bleyer, Willard Grosvenor. *Main Currents in the History of American Journalism*. Boston: Houghton Mifflin, 1927.

*Boston Evening Transcript*. "Deadlines." Jan. 13, 1923, 4.

———. "Ink: A Fearless Newspaper Editor in a Western Town." June 28, 1930, 2.

Brennen, Bonnie. "'Peasantry of the Press': A History of American Newsworkers from Novels, 1919-1938." Ph.D. diss., University of Iowa, 1993.

Brier, Royce. *Reach for the Moon*. New York: Appleton-Century, 1934.

Brush, Katharine. *Young Man of Manhattan*. New York: Grosset & Dunlap, 1930.

Bugbee, Emma. *Peggy Covers the News*. New York: Dodd, Mead, 1940. (Originally published 1936)

Butcher, Fanny. "Here's Story of News People, So Many Plan. But Katharine Brush Has Done Job Well." *Chicago Daily Tribune*, Jan. 11, 1930, 11.

*Christian Science Monitor*. "The Man Who Never Got Started." June 22, 1938, 11.

Claudy, Carl H. *The Girl Reporter*. Boston: Little, Brown, 1930.

Covert, Catherine L., and John D. Stevens, eds. *Mass Media between the Wars: Perceptions of Cultural Tension, 1918-1941*. New York: Syracuse University Press, 1984.

Current, Richard N. "Fiction as History: A Review Essay." *Journal of Southern History* 52, no. 1 (1986): 77-90.

Czitrom, Daniel J. *Media and the American Mind: From Morse to McLuhan*. Chapel Hill: University of North Carolina Press, 1982.

Davis, Clyde Brion. *"The Great American Novel."* New York: Farrar & Rinehart, 1938.

Dean, Graham. *Jim of the Press*. New York: Doubleday, Doran, 1933.

Dell, Floyd. *The Moon Calf*. New York: Knopf, 1921.

Dos Passos, John. *Manhattan Transfer*. Boston: Houghton, Mifflin, 1953. (Originally published 1925)

Douglas, Lloyd C. *Forgive Us Our Trespasses*. Boston: Houghton Mifflin, 1932.

Dreiser, Theodore. *Tragic America*. New York: Horace Liveright, 1931.

———. *An American Tragedy*. New York: Penguin, 1981. (Originally published 1925)

Emery, Edwin. *The Press and America: An Interpretative History of Journalism* (2d ed.). Englewood Cliffs, N.J.: Prentice Hall, 1962.

Emery, Edwin, and Henry Ladd Smith. *The Press and America*. Englewood Cliffs, N.J.: Prentice Hall, 1954.

Emery, Michael, and Edwin Emery. *The Press and America: An Interpretive History of the Mass Media* (7th ed.). Englewood Cliffs, N.J.: Prentice Hall, 1992.

Fiske, John. "British Cultural Studies and Television." In *Channels of Discourse: Television and Contemporary Criticism,* ed. Robert C. Allen, 254-80. Chapel Hill: University of North Carolina Press, 1987.

Flexner, James Thomas. "Tortured by Dreams." *New York Herald Tribune Books,* Apr. 13, 1930, 23.

Folkerts, Jean. *Media Voices: An Historical Perspective.* New York: Macmillan, 1992.

Folkerts, Jean, and Dwight L. Teeter. *Voices of a Nation: A History of the Media in the United States.* New York: Macmillan, 1989.

Fowler, Gene. *Trumpet in the Dust.* New York: Liveright, 1930.

Gauvreau, Emile Henry. *Hot News.* New York: Macaulay, 1931.

Gavit, John Palmer. "A Newspaper Story." *Literary Review,* Oct. 29, 1921, 115.

Gordon, George N. *The Communications Revolution: A History of Mass Media in the United States.* New York: Hastings, 1979.

Gottschalk, Louis Reichenthal. "Where Does Historical Information Come From?" In *Understanding History,* 86-117. New York: Knopf, 1950.

Haddock, Hugh V. *City Desk.* New York: Speller, 1937.

Hardt, Hanno. "The Foreign-Language Press in American Press History." *Journal of Communication* 38, no. 2 (1989): 114-31.

———. *Critical Communication Studies: Communication, History and Theory in America.* London: Routledge, 1992.

Hart, James S., and Garrett D. Byrnes. *Scoop.* Boston: Little, Brown, 1930.

Hecht, Ben. *Erik Dorn.* Chicago: University of Chicago Press, 1963. (Originally published 1921)

Hemingway, Ernest. *The Sun Also Rises.* New York: Macmillan, 1954. (Originally published 1926)

Hungerford, Edward. *The Copy Shop.* New York: Putnam, 1925.

Jones, Robert William. *Journalism in the United States.* New York: Dutton, 1947.

Kaul, A. J. "Ben Hecht." In *Dictionary of Literary Biography* (Vol. 9), *American Novelists, 1919-1945,* ed. James J. Martine, 116-124. Detroit: Bruccoli, Clark, 1981.

Kelland, Clarence Budington. *Contraband.* New York: Harper, 1923.

Kramer, Lloyd S. "Literature, Criticism, and Historical Imagination: The Literary Challenge of Hayden White and Dominick LaCapra." In *The New Cultural History,* ed. Lynn Hunt, 97-128. Berkeley: University of California Press, 1989.

Lee, Alfred McClung. *The Daily Newspaper in America: The Evolution of a Social Instrument.* New York: Macmillan, 1937.

Levin, Meyer. *Reporter.* New York: John Day, 1929.

Lewis, Edwin Herbert. *Sallie's Newspaper.* Chicago: Hyman-McGee, 1924.

Lord, Chester S. *The Young Man and Journalism.* New York: Macmillan, 1922.

Lowenthal, Leo. "Scholarly Biography." In *An Unmastered Past,* ed. Martin Jay, 111-38. Berkeley: University of California Press, 1987.

Lule, Jack. "Historiographical Essay: Telling the Story of Journalism, Journalism History and Narrative Theory." *American Journalism* 7, no. 4 (1990): 259-74.

Mallette, Gertrude Ethel. *Private Props.* New York: Doubleday, Doran, 1937.

Marx, Karl. "Economic and Philosophical Manuscripts." In *Marx's Concept of Man,* Erich Fromm, 85-196. New York: Ungar, 1966.

Marzolf, Marion Tuttle. *Up from the Footnotes.* New York: Hasting, 1977.

Mellett, John C. *Ink.* Indianapolis: Bobbs-Merrill, 1930.

Meltzer, Milton. *Brother, Can You Spare a Dime? The Great Depression 1929-1933.* New York: Knopf, 1969.

Mills, Kay. *A Place in the News: From the Women's Pages to the Front Page.* New York: Dodd, Mead, 1988.

Milosz, Czeslaw. *The Collected Poems, 1931-1987.* New York: Ecco, 1988.

Morley, Christopher. "Homer Zigler Goes Home." *Saturday Review of Literature,* June 4, 1938, 5.

Mosco, Vincent, and Janet Wasko. *The Critical Communications Review* (Vol. 1), *Labor, the Working Class, and the Media.* Norwood, N.J.: Ablex, 1983.

Mott, Frank Luther. *American Journalism.* New York: Macmillan, 1941.

———. *American Journalism: A History 1690-1960.* New York: Macmillan, 1965.

Nevins, Alan. *Gateway to History.* Chicago: Quadrangle, 1963.

*New York Times.* "Ben A. Williams, 63, Novelist, Is Dead. Author of 'House Divided' and 'Strange Woman' Succumbs During Curling Contest. Sold 400 Short Stories. Started to Write Books in His Thirties and Produced One a Year in the 1920's." Feb. 5, 1953, 23.

———. "Samuel Hopkins Adams Is Dead; Novelist and Biographer Was 87. Chronicler of Erie Canal Also Wrote Crusading Magazine Articles." Nov. 17, 1958, 31.

*New York Times Book Review and Magazine.* "Erik Dorn." Oct. 9, 1921a, 12, 18.

———. "Success." Nov. 6, 1921b, 16, 30.

*New York Times Book Review.* "Deadlines." Jan. 7, 1923, 17.

———. "A Batch of Theories." Aug. 17, 1924, 9.

———. "A Newspaper Story." Nov. 20, 1927, 6.

———. "A Roving Reporter." Mar. 30, 1930, 21–22.

———. "Newspaper Romance." June 3, 1934a, 7.

———. "Latest Works of Fiction." Nov. 11, 1934b, 26.

———. "The New Books for Boys and Girls." Dec. 6, 1936, 14.

———. "Newspaper Work." Dec. 5, 1937, 12.

*Outlook.* "New Novels with a Special Interest." Nov. 23, 1921, 486.

Rideout, Walter B. *The Radical Novel in the United States 1900-1954: Some Interrelations of Literature and Society.* New York: Columbia University Press, 1992.

Rogers, Charles Elkins. *Journalistic Vocations.* New York: Appleton, 1931.

Ross, Ishbel. *Ladies of the Press: The Story of Women in Journalism by an Insider.* New York: Harper, 1936.

Rosten, Leo C. *The Washington Correspondents.* New York: Harcourt, Brace, 1937.

Salcetti, Marianne. "Competing for Control of Newsworkers: Definitional Battles between the Newspaper Guild and the American Newspaper Publishers Association, 1937-1938." Ph.D. diss., University of Iowa, 1992.

*Saturday Review of Literature.* "In Tabloidia." Aug. 15, 1931, 57.

Schudson, Michael. *Discovering the News: A Social History of American Newspapers.* New York: Basic Books, 1978.

Seldes, George. *Lords of the Press.* New York: Julian Messner, 1938.

Shafer, Robert Jones. *A Guide to Historical Method.* Homewood, Ill.: Dorsey, 1974.

Sholle, David. "Resistance: Pinning Down a Wandering Concept in Cultural Studies Discourse." *Journal of Urban and Cultural Studies* 1, no. 1 (1990): 87–105.

Sloan, William David, James G. Stovall, and James D. Startt. *The Media in America: A History.* Worthington, Oh.: Publishing Horizons, 1989.

Smith, Henry Justin. *Deadlines.* Chicago: Covici-McGee, 1923.

———. *Young Phillips, Reporter.* New York: Harcourt Brace, 1933.

Smythe, Ted Curtis. "The Reporter, 1880-1900: Working Conditions and Their Influence on the News." In *Media Voices: An Historical Perspective,* ed. Jean Folkerts, 214–31. New York: Macmillan, 1992.

*Springfield Republican.* "Deadlines: Life and Spirit of American Newspaper Office." Jan. 7, 1923, 7a.

Tebbel, John. *The Compact History of the American Newspaper.* New York: Hawthorn, 1969.

———. *The Media in America.* New York: Crowell, 1974.

———. *A History of Book Publishing in the United States* (Vol. 3), *The Golden Age between Two Wars, 1920-1940.* New York: R. R. Bowker, 1978.

Tracy, Don. *Round Trip.* New York: Vanguard, 1934.

U. S. Department of Commerce, Bureau of the Census. *Statistical Abstract of the United States, 1938.* Washington, D.C.: U.S. Government Printing Office, 1939.

———. *Historical Statistics of the United States.* Washington, D.C.: U.S. Government Printing Office, 1975.

Van Gelder, Robert. *Front Page Story.* New York: Dodd, Mead, 1946. (Originally published 1936)

White, Hayden. *Tropics of Discourse: Essays in Cultural Criticism.* Baltimore: Johns Hopkins University Press, 1978.

———. *The Content of the Form: Narrative Discourse and Historical Representation.* Baltimore: Johns Hopkins University Press, 1987.

Whitman, Alden. "Floyd Dell, Novelist of 1920's and 'Village' Figure, Is Dead. Leading Rebel of the Period Was Author of 'Moon-Calf'—Fought with Mike Gold." *New York Times,* July 30, 1969, 39.

Williams, Ben Ames. *Splendor.* New York: Dutton, 1928.

Williams, Raymond. *Politics and Letters: Interviews with New Left Review.* London: Verso, 1981.

———. *The English Novel from Dickens to Lawrence.* London: Hogarth, 1987.

———. *Marxism and Literature.* Oxford: Oxford University Press, 1988.

Williams, Sidney. *An Unconscious Crusader.* Boston: Small, Maynard, 1920.

Wilson, Christopher P. *The Labor of Words: Literary Professionalism in the Progressive Era.* Athens: University of Georgia Press, 1985.

# 5 / The Site of Newsroom Labor

## The Division of Editorial Practices

William S. Solomon

Today the United States corporate sector owns most U.S. newspapers, the result of a trend that began early in this century and accelerated during the 1980s (Bagdikian 1992). "The impact of trading newspaper securities on the stock market," press critic Ben Bagdikian (1979) writes, "has meant that news companies must constantly expand in size and rate of profits in order to maintain their position on stock exchanges" (24). Yet, in today's structurally based economic downturn, newspapers face considerably lower rates of profit than those of the Reagan administration's "boom" years. Further, amid a continuing societal shift in "the distributive forms of the mass media" (Elliott 1982, 243), newspaper companies, in the view of some financial analysts, need to invest in electronic information services in order to avoid "becoming 'road kill' on the information highway" (Glaberson 1994, D-6).

Nonetheless, a measure of newspapers' continuing prosperity is that, even in lean times, it is estimated that from 1994 to 1998, "the Gannett Company, the largest newspaper company in the country, was likely to have about $1 billion in cash available for investment . . . the Tribune Company . . . about $700 million and Knight-Ridder about $600 million" (Glaberson 1994, D-6). Such wealth is the result of the steadfast pursuit of capital accumulation strategies. In the present recession, such strategies are driving corporations' newspaper subsidiaries to reduce labor costs through the use of new technologies, temporary workers, part-time workers, hiring freezes, attrition, layoffs, and, most recently, buyouts of newsroom workers. This last policy has been painted as doubly positive, as aiding "newspapers struggling to cope with the recession" while freeing journalists to change careers or to travel (Chang 1993, 17). But buyouts should not be characterized so facilely. Rather, they represent a modern version of newspaper management's long-standing efforts to control labor and cut labor costs. Indeed, the U.S. daily press's drive to "keep operating expenses low" was well established by the 1880s (Baldasty 1993, 99).

The roots of this orientation lie in the rise of a commercial model of U.S. journalism in the latter half of the nineteenth century, "a period of industrial and continental expansion and political conservatism" (Hofstadter 1955, 3). This era also solidified two basic changes in journalism: a shift in emphasis from editorials to news and an increasing focus on advertising revenues. The former was a cultural shift and the latter a shift in political economy; together they formed modern journalism's enduring ideological premise: the unity of commercialism and political independence (Nerone 1987, 401). This capitalist development of U.S. daily newspapers has had long-term consequences for newspapers' content, business practices, and work routines. Indeed, journalism work from the 1860s through the 1890s may be seen as an early form of labor for the culture industry, in that the development of newspapers during this era was a precursor of "one of the main trends of contemporary capitalist societies," the "synthesis of advertising, culture, information, politics and manipulation" (Kellner 1989, 132).

This essay deals with newsworkers of the U.S. commercial or "mainstream" press in the second half of the nineteenth century. The focus is the growth of a hierarchical division of newsroom labor, a hierarchy that persists to this day. The chapter examines the status and working conditions of newsworkers, linking the newsroom hierarchy to cultural, political, and economic developments in the wider society. It begins with an overview of the commercial press's development, in the context of several models of journalism in the early national and antebellum periods, and then outlines the consequences of this development, in terms of press coverage of class and labor issues, from the antebellum period to late in the nineteenth century. Finally, the essay addresses the evolution of newsroom work and the consequences for that work as it relates to the rise of a commercial model of journalism. It documents the experiences of newsroom workers and the development of a middle-class ideology of newswork.

Although some histories of labor/management relations tend to portray conflict between these two groups as shaping workplace conditions in any given era (see, e.g., Edwards 1979; Gordon, Edwards, and Reich 1982), news-workers in the late nineteenth century did not, as a rule, confront management. Rarely did they withhold their labor. Unlike typesetters and other printing crafts workers, their efforts to form labor unions were minimal and short-lived. Rather, their history is one of grudging accommodation to unpleasant circumstances. It is a history of collectively felt oppression most often expressed in individual acts of defiance—usually, quitting one newspaper to seek work at another or else leaving journalism altogether. It is not a history of collective action. Still, "the very right to organize is an effect of struggles" (Przeworski 1977, 372), and newsroom workers' experiences in this era may well have contributed to a growing awareness of class that did manifest itself, during the Depression of the 1930s, in the formation of the American Newspaper Guild.

In the early national period, the most prominent ideology of U.S. journalism was that of impartiality in the name of public service. The most common newspaper was the country weekly; after a visit to the United States in 1831-32, Tocqueville (1945) wrote that "the number of periodical and semi-periodical publications . . . is almost incredibly large. . . . there is scarcely a hamlet that has not its newspaper" (193-94). There also were partisan papers, founded and supported by political parties, and these did not aspire to impartiality: "Journals did not aspire to be 'newspapers'; they were mere personal or political organs, and aimed to influence public opinion by arguments—not to enlighten the public mind with facts" (Shanks 1867, 512; also see Parton 1866, 387). Although very different in content and readership, neither the country weeklies nor the partisan papers were particularly profitable. "In 1800 there was no good reason to suppose that a newspaper could support a young proprietor even into middle age" (Leonard 1986, 54). Similarly, Tocqueville (1945) found U.S. journalists to be "generally in a very humble position, with a scanty education and a vulgar turn of mind" (194). The economics of journalism, from the early national period to the antebellum era, would later be described as follows: "Most of the smaller dailies and a majority of the weeklies lived in a hand-to-mouth fashion" (King 1895, 588).

The key change came with "the integration of the newspaper into the market economy that itself was just coming of age" (Nerone 1987, 397). As the newspaper began to shift "from a craft to an industry" (397), a commercial model of journalism began to evolve. Its primary focus was neither impartiality nor public service, but profits. This new model had fundamental consequences for the practice of journalism; it treated news as a commodity and it rationalized production. Papermaking "shifted from handicraft to factory production" (Saxton 1984, 218). With technological improvements in printing, "capital became more crucial in the establishment of a successful printing shop" (Rorabaugh 1986, 77). Journalism work became more specialized: "The craft of printing became more and more separated from both publishing and editing" (77). Increasingly there appeared "'professional' or 'hireling' editors, who worked under contract to entrepreneurial publishers. Usually these new editors were lawyers. By mid-century, it had become rare for a printer in an urban center to edit a paper of his own" (Botein 1980, 52).

The rise of a commercial model of journalism altered the newspaper's social position, in that the commercial newspaper began to address more social classes. Whereas the partisan papers served the political elite, the earliest penny papers were a step toward addressing the whole populace.[1] The penny papers were arguably the most successful example of the commercial model of journalism in the antebellum period, if success is defined in terms of profitability and longevity. Ironically, this very success helped reorient the penny press away from the working-class interests that its earliest editors had tended to support (Saxton 1984). This shift is shown most dramatically in the rise of start-up costs. Horace Greeley started the *New York Tribune* in 1841 with "inconsiderable pecuniary resources, and only a promise from political friends to aid to the extent of $2,000, of which but one half was ever realized" (quoted in Bleyer 1927, 213-14). In 1840, Charles A. Dana, editor of the *New York Sun* from 1868 to 1897, would later estimate that $5,000 to $10,000 sufficed to start a daily (A. M. Lee 1937, 166). By 1850, that figure had risen to $100,000, according to Dana (1897, 166). "What was at the beginning of this century the occupation of gossips in taverns and at street corners," wrote E. L. Godkin (1890), founder of *The Nation* and an editor of the *New York Post*, "had by the middle of the century risen to the rank of a new industry, requiring large capital and a huge plant" (198). This transition greatly restricted entry into the field; as start-up costs soared, the class background of prospective publisher/editors rose. "Of the ten men listed as publishers of first wave penny dailies . . . eight began as artisans" and most had some involvement with working-class movements (Saxton 1984, 221). When the thoroughly middle-class Henry J. Raymond founded the *New York Times* in 1851, he had "the backing of a group of investors who subscribed $100,000 . . . before the first issue . . . came off the press" (222). When Dana bought the *New York Sun* in 1868, he paid $175,000. This was "a terrific bargain" (Steele 1993, 78) in the view of a recent biographer of Dana, which suggests how expensive entry into the daily newspaper field had become. In an 1894 address, Dana estimated that to start a daily newspaper would cost at least $1 million (1897,

80–81). Thus, in the space of some fifty-five years, start-up costs had risen from a few thousand dollars to $1 million. No wonder that after mid-century, artisan editors would be "limited to small circulation newspapers in western towns . . . or to the radical and labor press" (Saxton 1984, 222).

The shift in class background of publisher/editors may be gauged by changes over time in press coverage of labor and class issues. The earliest penny papers' editors supported "workingmen's and Jacksonian politics" and felt anger at "seeing upper-class dailies" being "subsidized by bank loans" (Saxton 1984, 221-22). In 1850, "the general tone of the public press was favorable to the endeavors that were being put forth by the workers" (Stevens 1913, 3). As late as 1860, long after the penny press had become established, the *New York Herald* would editorialize that the Lynn, Massachusetts, shoemakers' strike "is one of those cases which find a justification in the natural right of self-preservation" (*New York Herald* 1860). But, during the Civil War, aided by "a large section of the press" (Foner 1947, 353), employers' associations were formed to counter worker unrest. Reporting in 1872 on a victory celebration for the eight-hour day in New York City, the *New York Times* "wondered what proportion of the strikers were 'thoroughly American'" (quoted in Zinn 1980, 235). Reporting on a trades union meeting in 1873, the *New York Times* referred to banners such as "The Unemployed Demand Work, Not Charity" as being "decidedly communistic" (quoted in Foner 1947, 446). During coal miner unrest in the 1860s and 1870s, the commercial press's purpose "was to help the coal operators crush all organization in the mining industry" (460). In the railway strikes of 1877, "the commercial press . . . attacked the strikers with unprecedented fury" (465). During the railroad strikes, the *Chicago Times* fired and blacklisted a typesetter because he had spoken at a strike rally (Zinn 1980, 244). The basic outlook, the tone and substance of the commercial press's attitudes toward working-class movements, may be summed up as in a recent study of Chicago newspapers:

> In the 1870s, Chicago English-language dailies were uniformly hostile to strikes, picketing, class-based politics, and labor methods generally. . . . In the 1880s, these papers called for the suppression of militant labor tendencies and cheered the execution of the Haymarket martyrs. (Bekken 1993, 154)

That the commercial newspapers of this era did not stray beyond narrow characterizations of life under capitalism is illustrated in the following commentary by social critic Henry Adams, in his discussion of the 1884 presidential election:

> We are here plunged in politics funnier than words can express. Very
> great issues are involved. . . . But the amusing thing is that no one
> talks about real interests. . . . Instead of this the press is engaged in a
> most amusing dispute whether Mr. Cleveland had an illegitimate
> child and did or did not live with more than one mistress. (quoted
> in Zinn 1980, 252-53)

The roots of this policy lie in the commercial press's drive to maximize profits by avoiding political controversy. "Shaping the news with an eye to its
popularity meant that editors downplayed their political views lest they of-
fend readers" (Baldasty 1993, 107). Thus, while claiming impartiality, the
commercial press was hostile to working-class interests. This attitude helped
marginalize social reform movements, by asserting implicitly that to ignore or
trivialize them was an eminently fair and reasonable act, because they were
beyond the political pale.

In tune with its shifting coverage of labor and class issues, the commercial newspaper became increasingly autocratic and hierarchical internally. An
early 1850s daguerreotype of Horace Greeley and his editorial staff is a portrait of colleagues, similarly dressed and all looking equally formal and authoritative (Stevens 1913). By the turn of the century, the socioeconomic
differences between a publisher and his newsroom staff were such that the
president of the International Typographical Union (ITU) would describe
the working conditions in many newsrooms as "absolutely revolting to free
men" (Donnelly 1901, 275). This transformation in the labor process was a
basic part of the capitalist development of U.S. journalism, a trend that inten-
sified after the Civil War. Compared with other models of journalism, the
commercial model was best suited to benefit from economic growth. After
the Civil War, the United States

> was able to exploit [its] . . . rich agricultural land [and] vast raw
> materials . . . to transform itself at a stunning pace. [From 1865 to
> 1898] wheat production increased by 256 percent, corn by 222
> percent, refined sugar by 460 percent, coal by 800 percent. By
> 1914 . . . it was the largest oil producer in the world. . . . Its energy
> consumption . . . was equal to that of Britain, Germany, France,
> Russia and Austria-Hungary together. (Kennedy 1987, 242, 244)

This growth included the rise of standardized national brands, which
turned to advertising as a means of informing the population of the existence
of new products (e.g., Royal Baking Powder, Coca-Cola) and of persuading
people to buy one brand rather than another. Similarly, the rise of department

stores figured prominently in the growth of advertising. From 1867 to 1900, the annual amount spent on advertising in the United States increased from $50 million to $542 million (U.S. Department of Commerce 1975, 856). Mass media were an integral part of this process; newspapers and periodicals were ideal vehicles for such advertising, and from 1879 to 1909 the proportion of revenues they received from advertising rose from 44 percent to 60 percent (A. M. Lee 1937, 324). During this period, there also were many publications founded and supported by social reform movements, such as organized labor, suffragists, utopians, populists, and socialists. However, these did not receive the volume of advertising that enabled the commercial press to prosper and expand. They were not ideal vehicles for advertising because they did not strive to avoid giving offense. Quite the contrary, they existed in order to offer public discourse on often controversial issues (Armstrong 1981, 31-60).

In size, visibility, and influence, the newspapers that became dominant were those that catered to advertisers and treated news as a commodity. These "commercial" newspapers eagerly sought advertising; this meant avoiding political partisanship while "shaping the news to please advertisers" (Baldasty 1993, 113). The latter took two forms: publishing "puffs," favorable mentions of advertisers in news stories, and publishing favorable profiles of "businesses or businesspeople" (113). In contrast to the early national period, in this era newspaper publishing was becoming quite profitable; from 1870 to 1900, the number of daily newspapers increased from 574 to 2,226, while the U.S. population increased from 39.9 million to 76 million (A. M. Lee 1937, 718; U.S. Department of Commerce 1975, 810, 8). By late in the century, the managing editor of the *New York Mail and Express* would write that "the most important part of the newspaper . . . is the writing of advertisements. . . . The advertising department of a newspaper offers more rich rewards than any other" (Coates 1892, 3).

The pursuit of advertising brought prosperity to the commercial press, but it also laid the foundations for two basic changes in the political economy of U.S. journalism. One was a gradual attrition in the number of daily newspapers. Just as the capitalist development of daily newspapers had barred artisanal editors, in time it discriminated among capitalists. "Ads swelled the size of the paper each day, requiring larger plants, more paper and ink, and bigger staffs" (Bagdikian 1992, 176). In the early 1830s, Tocqueville observed that "the facility with which newspapers can be established produces a multitude of them" (1945, 194).

By 1918, Oswald Garrison Villard, editor of *The Nation* and the *New York*

*Evening Post,* would write that "the decreasing number of newspapers in our larger American cities is due to the enormously increased cost of maintaining great dailies" (62). The number of U.S. dailies peaked in 1909 at 2,452, when the U.S. population was 90.5 million (A. M. Lee 1937, 718; U.S. Department of Commerce 1975, 8). By contrast, in 1992 there were 1,570 dailies for a population of 255 million (Newspaper Association of America, 1993; U.S. Department of Commerce 1993, 1).[2]

The decrease in newspapers was accompanied by an increase in size and prosperity for the remaining dailies, which brought another basic change in the commercial press—the development of a corporate structure of ownership and management. By late in the century, U.S. capitalism was in transition from a proprietary form to a corporate form (Sklar 1988). Whereas this created far greater advertising revenues, the consequent rise in the costs of starting and running a daily newspaper necessitated changes in ownership. As Nerone (1987) has noted, the incorporation of newspapers has received "virtually no" study (397). One can note, however, that in 1849 Horace Greeley offered stock in the *New York Tribune* to his employees (Bleyer 1927, 220, 211), and that the *New York Times* was founded in 1851 "as a company with a capitalization of $100,000" put up by "half a dozen 'upstate' business men" (239). When Dana bought the *New York Sun,* he did so with the financial backing of a group of twenty-nine investors. "The stock of our company," he wrote a friend, "is increased to $350,000 in order to pay for this new acquisition" (quoted in Stone 1938, 30–31). These examples suggest that by mid-century, commercial newspapers were starting to move away from the situation where one person was the sole owner. By late in the century, incorporation clearly had arrived; a veteran journalist would refer in passing to "the great corporations now controlling the leading newspapers" (Shanks 1892).

This organizational shift also is suggested by the establishment, in 1887, of the American Newspaper Publishers Association (ANPA) (Emery 1950). A report of its founding focused on publishers' desire to avoid "irresponsible advertising agents" and to learn of "developments and improvements" in machinery such as printing presses, typesetting equipment, and the typewriter (*Journalist* 1892d). But the ANPA was in no small way a response to labor unions. At its founding conference, one publisher stressed that an employers' association could stand up to unionized printers who "think they can move the world" (quoted in Emery 1950, 24). The editor of the trade publication the *Journalist,* who was by no means an advocate of working-class solidarity, noted with amusement that some ANPA members viewed him as "a labor agitator and incipient Anarchist" (Forman 1891). Yet his views, and one of the ANPA's main purposes, were apparent in the tone of his comment on a type-setters' strike at the *Chattanooga Times:* "There is a general impression, be-coming more and more solidly fixed in the compositorial mind, that a strike on an ANPA paper does not pay" (*Journalist* 1890).

Begun during a time of labor unrest in society, the ANPA was a step to-ward marking the class lines more clearly within the newspaper world. A complement of the trend toward incorporation, the association reflected management's increasing wealth and power relative to unorganized news-room workers. Typographical workers had organized in various unions since the late eighteenth century, with the ITU appearing in 1852 (Stevens 1913, 34-207; E. Stewart 1905; Tracy 1913, 17-113). Yet, in the latter half of the nineteenth century, newswork did not evolve within a context of collective action. By the time that newsworkers began to organize, in the 1890s, the basic structure of newspaper management and of the division of newsroom labor had been set. It is to this evolution of newswork, that is, the develop-ment of a division of newsroom labor, that this essay now turns.

In today's newsrooms, the nature of work and the structure of power re-semble the circumstances that were emerging in the first few decades after the Civil War. A comparison is instructive. Characterizing modern U.S. jour-nalism, Bagdikian (1992) has noted, "The taboo against criticism of the sys-tem of contemporary enterprise is, in its unspoken way, almost as complete within mainstream journalism . . . in the United States as criticism of com-munism is explicitly forbidden in the Soviet Union" (155). A parallel to this control over news content exists in the contemporary newsroom's hierarchy of power, as suggested by the following letter to the editor published in the trade magazine *Editor & Publisher:*

> As an ex-newsman, I was amused by the recent flap in Miami about the publisher of the *Miami Herald* overruling his editorial board and endorsing Reagan for President. A fundamental question seems to have been overlooked. Who works for whom at the *Miami Herald?*
>
> My basic sympathies are with the publisher. His financial investment, or the investment he represents, gives him greater rights than the editorial workers.
>
> High-flown journalistic theories to the contrary, a newspaper is a business. It can't be run by consensus like a democracy, not if the rights that accrue to property are to continue to have meaning. (Gildea 1985)

This attitude was equally entrenched in the commercial press more than a century ago, as illustrated in an address to the Social Science Association in 1881:"The newspaper is a private enterprise. Its object is to make money for its owner" (Warner 1881, 5).

In the early national period, most country weekly editors had little or no staff; for that era's partisan papers, "the editorial force . . . consisted of two or three political writers and one news editor, who was at the same time general reporter, 'paste and scissors,' and money editor" (Shanks 1867, 512). As the commercial press began to emphasize news gathering, staffs increased, and this fundamental change required some way to control the labor force that was being created.

The solution was a hierarchy of power in the newsroom. "Simple control" was typical not just of newspapers but of most enterprises until late in the nineteenth century—a single entrepreneur, "usually flanked by a small coterie of foremen and managers" who "exercised power personally" (Edwards 1979, 18-19). For the commercial newspaper, the editor/publisher was indeed an autocrat who would "exhort workers, bully and threaten them, reward good performance, [and] hire and fire on the spot" (18-19). But, unlike other business ventures, the newspaper could claim a public service mandate that allowed publishers to submerge their profit motive within an appeal to their newsworkers' sense of public duty. Consequently, the development of a division of newsroom labor occurred within a strict hierarchy of power that was justified by a premise of public service. An initial step in this development was the establishment of the position of reporter, a process enabled by "the evolution of the social organizations that produced news" (Nerone 1987, 396). In 1840, "the staff of the larger daily had been increased from an editor who wrote the leaders, corrected the communications and read the proofs, with an assistant who did the local work, to two editors and two reporters" (King 1895, 588). The Mexican War and later the Civil War supplied impetus for more systematic news gathering (O'Brien 1918, 168, 188), which the advent of the steamship, the railroad, and the telegraph helped make possible (Shanks 1867, 514-18; Smith 1891). By 1843, the *New York Sun* employed "eight editors and reporters" (O'Brien 1918, 157). By 1850, the staff of the *New York Tribune* "consisted of 12 editors and reporters" (Bleyer 1927, 221).

As newspapers added more reporters and editors, the division of newsroom labor increased as the editor/publisher needed managerial help. The appearance of the positions of city editor and managing editor, in the 1850s, signaled that more tasks were being separated from the editor's work. The city editor would supervise the reporters, while the managing editor would "act as a link" between the editor and the various "subeditors" (O'Brien 1918, 262). While reporters had always been regarded as laborers, editors were not. In time, however, the addition of more editorial positions gradually led to their shift in status from manager to worker. This process preserved the hierarchy of newsroom power, maintaining "simple control" by keeping to a minimum the size of the managerial coterie. The shift in the status of some editing work is illustrated by the emergence and subsequent evolution of the position of copy editor (Solomon forthcoming). After the Civil War, tasks today associated with copyediting began to appear as a separate work position:

> At the desk near the door we find Dr. John B. Wood . . . through whose hands passes all the telegraph and news matter. . . . The doctor prides himself as a thorough grammarian, and his brilliant feats with the blue pencil have frequently gashed long reports and letters to the consternation of their authors. (Cummings 1868, 108)

Increasingly it was the case that, rather than the managing editor or the city editor, another editor would edit the copy. At this point virtually all editing jobs were considered managerial work. When Edward P. Mitchell, later an editor for the *New York Sun,* arrived in New York City in 1875 for a job interview at the *Sun*, he first watched the paper's newsroom from his hotel window and mistook John Wood, the night editor, for Charles A. Dana (Mitchell 1924, 122, 124). But, as commercial papers continued to grow, the division of newsroom labor that had created the position of night editor in time brought further specialization and separation of this position's tasks. Judging the worth of all news stories remained the work of the night editor or city editor, who also made changes in content, tone, and structure. Any remaining such changes, but primarily headline writing and technical editing—correcting grammar, spelling, factual errors, and so on—became the work of a separate editor who was considered an assistant to a senior editor, usually the city editor, the night city editor, or the night editor. With this change came the name of copy editor, or, at first, copyreader.

Initially, the copy editor had two claims to status and authority. First, the copy editor worked closely with a senior editor, often the city editor, who typically had the authority to hire staff and decide what was newsworthy. Second, the copy editor trimmed reporters' copy, at a time when many, if not most, reporters were paid by the word. Under the "space and time" system, reporters were paid largely according to how many of their words were published (Smythe 1980, 2). Both of these bases for status and authority proved transient. The "space and time" system faded after World War I; also, as newspaper staffs grew, copyediting became the work of a distinct department. By 1884, it was common practice that "a special department condensed and prepared news and wrote headlines, distinct from one that edited telegraphic reports and correspondence" (A. M. Lee 1937, 629).[3] The term *copy desk* soon came into use: for example, a young woman joined the *Chicago Tribune* staff as a reporter in 1893, and the next February "the boys on the copy-desk sent her a joint valentine" (Linn 1937, 53).[4]

With the establishment of a separate "copy desk," with its own head copyreader, or "slotman," the copy editor's authority and status now derived from the slotman, who typically played no part in the other stages of the news gathering or editing process (Bleyer 1913, 258-59). The copy editor had been shorn of direct links with the city editor or the night editor and had become one of a number of anonymous editors whose "bundle of tasks" had been narrowed to writing headlines and doing a restricted version of final editing.[5] The copy editor judged not all news stories but only some, and thus saw only part of a larger picture. Assessing a story only after a more senior editor had judged it, the copy editor performed tasks that were, essentially, supplementary:

> It becomes the copy reader's duty to assure that every "story" . . . is written in good English, is clear, concise and consecutive in statement, with all its features given appropriate weight; that the policy of the paper is conserved; that all libelous phrases are eliminated; that attractive, telling headlines are written, and . . . that the points and the symmetry of the article are not lost in the condensation necessitated by the exigencies of space. (Bridge 1892)

This work was the final polishing, "the decorative touches which dress the paper, attract the reader's eye, and round off the work of the editor and the reporter" (Bridge 1892). Its status was much lower than that of deciding which topics were newsworthy or which reporter would cover a story. The latter tasks guided the news-gathering process. By contrast, the copy editor's tasks lacked any such measure of authority and status. In effect, the class position of copyediting work was transformed from that of manager to laborer. A trade journal reported in 1892 that at the *New York World* "the fate of the copy readers is . . . doleful. A time clock is to be used, to keep tabs on them like so many day laborers. Copy is to be stamped when handed to a man, and stamped when returned" (*Journalist* 1892c).

The increasing division of newsroom labor illustrated the increasing rationalization of the production process in the commercial press. With the evolution of more editing positions, each with a more restricted set of tasks, newsroom work became more akin to work on an assembly line. In such a workplace, status and authority were reserved for the managers. Two themes suggest the copy editor's descent within this increasingly stratified newsroom hierarchy of power. First, the nature of the tasks assigned to copy editors was viewed as lackluster, if not unpleasant, when compared with reporting or other editing work. Repetitive and narrowly focused, copyediting was "in many respects . . . akin to literary drudgery" (Bridge 1892). A reporter described the *New York Herald*'s night desk: "Oh, what a dreary spot it is" (Howard 1891a). The *Journalist* (Oct. 8, 1892) described the night desk of the *Brooklyn World:* "Night toil is 'hard beyond picturing,' the responsibilities great, and the shekels generally few" (13). Second, copyediting was described as being thankless work: "The post of copy reader on the [San Francisco] *Examiner* is a thankless job and there has been a still hunt for some one to fill that position. . . . Al Murphy said that there were four men whose sole duty was to read the paper and find mistakes, and the copy reader got blamed for every mistake, and he wasn't going to have it" (*Journalist* 1892a). Will Irwin (1911b) lauded Selah M. Clarke for having "put genius into the ungrateful task of copy-reading."

The copy editor's transition reflected newsroom management's ability to define and redefine a job's tasks, skills, status, and authority in the absence of sustained worker resistance. The resulting structure of newswork has endured into the twentieth century, as has the grim status of copyediting. Recalling his experiences on a copy desk in the mid-1920s, one journalist wrote that the copy editor "seldom held his head high. . . . he had been called the old maid of the profession, he had been accused of murdering the creative talent" of reporters (K. Stewart 1943, 44). Some newsworkers transferred the copy editor's unattractive work to the personalities of those who did it. A biography of the *New York Times,* Talese (1969) describes copyediting as

> probably the most tedious and unheralded craft in the newsroom. Copyreaders were a special breed of journalists. They were indoor creatures, retainers of rules, anonymous men. Educated men, well-read travelers, they were ideally suited for the work, though few would admit it. They had not planned on that. . . . [Copy editors were] introspective men, careful men, dreamers, not doers. (61-62)

A former reporter, recalling the early 1960s at the *New York Times,* noted that, concerning the copy desk, he was advised, "The game is to sneak some color or interpretation past that line of humorless zombies" (Darnton 1975, 180).

In 1993, the editor of a Catholic newspaper in Hartford, Connecticut, resigned after accusing the local archbishop of censorship tantamount to direct control, and said, "I was reduced to a glorified copy editor" (quoted in Goldman 1993).

The copy editor's history also illustrates the forming of divisions among newsroom workers. Reporters and copy editors developed somewhat different and opposed identities, in good part because of their respective tasks: editing someone else's work often means second-guessing him or her. In an atmosphere where deadline pressures are routine, such decisions became contested and resented often enough to become entrenched in an enmity that exists to the present day. "A colleague-group," noted sociologist Everett C. Hughes (1984), "will stubbornly defend its own right to define mistakes, and to say in the given case whether one has been made" (319). Especially under the "space and time" system, which linked pay to the number of published words, reporters not only competed among themselves but then submitted their work (and hence their prospects for pay) to the copy editors. This method of securing surplus labor from newsworkers, under the guise of public service, contributed to an atmosphere hostile to the fostering of collective identity.

The evolution of newswork occurred as the commercial model of journalism increasingly emphasized news, the product of its newsroom workers' labors. By late in the century, E. L. Godkin (1890) would reflect that "the role of the American press in the growth of journalism has been distinctly the development of news-gathering as a business, leaving to the work of comment only a subordinate place" (201; also see Ottarson, 1869). Similarly, John Cockerill (1892), editor of the *New York Advertiser* and president of the New York Press Club, wrote that "the most important contents of a newspaper are its news. . . . The day of the editorial page is past" (12). Ironically, the commercial press's emphasis on news did not mean that its newsworkers were treated well. Quite the contrary, their wages and working conditions are the clearest indicator of their failure to contest managerial control effectively.

Their plight was sufficiently poignant as to be well known outside the newsroom. In particular, their low wages received attention. As early as 1873, *The Nation* (1873) editorialized about journalism that "there is probably no industry of modern times in which the part played by labor is so large, and the share in the profits received by labor so small" (38). A government study a decade later reached a similar conclusion: "I find the . . . wages paid ($32.09) for each $100 of gross product to be considerably lower than it then was in industries of this group ($51.30), while the product per capita, gross, in the same comparison is much higher . . . ($843.51)" (North 1884, 83). These findings reflect commercial newspaper management's success at securing surplus value from their newsroom workers. Given this ratio of profitability, it is not surprising that the price of buying or starting a daily newspaper would rise sharply, even as the number of dailies rose dramatically.

Yet the debate about newsworkers' wages was not one-sided. As a benchmark, one may note that in 1895 the average annual pay for federal employees in executive departments, the highest figure among eleven work categories listed, was $1,104 (U.S. Department of Commerce 1975, 168). The editor of the *Journalist* contended that a journalist, "until he reaches forty, if he be worth his salt . . . is making much more money than the average doctor or the average lawyer" (Forman 1900). Still, a critic noted that it was "manifestly unfair and illogical to compare" journalists' pay with "the earnings of the learned professions of law and medicine" (De Weese 1898, 444). Also, one should note that physicians in the United States did not gain high social status and high income until the twentieth century (Starr 1978, 179-80). A national survey put the annual salary of "news editors, copy-readers, and space-writers" at $1,800, "matching the pay of a captain in the army or a junior lieutenant in the navy"; reporters averaged $1,200, "as much as the average income of the majority of those engaged in any commercial pursuit" (King 1895, 593). This study estimated "the average pay of journalists of all kinds on all of the dailies" at $1,500 (593). Yet three years later, another study placed that figure at $1,109, and it contended that journalism was not worthy of "serious attention of educated young men seeking a permanent occupation that will yield an income sufficient for present needs and the necessary provision for old age" (Avenel 1898, 366-67). A similar thought was put more succinctly by one newsworker: "No matter how bright you may be, how loyal you may have been, there is nothing but a bare existence in the business unless you have a proprietary interest in the paper you are working for" (J.K. 1890). A loftier view acknowledged that "the pecuniary rewards of journalism are inadequate," but concluded that "the man who enters journalism . . . adopts [it] . . . as an intellectual calling" (De Weese 1898, 441, 451). Still, it is hard to get past the description given in 1900 by the ITU president:

> I have known newspaper writers to almost starve to death on the streets of New York. Men of education who were in the position . . . of a vagrant, the field in which they were employed being overcrowded. . . . The editors and managers being entirely too busy to converse with them on questions of employment, their only op-

portunity . . . [was] offering to do the work of some other man, and displace him, at a lower rate of wages. (Donnelly 1901, 275)

Another crucial factor was job security, which was virtually nil. There were two key aspects to this condition. One was a theme prominent in intellectual journals and trade magazines during the latter half of the nineteenth century, that daily journalism was a young man's work. "Beyond question," wrote a reporter touting journalism as a career, "the work on the newspapers is done by very young men," from eighteen to twenty-five years of age (Howard 1891b, 5).

> The most pathetic figure in journalism is the man who has grown old in its service. . . . In any other business, his experience would be of value. . . . Here it is valueless. Ninety percent of the men who enter journalism leave it before they become old. . . . On the staff of the daily newspaper with which I am connected there is only one man over fifty years of age, and the average age of the employees in the editorial department is less than thirty-five. A canvass of other metropolitan newspaper-offices will show but a slight variation from these figures. (Keller 1893, 693)

The demanding conditions of journalism work contributed to the preference for young newsworkers. For reporters, there were "long hours, arduous working conditions, lack of sick leave and vacation time" (Smythe 1980, 5). It was more difficult for older people to keep up the physical pace that reporting work then required. The telephone was not so widely used, and newsrooms did not have highly specialized "beats" that would enable an older reporter to do good work without having to rush all over the area. Furthermore, the grueling pace and the lack of job security applied to virtually all of the editors as well. Perhaps one of the saddest testimonies to this harsh reality was the story of Dr. John B. Wood, the forerunner of the copy editor:

> A man had held for years the post of city editor on a large New York daily. He had become famous throughout the world of journalism as the greatest news-condenser of his time. The newspaper he had served so long suddenly dropped him . . . [because] he had grown old. . . . No position similar to his old one was open to him, and he was forced . . . to start again as a reporter. . . . One night he was sent out on a river-front assignment in the cold and wet and darkness of a winter storm. That night he met his death amid the floating ice of the Hudson. (Keller 1893, 694-95)

Another key aspect of job insecurity was the ease with which newsroom managers fired or reassigned people on the spot; journalists often could not count on a job from one day to the next, much less a regular paycheck until they retired. Writing about reporters' work conditions in smaller cities, one newsworker wrote that "sudden and sweeping changes are liable to occur in the local force" (O'Shaughnessy 1892, 13). The *Fourth Estate,* a trade publication, wrote in 1898:

> The chief fault with journalism in the large cities is the insecurity felt by the workers in their positions. . . . Reporters are discharged upon the slightest pretexts. Desk men who have a reasonable right to believe their positions secure as long as they do conscientious work suddenly find themselves thrown out in the street without warning. (quoted in Smythe 1980, 5)

An example of this volatility is the experience of Moses Koenigsberg, who, when he became city editor of the *Chicago Evening American* in 1903, was the twenty-seventh person to hold that job within thirty-seven months (Smythe 1980, 5). Similarly, Will Irwin (1911a) reported: "Some one met 'Cosey' Noble, Hearst man, in a restaurant. 'What are you doing now, Noble?' he asked. 'When I left the office,' Noble replied, 'I was city editor'" (17).

Lack of job security was an effective means of exercising managerial control; newsworkers could be directed, evaluated, and disciplined at a boss's will. They had little autonomy in their work. Moreover, some publishers, such as James Gordon Bennett Jr. and Joseph Pulitzer, spied on their newsroom workers (Smythe 1980, 5). "The whole tendency of the policy of the most successful journals . . . is to foster this spirit of distrust . . . not only between its own staff and the staffs of its rivals, but actually between the members of its own staffs" (Cockerill 1892, 13).

Taken as a whole, these conditions describe a grim reality. As part of "publishers' strategies to keep operating expenses low," they "drove seasoned reporters out of the newspaper industry" (Baldasty 1993, 101). This would appear to have been a strange system for a social organization constitutionally protected, as a vital part of a democracy, and charged with contributing to an "open marketplace of ideas." But it made perfect sense as a method of securing maximum surplus labor from newsroom workers while maintaining virtually total control, all under the guise of public service. Given the prohibitive cost of starting or buying a daily newspaper, nearly all journalists faced the choices of quitting, accepting the oppressive conditions of newsroom work, or organizing.

Labor was an increasingly prominent issue for newspaper managers in the late nineteenth century. The capitalist development of newspapers drove technological changes in various aspects of the printing process, including presses (Moran 1973) and typesetting. Printing crafts workers had long since unionized, and they were alert to and active concerning potential threats to skills, pay, work conditions, and job security (Mendel 1991, 359-62). On occasion they were, in the 1887 view of one publisher, able to place newspapers "in peculiarly unpleasant situations" (quoted in Emery 1950, 24). The ANPA responded in 1899 by forming a labor relations committee (Emery 1950, 65) and starting a "systematic labor relations program" (A. M. Lee 1937, 670). Overall, however, the ITU was both active and successful in protecting its members' jobs and improving their pay. In the late nineteenth century in New York City, "the comparative absence of strikes in the printing trades was a measure of the strength of the unions representing compositors and pressmen" (Mendel 1991, 371). Compared with typesetters' wages, those of newsroom workers were "very much lower," the ITU president told Congress (Donnelly 1901, 275).

In 1891 the ITU amended its constitution to authorize "the issuance of charters to unions of editors and reporters" (Tracy 1913, 452). In 1893 it "dispensed with the four-year apprenticeship rule in the case of newswriters" (A. M. Lee 1937, 670). Leab (1970) suggests three motives in all this. First, the ITU was concerned that "its strikes often were hindered" (12-13) by newsroom workers. "There was a strike in the composing room of the *Chattanooga Times* last week. The editors, reporters, and a few friends went to the cases at night, and the paper was issued as usual" (*Journalist* 1890). The ITU also hoped to "improve its image in the press," and, finally, some of the union's leaders saw newsroom workers as simply "one more specialty to organize" (Leab 1970, 12-13). From 1891 until the start of World War I, the ITU issued forty-four local charters of newsroom workers (U.S. National Labor Relations Board 1939, 108), although the bulk of this activity had occurred by 1904 (A. M. Lee 1937, 670). In 1892 an ITU official said that "there were now big unions of reporters and editors under the I.T.U. in Pittsburgh, Denver and Sacramento" (*Journalist* 1892b). The *Journalist* reported in 1892 that "representative working newspaper reporters and copy editors" in New York met, listened to speeches from union officials, and "unanimously decided to organize a local union . . . under the I.T.U." Several journalists described "details of some of the injustices under which they suffer and the abuses to which they are subject" (*Journalist* 1892b). Again in 1892, protesting the policies of a new city editor, the reporters of the *New*

*York Recorder* struck—"a decided novelty . . . among reporters in New York" (*Journalist* 1892e).

Overall, most of the ITU's "newswriters' locals" did not last for more than a few years, and often they had small memberships (A. M. Lee 1937, 666-73; U.S. National Labor Relations Board 1939). The reasons are complex, involving politics and ideology. Politically, there was an element of intimidation. One journalist wrote that "legal insistence on his rights . . . will not only cost him his place on the newspaper immediately concerned but will prove a serious obstacle to employment on any other newspaper" (Keller 1893, 699). In addition, because the field was "overcrowded" (Donnelly 1901, 275), organizing likely appeared as highly problematic. Over and above these problems, however, was what may be termed the ideology of newswork. The public service ethic militated against any idea of going on strike. Like many college and university professors today, newsworkers saw their work as being sufficiently intellectual and individualistic as to preclude any collective identity and behavior. In the words of a 1900 report by the ITU vice president for the newswriters' locals, "In nearly every instance the general principles of organization as applied to our calling are agreed to, but the principal objection to joining with us . . . seems to be that it is not a practical proposition" (quoted in Tracy 1913, 630). Journalists, a newsroom worker wrote, "hold themselves on a plane high above that where the self-preservation of labor has made trades-unions imperative" (Keller 1893, 700). Many "considered it beneath the dignity of a newspaperman to join a labor union" (quoted in Leab 1970, 15). In addition, there was a popular notion of "the romance of newspapering," rooted in "myths that the newspaper business was a game . . . and that wages, hours and conditions did not count. What really mattered was high adventure and being 'on the inside'" (Leab 1970, 8-9). This view was actively promoted by newspaper publishers, as was a related outlook, that newsroom workers should seek individual solutions to their oppression, through upward mobility:

> They, like most "white collar" workers, intended to find financial relief through individual advancement, through taking a place among the executives, the employers, in the newspaper industry or elsewhere. Reporting was merely a means to an end; typesetting and press operation was, for many, an end in itself. (A. M. Lee 1937, 667)

Ironically, in terms of pay, working conditions, and job security, newswork appears to have been more blue-collar than was typographical work. Newsworkers' white-collar identity, then, may be explained in part by the fact that the work did not involve manual labor and dirtying one's hands. In this vein, the determinants of newsroom work's ideology and social status were rooted in a long-standing distinction between editor and printer. With the separation of these two tasks earlier in the century, the position of editor—and that of all newsroom work—came to carry a more intellectual aura than did typographical work. But newspapers' capitalist development brought such growth in newsroom staffs that most newswork positions became in many respects proletarian in nature. In effect, the work retained its intellectual nature as the main determinant of its identity, even as its material circumstances deteriorated.

These shifts were fairly gradual. The growing division of newsroom labor took place amid an increasing differentiation in the class backgrounds of newspaper workers. A college graduate was "a rather rare bird in American journalism" (Baehr 1936, 83) when Whitelaw Reid joined the *New York Tribune* in 1869. But by 1900 the *Journalist* would declare, perhaps with some exaggeration, that "today the college bred men are the rule" (quoted in Schudson 1978, 68). To a congressman's query on this trend at a 1900 hearing, the ITU president replied:

> For the past few years there have come into the newspaper profession many college graduates and sons of rich men, who take their places directly in the editorial room, on account of political influence or ownership of stock. This has a tendency to change the old democratic traditions as they existed in the newspaper trade or profession 25, 30, or 40 years ago. (Donnelly 1901, 276)

This comment harkened back to an era marked by less sharp distinctions among newspaper workers, when most lacked college degrees or solidly middle-class backgrounds. Most who ended up in the newsroom had some typesetting experience and were unlikely to cross printers' picket lines. The loss of "old democratic traditions," then, may be seen, in part, as a crucial shift in the identity of newswork; increasingly it belonged to "college graduates and sons of rich men." For these people, such work could reasonably combine a notion of a sacred public trust with that of an exciting but insecure and poorly paid job—precisely because it was only temporary work. These were indeed difficult conditions for organizing.

Journalists long have tended to be motivated primarily by a sense of public service (Johnstone, Slawski, and Bowman 1976, 229; Weaver and Wilhoit 1991, 93-94). Yet, the reality of newswork for the commercial press has virtually always belied its noble ideology as voiced by publishers. In

1937, long after many of the grim conditions described in this essay had been eliminated, a copy editor for the *Chicago Tribune* testified before the National Labor Relations Board:

> Nobody said lousier things about Roosevelt than I did in certain headlines. If the *Tribune* had ordered me to say that Roosevelt was illegitimate, I would have done so. To refuse would have been impossible. To hold a job I had to obey my boss's wishes. (quoted in Dreier 1978, 75)

A similar description of publishers appeared in the nineteenth century, made by an Englishman who visited the United States in 1833:

> The conductors of American journals are generally shrewd but uneducated men, extravagant in praise or censure . . . and exceedingly indifferent to all matters which have no discernible relation to their own pockets or privileges. (quoted in Sanborn 1874, 61)

Thus, from well before newsworkers' wages were decried by *The Nation* in the 1870s to today's newsroom buyouts, the U.S. commercial press has shown a single-minded pursuit of profits. After the turn of the century, newsroom workers began to move more forcefully toward collective behavior. Increasingly they were prepared to treat management as an opponent, more than as a colleague with whom one put out the paper. In 1919 the *New Republic* editorialized, "From Copy Readers to Leg Men to Chief Editorial Writers, they have organized in Boston."[6] In 1933, newsroom workers formed the American Newspaper Guild (Leab 1970). But their lot has never been an easy one. To the present day, long-standing obstacles continue to hinder newsworkers' attempts to organize or to retain their union affiliation. Further, new technologies and media mergers improve newspaper corporations' leverage over newsroom workers. Today, the pay of newsroom workers gives them less "relative buying power" than they had "in the late 1960s" (Weaver and Wilhoit 1992, 8). Compared with ten years ago, a current study of newsroom workers found a sharp drop in morale and a sharp rise in turnover rates (8). And yet, studies of journalists are loath to link such findings to the policies of corporate owners, possibly because these owners often finance the studies.

In the late nineteenth century, U.S. capitalism's transition to a corporate phase drove the commercial press's development, enlarging newsroom staffs and fueling an increasing division of labor. At the same time, the rising costs of owning a newspaper were moving the ownership of the means of production beyond the financial reach of most newsworkers. Underlying these changes in political economy was a long-standing ideological component, one that infused newswork with a thoroughly individualist, middle-class ethos. Caught between their public service ethic and their self-image on the one hand and their employers' capital accumulation strategies on the other, newsroom workers suffered. Today, as corporate capitalism becomes increasingly global, newsworkers again face worsening work conditions. So, like their counterparts of more than a century ago, today's newsroom workers increasingly are coming to view their work as combining a sacred public trust with a temporary job. The consequences for the public sphere—in a country that identifies itself as having a well-informed citizenry that is becoming even more so, by moving onto an information superhighway—are unpleasant, at best.

## Notes

1. There has been considerable debate as to whether the advent of the penny press brought a major shift in the readership of newspapers. Some contend that the penny press did pioneer a focus on working-class readers (e.g., Bleyer 1927; J. L. Lee 1923; Schiller 1981), but Nerone (1987) argues convincingly that the penny press was simply part of an evolution toward newspapers' including more social classes among their readers.

2. The decline in the number of U.S. daily newspapers began well before the advent of commercial broadcasting in the mid-1920s (McChesney 1993), which, along with direct mail, today constitutes newspapers' and magazines' main competition for advertising revenue (Glaberson 1994, D-6).

3. A comprehensive survey of U.S. newspapers reported that editorial work was "divided between editorial writing, exchange reading, the condensation and preparation of news, the editing of telegraphic news and correspondence, etc." (North 1884, 83).

4. Will Irwin (1909) described the *New York Sun's* managing editor as "rising from his chair and walking over to the copy desk" (308).

5. Copy editors' anonymity and increasing numbers are suggested in a staff memo from Joseph Pulitzer (1897): "One really good one is worth three ordinary ones; we should pick out the best copy readers in the town and pay them the highest salaries."

6. "1919 was *the* great year of industrial unrest over wages, hours, and recognition of unions and shop committees" (Stark 1980, 111).

## References

Armstrong, David. *A Trumpet to Arms: Alternative Media in America.* Los Angeles: J. P. Tarcher, 1981.

Avenel, Walter. "Journalism as a Profession." *Forum* 25 (May 1898): 366-74.

Baehr, Harry W., Jr. *The New York Tribune since the Civil War.* New York: Dodd, Mead, 1936.

Bagdikian, Ben H. "More Mergers Mean Less News." *Journalism Studies Review* (July 1979): 21-24, 60.

———. *The Media Monopoly* (4th ed.). Boston: Beacon, 1992.

Baldasty, Gerald J. "The Rise of News as a Commodity: Business Imperatives and the Press in the Nineteenth Century." In *Ruthless Criticism: New Perspectives in U.S. Communication*

*History*, ed. William S. Solomon and Robert W. McChesney, 98-121. Minneapolis: University of Minnesota Press, 1993.

Bekken, Jon. "The Working-Class Press at the Turn of the Century." In *Ruthless Criticism: New Perspectives in U.S. Communication History*, ed. William S. Solomon and Robert W. McChesney, 151-75. Minneapolis: University of Minnesota Press, 1993.

Bleyer, Willard Grosvenor. *Newspaper Writing and Editing*. New York: Houghton Mifflin, 1913.

———. *Main Currents in the History of American Journalism*. Boston: Houghton Mifflin, 1927.

Botein, Stephen. "Printers and the American Revolution." In *The Press and the American Revolution*, ed. Bernard Bailyn and John B. Hench, 11-57. Worcester, Mass.: American Antiquarian Society, 1980.

Bridge, Charles A. "The Copy Reader." *Journalist*, May 15, 1892, 13.

Chang, Elizabeth. "The Buyout Boom." *American Journalism Review* 15 (July/August 1993): 16-21.

Coates, Eugene. "The Coming Newspaper." *Journalist*, Feb. 13, 1892, 2, 3.

Cockerill, John A. "Some Phases of Contemporary Journalism." *Journalist*, Oct. 22, 1892, 5, 12-13.

Cummings, Amos J. "How Newspapers Are Made: The New York Tribune." *Packard's Monthly* 1 (November 1868): 105-9.

Dana, Charles A. *The Art of Newspaper Making*. New York: D. Appleton, 1897.

Darnton, Robert. "Writing News and Telling Stories." *Daedalus* 104 (Spring 1975): 175-94.

De Weese, Truman A. "Journalism: Its Rewards and Opportunities." *Forum* 26 (December 1898): 441-51.

Donnelly, Samuel P. "Testimony." In *Report of the U.S. Industrial Commission on the Relations and Conditions of Capital and Labor Employed in Manufactures and General Business*. (Vol. 7), 268-92. Washington, D.C.: U.S. Government Printing Office, 1901.

Dreier, Peter. "Newsroom Democracy and Media Monopoly: The Dilemmas of Workplace Reform among Professional Journalists." *Insurgent Sociologist* 8 (Fall 1978): 70-86.

Edwards, Richard. *Contested Terrain: The Transformation of the Workplace in the Twentieth Century*. New York: Basic Books, 1979.

Elliott, Philip. "Intellectuals, the 'Information Society' and the Disappearance of the Public Sphere." *Media, Culture & Society* 4 (July 1982): 243-53.

Emery, Edwin. *History of the American Newspaper Publishers Association*. Minneapolis: University of Minnesota Press, 1950.

Foner, Philip S. *History of the Labor Movement in the United States*. New York: International Publishers, 1947.

Forman, Allan. "That Strike." *Journalist*, Feb. 21, 1891, 8.

———. "Make a Home for Yourself." *Journalist*, July 21, 1900, 108.

Gildea, Robert L. "You Can't Run a Newspaper by Consensus" (letter to the editor). *Editor & Publisher*, Jan. 12, 1985, 5.

Glaberson, William. "Newspapers Race for Outlets in Electronic Marketplace." *New York Times*, Jan. 17, 1994, D-1, D-6.

Godkin, Edwin L. "Newspapers Here and Abroad." *North American Review* 150 (February 1890): 197-204.

Goldman, Ari L. "Question of Censorship Shadows Catholic Paper." *New York Times*, May 19, 1993, B-5.

Gordon, David M., Richard Edwards, and Michael Reich. *Segmented Work, Divided Workers: The Historical Transformation of Labor in the United States*. New York: Cambridge University Press, 1982.

Hofstadter, Richard. *The Age of Reform: From Bryan to F.D.R.* New York: Vintage, 1955.

Howard, Joe. "The *New York Herald* under the Two Bennetts." *Journalist*, Aug. 8, 1891a, 4.

———. "Young Men in Newspaper Management." *Journalist*, Sept. 5, 1891b, 4, 5.

Hughes, Everett C. *The Sociological Eye*. New Brunswick, N.J.: Transaction, 1984.

Irwin, Will. "The *New York Sun*." *American Magazine,* Jan. 1909, 301-10.

———. "The American Newspaper—Part III: The Fourth Current." *Collier's,* Feb. 18, 1911a, 14-17, 24, 27.

———. "The American Newspaper—Part VII: The Reporter and the News." *Collier's,* Apr. 22, 1911b, 35.

J.K. "The Reporter." *Journalist,* Apr. 26, 1890, 5.

Johnstone, John W. C., Edward J. Slawski and William W. Bowman. *The News People: A Sociological Portrait of American Journalists and Their Work*. Urbana: University of Illinois Press, 1976.

*Journalist.* "In the A.N.P.A." June 7, 1890, 13.

———. "A Union Formed." Apr. 23, 1892b, 8.

———. "Free Lance." Oct. 8, 1892c, 4.

———. "The American Newspaper Publishers' Association." Dec. 17, 1892d, 60.

———. "New York." Dec. 24, 1892e.

Keller, J.W. "Journalism as a Career." *Forum* 15 (August 1893): 691-704.

Kellner, Douglas. *Critical Theory, Marxism and Modernity*. Baltimore: Johns Hopkins University Press, 1989.

Kennedy, Paul. *The Rise and Fall of the Great Powers*. New York: Random House, 1987.

King, Henry. "The Rank and Pay of Journalists." *Forum* 18 (January 1895): 587-96.

Leab, Daniel J. *A Union of Individuals: The Formation of the American Newspaper Guild, 1933–1936*. New York: Columbia University Press, 1970.

Lee, Alfred McClung. *The Daily Newspaper in America: The Evolution of a Social Instrument*. New York: Macmillan, 1937.

Lee, James L. *History of American Journalism* (rev. ed.). Boston: Houghton Mifflin, 1923.

Leonard, Thomas C. *The Power of the Press: The Birth of American Political Reporting*. New York: Oxford University Press, 1986.

Linn, James W. *James Keeley: Newspaperman*. New York: Bobbs-Merrill, 1937.

McChesney, Robert W. *Telecommunications, Mass Media, and Democracy: The Battle for the Control of U.S. Broadcasting, 1928-1935*. New York: Oxford University Press, 1993.

Mendel, Ron. "Cooperative Unionism and the Development of Job Control in New York's Printing Trades, 1886-1898." *Labor History* 32 (Summer 1991): 354-75.

Mitchell, Edward P. *Memoirs of an Editor: Fifty Years of American Journalism*. New York: Charles Scribner's Sons, 1924.

Moran, James. *Printing Presses: History and Development from the 15th Century to Modern Times*. Berkeley: University of California Press, 1973.

*The Nation.* "The Profession of 'Journalism.'" 17 (July 17, 1873): 37-38.

Nerone, John C. "The Mythology of the Penny Press." *Critical Studies in Mass Communication* 4 (1987): 376-404.

*New Republic.* "News Writers Union Local No. 1." Aug. 6, 1919, 8.

*New York Herald.* "The Massachusetts Labor Strike—Aid for the Sufferers." Feb. 29, 1860, 4.

Newspaper Association of America. *Facts about Newspapers, '93*. Reston, Va.: Newspaper Association of America, 1993.

North, Simon N. D. *Newspaper and Periodical Press of the United States*. Washington, D.C.: U.S. Department of Commerce, Bureau of the Census, 1884.

O'Brien, Frank M. *The Story of the Sun, 1833-1918*. New York: George H. Doran, 1918.

O'Shaughnessy, James, Jr. "The Reporter in the Smaller Cities." *Journalist,* June 4, 1892, 12, 13.

Ottarson, F. J. "The Press as Maker of Public Opinion." *Packard's Monthly* 2-3 (July 1869): 211-13.

Parton, James. "The *New York Herald*." *North American Review* 102 (April 1866): 373-419.

Przeworski, Adam. "Proletariat into a Class: The Process of Class Formation from Karl Kautsky's *The Class Struggle* to Recent Controversies." *Politics & Society* 4 (1977): 343-401.

Pulitzer, Joseph. Pulitzer Papers, Box 1 (May 28, 1897).

Rorabaugh, W. J. *The Craft Apprentice: From Franklin to the Machine Age in America*. New York: Oxford University Press, 1986.

Sanborn, F. B. "Journalism and Journalists." *Atlantic Monthly,* July 1874, 55-66.

Saxton, Alexander. "Problems of Class and Race in the Origins of the Mass Circulation Press." *American Quarterly* 36 (Summer 1984): 211-34.

Schiller, Daniel. *Objectivity and the News: The Public and the Rise of Commercial Journalism*. Philadelphia: University of Pennsylvania Press, 1981.

Schudson, Michael. *Discovering the News: A Social History of American Newspapers*. New York: Basic Books, 1978.

Shanks, William F. G. "How We Get Our News." *Harper's New Monthly Magazine,* Mar. 1867, 511-22.

———. "The Old-Timer." *Journalist,* Sept. 10, 1892, 12.

Sklar, Martin J. *The Corporate Reconstruction of American Capitalism, 1890-1916*. New York: Cambridge University Press, 1988.

Smith, William Henry. "The Press as a News Gatherer." *Century Magazine,* Aug. 1891, 524-36.

Smythe, Ted Curtis. "The Reporter, 1880-1900: Working Conditions and Their Influence on the News." *Journalism History* 7, no. 1 (1980): 1-10.

Solomon, William S. "Newsroom Managers and Workers." *American Journalism* (forthcoming).

Stark, David. "Class Struggle and the Transformation of the Labor Process." *Theory & Society* 9 ( January 1980): 89-130.

Starr, Paul. "Medicine and the Waning of Professional Sovereignty." *Daedalus* 107 (Winter 1978): 175-93.

Steele, Janet E. *The Sun Shines for All: Journalism and Ideology in the Life of Charles A. Dana*. Syracuse, N.Y.: Syracuse University Press, 1993.

Stevens, George A. *New York Typographical Union No. 6: Study of a Modern Trade Union and Its Predecessors*. Albany, N.Y.: Lyon State Printers, 1913.

Stewart, Ethelbert. 1905. "A Documentary History of the Early Organizations of Printers." *Bulletin of the Bureau of Labor* 10, no. 11 (1905): 857-1033.

Stewart, Kenneth. *News Is What We Make It*. Boston: Houghton Mifflin, 1943.

Stone, Candace. *Dana and the* Sun. New York: Dodd, Mead, 1938.

Talese, Gay. *The Kingdom and the Power*. New York: New American Library, 1969.

Tocqueville, Alexis de. *Democracy in America* (Vol. 1). New York: Knopf, 1945.

Tracy, George A. *History of the Typographical Union*. Indianapolis: International Typographical Union, 1913.

U.S. Department of Commerce, Bureau of the Census. *Historical Statistics of the United States: Colonial Times to 1970*. Washington, D.C.: U.S. Government Printing Office, 1975.

———. *Statistical Abstract of the United States: 1993*. Washington, D.C.: U.S. Government Printing Office, 1993.

U.S. National Labor Relations Board. *Collective Bargaining in the Newspaper Industry*. (Division of Economic Research, Bulletin No. 3, Oct. 1938). Washington, D.C.: U.S. Government Printing Office, 1939.

Villard, Oswald G. "Press Tendencies and Dangers." *Atlantic Monthly,* Jan. 1918, 62-66.

Warner, Charles D. *The American Newspaper*. Boston: James R. Osgood, 1881.

Weaver, David H., and G. Cleveland Wilhoit, eds. *The American Journalist: A Portrait of U.S. News People and Their Work* (2d ed.). Bloomington: Indiana University Press, 1991.

———. *The American Journalist in the 1990s*. Arlington, Va.: Freedom Forum, 1992.

Zinn, Howard. *A People's History of the United States*. New York: Harper & Row, 1980.

# 6 / Words against Images

## *Positioning Newswork in the Age of Photography*

## Barbie Zelizer

It is a commonly accepted, if little understood, truism that one picture is worth a thousand words. Yet how such a truism came to be incorporated into the practices of those responsible for the discourse surrounding images is a less developed dimension of our understanding. This essay addresses the collective response to photographs among American journalists during a time when photographs were a novel tool for documenting the events of public life. It considers how journalists of the 1930s and 1940s resisted, challenged, and adapted to the photographic image, ultimately accepting photography as an alternative but legitimate mode of newswork.

In considering discussions about the image in newspapers of record among reporters of the time, this chapter raises fundamental questions about the shape of technological adaptation—both among those who are in the position of accepting the new technology and among those who are seen as constituting it. It suggests that at the heart of such adaptation are long-standing issues of legitimacy, power, and authority that figure centrally into the negotiation of changing standards of practice.

As long as news has tried to tell the stories of "real-life" events, a legacy of images has accompanied its words. Long seen as secondary to words, images have changed in stature as evolving technologies of newsgathering and news presentation have made them more central. The past three decades in particular, with the ascendancy of television and development of cable-driven images, have greatly enhanced the authority of the visual image, making it a serious contender to the word preference of most members of the journalistic community.

The cogency of the visual image derives in part from the mythology that surrounds it. Roland Barthes (1977a, 1977b) and Stuart Hall (1973) have long held that the photograph fulfills both a denotative (or referential) and connotative (or interpretive) function. Rudolf Arnheim (1986) has argued that when interpreting an image's significance, one need look beyond it, even if its "glimpses of events show with immense authenticity what actually happened" (308). Allan Sekula (1984) has echoed the strategic nature of photography's functions, noting that "a photographic discourse is a system within which the culture harnesses photographs to various representational tasks. . . . Every photographic image is a sign, above all, of someone's investment in the sending of a message" (5). Yet it is the latter function, that of interpretation, that has long been underprivileged in discourse about photography's workings. Notwithstanding more recent attacks on the activity and authority of image making, attacks facilitated by the technologically sophisticated practices of the media and computer graphics (Jussim 1989), the general function of interpretation has rarely been incorporated into discourse about the photograph, which has tended instead to privilege the image as a "transcription from reality" (Ritchin 1990, 7).

Thus, news photography has been assumed to "tell it like it is" (Worth 1981, 175).[1] Its audience possesses an "insistent belief in [its] power to document things as they are" (Hardt and Ohrn 1981, 49). When seen from within journalism, the emphasis of referentiality over interpretation has had a more general resonance that upholds the structures of journalism. At some level, journalists have been expected to provide, realistically or not, a mirror on the world, and the "wedding of reporter's facts and statistics to the photographer's visual proof" has thereby been seen as the "total journalistic implement" (Rhode and McCall 1961, vii). Photojournalists have been thought to offer a "visual expansion" of journalistic practice (Gidal 1972, 5), one that appears to increase the truthfulness of news and extend the adage that "the camera does not lie" to journalism's primary authority, the reporters (Ritchin 1990, 1). In other words, emphasizing photojournalism's denotative function—and its concomitant traits of objectivity, transparency, and verisimilitude—helps to uphold the more general authority of journalism for reporting events of the "real world." Allowing the camera to function as a medium of denotation supports journalism's status as a major institution for reporting events in this way.

The recognition of photography as part of newswork has played off of such a mythology. As with other critical incidents in the annals of American journalism, in which journalists have attempted to generate consensual meanings about their profession by addressing them in discourse, here too reporters used discourse to address the changing pictorial technology of news and the photographers who came with it (Zelizer, 1992, 1993). In evaluating the burgeoning presence of photographers in their midst, journalists of the 1930s and 1940s at first eschewed the photograph's interpretive function to define the photographer's mission in hard news as a primarily denotative one. This had possibly unintended consequences for both reporters and photographers: By upholding one function of photography—denotation—over another—connotation—reporters persuaded photographers to adopt one of the professional goals by which the journalistic community had long defined its own boundaries of practice. Moreover, they upheld an unspoken rule in journalism itself, whereby tasks of interpretation tended to be reserved for newsworkers with high status, such as owners, editors, or senior columnists. This meant that journalists co-opted photojournalists within a certain strategically suitable understanding of photojournalism. But it was an understanding that restricted the authority of the image. Only when the circumstances of World War II allowed photojournalists to play a more interpretive role in documentation was that co-optation somewhat eased.

In looking back, the early 1930s should have promised a time of considerable advancement for most media workers. In the United States, the events of the Depression had enhanced the authority of those invested in recording the events of public life, and many media workers felt that their reportage—in word, image, or a combination of both—constituted the performance of an essential social duty. As one wire editor opined in 1932, "to dig themselves out of depression, people must think and they cannot think unless they are reliably informed" (Cooper 1932, 6).

Technological advancement came on many fronts. From a general perspective, radio experienced the greatest development, exemplified by a cacophony of voices trying to claim the airwaves for daily news forums and other kinds of broadcasting. Listeners trusted radio to such a greater degree than they did other media that the 1930s became known as the "golden age" for radio broadcasting (Stott 1973). In print journalism, extensive and faster wire connections, the addition of international news bureaus, especially in Latin America and Europe, and the growth of newspaper chains all extended the reach of the press. In photography, smaller cameras, better lenses, faster film, and better means of transmission made the image an increasingly viable tool for representing social life. Technologies of preparation, distribution, and reproduction took on degrees of sophistication that facilitated the reportage of current events through the camera, as did the development of long-range airplanes and the beginnings of wirephoto technology (Stapp 1988, 2). All of this made the photograph of the 1930s a potential "everyday newspaper attraction" (Cooke 1931, 313). Other media technologies cut across simple distinctions between word and image: sound movies were introduced to the public in 1927, and newsreel houses sprang up throughout the following decade. From the mid-1920s to the mid-1930s, Americans were bombarded with new magazine formats—ranging from the compartmentalized newsmagazines of *Time* and *Newsweek* to the picture magazines of *Look* and *Life* (and the shorter-lived *Click, Focus, Picture,* and *See*).

The potential for advancement, however, was unevenly spread across different kinds of newsworkers. Coming off of what in one view constituted a general "repudiation of the press," reporters appeared to suffer the most (cited in Stott 1973, 79; see also Olson 1935). Looking ahead into the 1930s, the editor of *Editor & Publisher* predicted a time "filled with doubt and insecurity" (Pew 1930, 29). His assessment was based in part on past performance, in part on journalism's continued ability to document the events of the day. In the views of some, not only had the press belittled evidence of the Depression, but its experiments with tabloidlike journalism and excessive commercialism constituted what one critic later called "playing for the crowds" (Marzolf 1991, 76). Coverage of the Lindbergh baby kidnapping in 1932 posed particular problems, in that the press "outdid themselves and one another in verbosity and vulgarity" (Bent 1932, 212). Because of fallout from the Depression, journalists were financially not much better off: in the best of cases newspapers reported falling revenues; in the worst, they faced folding and merging news organizations (Cooper 1932, 6). Finally, journalism was unclear about its priorities. Journalists and journalism educators "were squeezed by both sides": conservatives wanted better and stronger censorship, and progressives were bothered by the big business interests of the press (Marzolf 1991, 134). Reporters were also concerned about what constitutes appropriate journalism—interpretive, personalized, or objective reporting. Some high-ranking journalists called for more interpretation (e.g., Brucker 1937, 229; Olson 1935), with even the wire services reporting a demand among member newspapers for more interpretive material (Cooper 1933, 9); others demanded more bylines and compartmentalized newspapers so as to lend the news a more personal demeanor (Watson 1937, 254); yet others found objectivity the only way to maintain good journalism (Gannett 1931; Lippmann 1931). All of this meant that journalistic professionalism, until then on the rise, "suffered a loss of momentum" (Marzolf 1991, 134). It is thus perhaps no surprise that journalists suffered a loss of credibility in the public eye. The end of the 1930s was marked by distrust of the press, and public opinion polls reported that at least one in three people disbelieved what he or she read in the newspapers (cited in Stott 1973, 79; see also Olson 1935).

At the same time, however, journalism showed considerable staying power in the face of adverse circumstances. There was a "perceptible growth in the field of practical education in journalism" (American Society of Newspaper Editors 1928, 45). Newly founded organizations, unions, and professional forums—such as the American Society for Newspaper Editors (ASNE), the American Association of Schools and Departments of Journalism (AASDJ), and the American Newspaper Guild—were taking hold, and membership was at a high (Cooper 1931; Keating 1935). Journalists were moving toward the accoutrements of professionalism, and they began discussing ways of accrediting journalism schools, adopting codes of ethics, and improving journalism education. In 1932, the Associated Press reported "handling more wordage per hour per wire than at any previous time," making that year "one of the heaviest producers of news in the history of the Associated Press" (Cooper 1932, 9; 1933, 9).

For most kinds of photographers, the road to advancement seemed slightly more certain than it did for most journalists. Although the photograph's first hundred years have generated conflicting views of the meaning of expansion in photographic practice, most traditional overviews underscore a growing recognition of the image's use as a tool of documentation.[2] Arenas of visual documentation were supported by inroads generated by both Depression photographers and military photographers during the early 1930s. The possibility of documenting social problems through images, which dated back to the work of Jacob Riis in the 1890s and of Lewis Hines in later years, was enhanced when the federal government employed photographers such as Dorothea Lange and Walker Evans to document social conditions during the Depression. Although their emphasis on human misery—exemplified by the visual records of the lives of sharecroppers and migrant workers—earned them the name of the "ashcan school of photography" (Rhode and McCall 1961, 27), these documentary photographers considerably enhanced the general status of photography by showing that it was possible to use images for important social aims, a notion with direct bearing on news photography. A similar effect was generated by military photographers, who found the image an increasingly useful tool for intelligence, recording, and reconnaissance. Although depictions of battle scenes had accompanied the major wars of earlier years, the photograph of the 1930s and 1940s considerably improved on the carvings, woodcuts, and drawings used until then. Although faster lenses and emulsions had made the visualization of battle scenes possible already during earlier wars, it was not until World War II that

> the livid flash of gunfire is captured in color while the sound-on-film records the thundering roar. Photographers follow every activity from camp to front. . . . Movies have come into their own both on land, sea and in the air. . . . Improvements in camera design and lenses mean pictures under almost impossible conditions. Aerial photos show every crosstie in tracks, every fence and post down to the smallest detail. . . . World War II promises to be not only the most photographed war in history but the best photographed. (*Camera* 1943, 39)

Advances in technology made photographers increasingly competent at recording the wartime experience. Using the camera as an aid to the military allowed photographers to use visual images as documentation at the same time they served their country.

This use of photography had direct bearing on the incorporation of the image in hard news. During the early 1930s, photojournalism was just beginning to come into vogue. Photojournalists were still called "newspaper illustrators" or "pictorial reporters." Early attempts had produced engravings of Civil War scenes that appeared in *Harper's Weekly* and *Leslie's,* or tabloidlike efforts that used photographs in sensationalistic ways. Photographs appeared widely on sports pages, society pages, and women's pages, but rarely in the hard news sections of newspapers of record. In American dailies in particular, the use of the photograph had long been associated with yellow journalism, and it was not until the early 1930s that the camera began to be seen as "a crucial reporting tool" (Stott 1973, 76).[3] Although modern photojournalism had already begun to take shape in Germany by 1929, when photoreportage, or the inclusion of photographic series, had become an increasingly frequent staple of German magazines (Gidal 1972; Hardt and Ohrn 1981), only in the mid-1930s did the American picture magazine, exemplified by *Life* and *Look,* and its main form of expression, the picture essay, come into being (Fulton 1988; Newhall 1982). These illustrated magazines, using what *Life* (1939, 81) called their "new picture-and-word editorial technique," enhanced the option of applying photographic skills to reporting.

It took an experience in need of documentation through images to rattle the staid institutions of journalism, however. The dailies and weeklies became particularly interested in the image's role in documenting news when they witnessed the photographic recording of the Hindenburg explosion of 1937. At the time, journalists proclaimed photographic coverage of the disaster a "spectacular achievement," its pictures winning acclaim from the trade forums (Associated Press 1938, 3; *Editor & Publisher* 1938). Years later, claims were made that in responding to the explosion a wide range of newspapers "told the story not in words but in pictures, which were often enlarged half a page in size. . . . Never had a disaster been so thoroughly covered by photography" (Newhall 1982, 258). This suggested that the Hindenburg incident underscored the advantages to be had in making the photograph a part of daily news. The work of other news photographers, such as Weegee and Joe Costa, further convinced the American public that photographers—though still "journalism's poor relation"—deserved more attention (Fulton 1988, 118). The increasing popularity of photographs made them even more a force that deserved attention (*Editor & Publisher* 1937, 5).

So it was that two professional groups—photographers and reporters — faced each other as potential allies created by the rising use of the photographic document in news. This is not to say that either group approached the impending proximity without some trepidation. In fact, reporters debated extensively the redefinition of professional boundaries that the incorporation of the photograph and photographer in news seemed to entail. Their discourse showed the extent to which the incorporation of the photographic image in news appeared to challenge the long-held authority of the word. It promised to push reporters and photographers into new, and unknown, horizons that would force them to consider each other not only in discourse but in practice as well.

The early integration of images in hard news had much to do with the efforts of the Associated Press. Although certain services were distributing photos earlier and wirephotos were hardly necessary to the use of images in local news, the Associated Press did much to systematize the new medium of dissemination. Associated Press general manager Kent Cooper had long been interested in promoting images as part of newswork. He figured that images provided the vehicle for the Associated Press to maintain its lead as a news organization, and he argued to his board in 1927 that it had "to take the step of coordinating delivery of news in pictures with delivery of news in words" (cited in Cooper 1959, 136). Largely due to his efforts, the Associated Press established its News Photo Service, a decision that Cooper (1932) predicted would make "news picture distribution a vital and integral function of the Associated Press" (9). In 1931, the Associated Press's New York photography plant was moved from outside general headquarters to the service's main plant, underscoring the "soundness" of the link between pictures and words (Cooper 1931, 9). Citing "a new epoch in American journalism brought about by the widespread use of pictures by newspapers," as early as 1932 Cooper was able to claim definitively that "pictures are news today" (9).

Although other news organizations may not have shared Cooper's enthusiasm, they began to follow the lead of the Associated Press once it systematized the introduction of the wirephoto to American journalism in 1935. By substantially quickening the transmission of photographs by mail, wirephoto constituted a technology that ensured the delivery of photographs in as rapid a fashion as words. For the first time, pictures could be sent as quickly as their primary competitor for documentation, words (Zelizer, forthcoming).

Many journalists recognized that this new technology for transmitting photographs would change the shape of journalism, and they saw that the status of images was on the rise. As one leading news editor of the 1930s said:

> The old forms are breaking up and new ideas are coming in, and the big thing, until television comes and blows us all out of the water, is the development of that completely new technique of photography combined with newspaper stories. It is an idea, it is a theory. Nothing is yet factual. I haven't seen a newspaper in the United States, including my own, that has yet caught what is coming. (Bingay 1935, 53)

With the ascent of the photograph in news, many journalists scrambled to figure out how best to accommodate the image without harming their own authority.

Journalists regarded the rising presence of photographs in news with considerable ambivalence. While they knew that images enhanced the readability of the news and that in many cases they needed images to help establish an authoritative voice in reporting, they were unclear about the value and power of the photograph. In fact, many trade articles at the time avoided the issue of expanding news to include photography. One article considered the future of journalism under the title "Who's a Journalist? Writers No Longer Have Sole Claim to Title Many Have Scorned in Past" (Pollard 1937, 9). The article, however, dealt with expanding definitions of journalism not to photographers, but to business personnel.

From the beginning, recognition of the image generated professional anxiety for many journalists, who perceived it as the unwanted beginning of another language in journalism. At the heart of their anxieties was a concern that the image had the potential power to circumvent the power of the word. Journalists responded to this dilemma by constructing a view of photography that admitted its partial authority. Although they recognized that their narratives could benefit from images, they knew that their own authority depended on the degree to which they could constrain the image's presence in news. Possessing what appear to be few clues about how to relate the two, they began to recognize the image and the photographer in news in contained ways.

On the one hand, journalists recognized the potential value to be had in adjoining words with pictures in daily news, and many were cognizant of and vocal about the value of the photographic image. The move to accommodate the image was thereby hailed by the trade journals, whose editors recognized that photography deserved discussion. In August 1935, *Editor & Publisher* began regularly publishing a new feature called "Eyes of the Press," which was slated to track the "triumphs of press photographers" (Price 1935). Two years later, the trade journal the *Quill* (1937) decided, because of "the current furor over pictures, their treatment and handling," to run a series of features on photographs. The series offered to bring "helpful, interesting articles on pictorial subjects from month to month." That same year, the editor of the Associated Press's News Photo Service proclaimed that "photos now ride the wires with text," adding, "They often tell the story better than words" (Stanley 1937, 5). Claiming that news photography was "the most effective implement that editors have at their command today for conveying information quickly and forcefully," he stated that it is "up to this generation of newspapermen to . . . show the text side how to tell the news":

> It seems to me that these many months of wire photo operation have demonstrated to any Doubting Tom that pictures assist the clarity of any story, and that they inform the reader more succinctly, and more vividly and more completely than words in far more instances than generally believed. (5)

At about the same time, the ASNE called for the "creation of a new breed in the newspaper business," one that would be in keeping with "the new value of pictures in newspapers" (Bingay 1935, 50).

By the late 1930s, accommodating the image was more than just a topic of discourse. Dailies reported an increase of nearly 40 percent in the use of photographic cuts since the beginning of the decade (Brandenburg 1938, 8). In 1937, reporters were being urged by leading news editors to maintain adequate picture files for their archives (Drummond 1937, 11). Different photographic services added new beats, new photographers, and new bureaus. News organizations opened subsidiary photographic agencies, including World Wide Photos, ACME Newspictures, United News Pictures, and International News Photos, and the reports of the in-house organs of many news organizations began to include sections on news photography regularly. In February 1938, the *Quill* decided to substitute its bland cover design with a cover photograph, calling the new feature "Cover Picture." Later that same year, *Editor & Publisher* shaped its own full-page advertisement into a drawing of a man taking a picture. The headline read, "Candid Camera Close-ups of Ideas," and three paragraphs of text went on to explain how in the "age of pictures," it was still possible to offer "factual close-ups" through words (*Quill* 1938b). By the early 1940s, issues of photographic representation were being addressed in trade forums such as the annual meetings of the ASNE (Peters 1941). All of this suggested not only that photographs were very much on the agendas of journalists of the time, but that the photographic image was being emulated in many types of mediated discourse.

Early in 1938, the issue of academically training news photographers began to rattle the community of journalists. At the same time the *Saturday Review of Literature* (1938) proclaimed that photography textbooks were "useless," the *Quill* began to debate whether or not courses in photojournalism should be introduced into schools of journalism. One early discussion about the introduction of photojournalism classes was interesting because it was articulated by a "lecturer at the University of Wisconsin who has been giving a course in news photography for more than a year" (Smith 1938a, 5). Claiming that "only seven of the leading schools of journalism were making even feeble attempts to teach the fundamentals of this fascinating new phase of journalism," the author began with the somewhat aggressive statement that

> you may not agree with a recent statement that the news picture has become as important as the news story, but the fact that the various services are spending enormous amounts of money to perfect picture coverage to the same extent as their reporting would seem to indicate that pictorial journalism is at least challenging reportorial journalism. (5)

Resting on the premise that financial expenditures proved the value of photography, the article claimed that "only the schools of journalism have lagged in their recognition of pictorial journalism." Other observers, lamenting the lack of photographic equipment in journalism schools, adopted a more conciliatory tone to claim that it was time to begin incorporating photography in journalism schools (Price 1941).

Underlying what appeared to be an outright validation of photography, however, was a simultaneous undermining of the authority of the image. The proliferation of activities that appeared to embrace wholeheartedly the coming of the image in news in fact concealed a fundamental ambivalence toward the image among journalists. As usage of this new technology grew in the practice of journalism, reporters began to recognize it as a threat of no small degree. Tensions reached a particular high with the coming of the wirephoto, which, in giving the photograph a vessel for immediate delivery, facilitated the rapid incorporation of images into hard news. At the same time, however, wirephoto technology equalized the circumstances for using the two tools of documentation, thereby neutralizing the long-held edge that had belonged to words. Journalists thus somewhat predictably reacted to the growing presence of photographers in their midst by attempting to contain the authority of the photograph within prescribed parameters, even when it faced them with increasing frequency.

Evidence of journalists' ambivalence was widespread, though subtle. As the Associated Press made possible the transmission of photographs over telephone wires, there were suggestions that journalists failed to take the development seriously. One reporter scoffed at the idea, claiming as late as 1935 that "no one believed in the coming wire transmission of photos" (cited in Stouffer 1949, xvii). Other objections had what appeared to be monetary reasoning behind them. Decrying what they proclaimed to be an erosion of professional standards, editors wondered whether photographs were worth the money it cost to produce them ("The News and Pictures" 1935, 69; *Newsweek* 1932). One New York editor argued against the increased costs of printing wirephotos, pictures that "would have been discarded without a second glance had they come by mail" (Blanchard 1935, 54). The irony, he continued, is that "the paper could have used the captions and pictures interchangeably throughout these months with no one the wiser."

All of this meant that journalists, at least initially, referenced news pictures in a way that continued to underscore their own authority for telling news. They did so by deflating the threat of the pictorial reporter, with reporters subscribing to an expectation that photographers were useful only insofar as they could provide adjunct documentation to accompany the grander interpretive narratives of journalists. In other words, reporters structured their discourse about the appropriate boundaries of this new technology in news by preferring the "small" view of the craft of photography to its "large" one. Although this initial thrust toward referentiality over interpretation would be somewhat dismantled over the course of the Second World War, it nonetheless set up a certain aura around photojournalism that lingered in various forms throughout the years that followed.

Journalists deflated the authority of photography in two main ways—by constructing photography as a medium of record and by constructing the photographer as a disembodied figure. Both views underscored the perspective that photography needed print journalism in order to make sense. News photography was constructed as a craft that was adjunct to journalism, and it needed words, and reporters, to be regarded as a complete tool of documentation.

One way of deflating the authority of the image was by constructing a vision of photography as primarily a medium of record. In appealing to the denotative function of the photograph, bypassing its potentially threatening connotative role, journalists were able to fasten photography within its position as an adjunct, rather than primary, tool of documentation.

In some cases, photographs were explicitly labeled an "adjunct of the daily news" (Cooper 1935, 8). "Picture-getters" were "not required to be picture-makers" (Cooke 1931, 315). In most cases, however, the discourse was far subtler: one way the image's dependence on words was underscored was by running a comparison of the two tools of documentation, a comparison that both undermined and restricted the image's authority in lieu of that of the word (Blanchard 1935; Cooper 1935). One editor suggested that "if newspapers were to become so foolish as to reduce [the remark that one picture is worth a thousand words] to a formula, the rule probably would be that a picture should be worth at least as many words as it displaces" (Blanchard 1935, 53). Such comparisons between word and image inevitably worked to the image's disadvantage, in that they found images lacking. Although images were thought to enhance a newspaper's readability, they did so only when they were used to support the words that grounded them.[4] One editor, addressing the ASNE, argued that it was "the happy combination" of pictures and stories that would convince the American public to read news and not just skim its headlines (Bingay 1935, 53). In short, the running comparison with words generally worked against a recognition of what photographs could do that was different from what could be accomplished with other tools of documentation.

The construction of news photography as a medium of record was facilitated by the imitation of a highly technical mode of discourse that had long characterized discussions of photography in the photographic trade journals.

Photographic evidence, said one such journal, should be "scrupulously honest" and "accurate." It is "as dependable as are the laws of chemistry and physics upon which it is based" (Meyers 1943, 20). Written largely by photographic editors, many early articles on photography that appeared in the journalism trade literature offered detailed descriptions of different photographic processes, discussions of the largely denotative function of photographs, or discussions of how photographs and photographic work could be incorporated into the newspaper (Hammesfahr 1936; *Life* 1937; Mahoney 1938). Even here the image was sometimes measured through a comparison with words: Rotogravure, said the president of one newspaper chain,

> calls for a program of stories in pictures, and pictures in stories. . . . In doing this, rotogravure . . . is returning to the basic formula of the printed word, or the appeal of the magazine section that tells its stories in words instead of pictures. . . . Roto, however, does it in pictures. (Hammesfahr 1936, 15)

When they did assess the general role of photography in news, journalists focused not on the everyday dimension of journalistic photography, but on the high moments of the trade (e.g., *Time* 1935b, 1937). One typical article, titled "Death Pictures," hailed photography for visually capturing an electrocution with cameras, but blunted its praise with comments about how the photographs had failed to play in different newspapers. "Every paper in New York," it said, "found some reason not to run the pictures" (*Time* 1935a, 47). This suggested that although the journalists recognized that photographs offered valuable information about events of everyday life, they felt that the image was incapable of making itself coherent as an autonomous chunk of discourse. To make sense, the photograph needed, in a word, the intervention of the reporter. Moreover, as late as 1937, references to news, when they were intended to include pictures, still included a phrase such as "and pictorial events" to signify that the visual element was pertinent to the discussion (Cooper 1937, 5). Thus, even in the late 1930s, the photograph remained an additive to words that constituted the primary documentation of real-life events. Its entry into news depended largely on its construction as a medium of record.

Significantly, however, the predominant view of news photography as a medium of record was somewhat countered by discussions about the ascent of the picture magazine. Unlike reporters who worked for the dailies and weeklies, practitioners of the picture magazine recognized early on the significance of the photograph's interpretive role. As early as 1938, the establishment of *Life* was claimed to operate on "the journalistic principle of reporting objectively the folk and folkways of the world—in pictures" (*Quill* 1938a, 10). It was "not until the birth of *Life* that pictorial journalism—informing through pictures—attained its present status." In one view, the "camera surpasses the typewriter" in telling a story (Mahoney 1938, 17). Editors of the picture magazine argued that it pledged to "increase the readers' total knowledge not only of things seen but of things understood" (*Quill* 1938a, 19).

The editorial staffs of the picture magazines were also more direct about challenging the tension between image and word in journalism. One picture magazine editor lauded the ability to develop "pictures which told stories themselves rather than merely [supplemented] the text" (Mahoney 1938, 8). In one early article titled "The Camera as Essayist" *Life* (1937), noted that "when people think of the camera in journalism, they think of it as a reporter—the best of reporters, the most accurate of reporters, the most convincing of reporters" (62). Elsewhere, *Life*'s pictures were called "the most remarkable reporters of all time" (*Quill* 1938a, 10). Words "give you a picture," said one editor, "which can never be as faithful as the picture made by the camera" (quoted in Mahoney 1938, 17). A few years later, it was an editorial in *Life* that addressed the need for photographic images to supplement, even supplant, words. In this case, the issue surrounded the decision to allow photographs of dead American soldiers, and in reviewing the decision, *Life* (1943) proclaimed that words were "never right." It proclaimed that "the American people ought to be able to see their own boys as they fall in battle; to come directly and without words into the presence of their own dead" (34). Unlike other forums, the comments here went on to claim a more interpretive role as well: the camera, said *Life* (1937), "is not merely a reporter. It can also be a commentator. It can comment as it reports. It can interpret as it presents. It can picture the world as a seventeenth century essayist or a twentieth century columnist would picture it" (62).

Yet, even if the comments by the editors of the picture magazines proved more accurate than other discourse in predicting the eventual interpretive force of the photograph, they were not representative of discussions at the time about the denotative function that the photograph was expected to fulfill. The photograph was seen as a tool of reportage that helped underscore the referentiality of news. Most discussions thereby regarded photography's recording function as a trait that made it valuable to the larger community of journalists. Photographs were codified as adjuncts to, not substitutes for, the written word, and it was assumed that they needed the intervention of reporters to make sense.

Another way that journalists deflated the authority of the photograph was by disembodying the photographer. They generated discourse about photography as if it operated without full-blooded human beings who were necessary to make it work. Articles proliferated that told of the role of the camera as a tool of documentation, but without mention of the individuals on whom it depended. Such discourse appeared to presume that photography worked without human hands.

When journalists did address the photographer, it was in unrealistic terms. As one news editor told the assembled body of the ASNE in 1935:

> The ideal modern newspaper photographer has got to be both an artist and a fighter. He has got to have that all-seeing eye of the reporter in our popular fiction magazines. He has got to have the genius for composition of Leonardo da Vinci, the speed and stamina of Jack Dempsey; he has got to be a pugilist and an artist. He has got to have the patience of an American taxpayer and the endurance of a political fallacy. Create such a synthesis of a human being and put him on your photographing staff, and he may meet the requirements of a good editor. (Bingay 1935, 50)

Other articles reproduced such a view, calling for "a photographer with a painter's vision" (Drummond 1937, 20). This romanticized perspective of the photographer suggested how underdeveloped the discourse was among journalists toward practitioners of the camera.

However, discourse concerning the photographer was no accident. Although journalists were ambivalent about the image and image-making technology, they were particularly resistant when faced with recognizing the human body who operated the camera—the photographer. Discourse about the photographer thus took on a distinctly disembodied character. It served to deflate the authority of the photographer, as pictures and images began to be discussed as tools that operated in an apparent void of human presence.

One of the first ways of disembodying the photographer was to argue that reporters themselves could take on the photographic function in news. Some editors argued that they themselves were well qualified to master the art of photographic documentation:

> Reporters can be taught to make good pictures. A reporter who takes an interest in his camera has a background that the ordinary photographer must acquire by painful and profane experience. He is accustomed to meeting people and getting them to do what he wants done. He is supposed to know news and he should translate

that news through pictures as readily as through the written word. (Blanchard 1935, 56-57)

"The reporter-cameraman," this author continued, "is a combination much to be desired." Journalists regarded the small and portable size of the newer cameras as proof of the fact that they could carry out photographic as well as reportorial responsibilities. Advertisements in the journalism trade literature begin to suggest that reporters themselves could carry cameras and easily learn to use them.

In 1932, the Gannett Newspaper chain became the first news organization to advise its members to begin carrying cameras (*Editor & Publisher* 1932). That decision was chided as having much to do with the general manager's own reputation as a "camera enthusiast," yet was regarded as a positive development for reporters. The "day is coming," said one observer, "when a reporter who can't operate a camera will be as helpless as one who can't use a pencil" (Blanchard 1935, 57). By 1938, the fact that "reporters carry pocket cameras" was seen as an index of the growth of photography in news (Mahoney 1938, 8).

But early photographic attempts by reporters produced products that did not meet photographers' standards. They generated scores of "chinless women, headless men, and tipsy buildings." With editors admitting that training reporters to use the camera and "add photographic ability to reportorial is a bit more difficult than it might seem," reporters were told to snap three shots of everything in hopes that one shot would succeed (Blanchard 1935, 50, 57-58). Certain types of cameras were discarded as reporters' cameras because they proved too complicated for the newsworkers to handle (58).

Yet the disembodied presence of the photographer persisted in journalists' discussions of the image. In 1935, a symposium titled "The News and Pictures: Cameras and Reporters" was held at the ASNE's annual meetings. The title of the symposium, transcription of which stretched over more than twenty pages of the conference proceedings, was revealing: the camera, as a tool of documentation, was held on an equal par with the journalists, seen at that point to be the camera's practitioner. The title bore no mention of the photographer.

The disembodied photographer also showed up in discussions of the use of cameras during court trials. One such trade discussion, presented at a 1939 ASNE editorial roundtable, addressed the use of the camera during court trials (Grier 1939). It discussed the issue of receiving consent to photograph parties in a courtroom. Interestingly, the professional organization set up a standing committee to deal with the problem called the Committee on Cooperation between the Press, Radio, and Bar. Nowhere in the committee's name was the photographer mentioned as having an equal, or even relevant, voice in the issue under discussion. Similarly, an article on the same topic ran in *Forum* magazine under the telling title "The News Camera on Trial" (Smith 1938b).[5] In both cases, it was as if journalists would accept only a disembodied photographic presence—the photograph without the photographer.

In discourse, the disembodied presence of the photographer was strategically correct for journalists, for it allowed them to claim and maintain their own presence in discussions about the photograph. It showed that they recognized the value of the photographic image even if they disputed who was best qualified to produce such an image. This is not to say that they necessarily recognized what they were doing, for the relevant schemes for interpreting the value of the photograph went far beyond any specific negotiations between certain photographers and journalists.

This insistence on the disembodied photographer, or at the very least the devalued photographer, persisted until the early 1940s, when one editor justified to the ASNE his newspaper's decision to use the photographic process of rotogravure. He claimed: "We had to put reader interest into our sections, to give them something to turn the scanners and the skimmers into readers. . . . We had to tie our pictures and text together, to present picture stories and pictorial features. We had to get the best pictures possible" (Peters 1941, 114-15). It was somewhat in keeping with a more general dismissal of photographers, however, that in the next sentence he complained about how long it had taken the editorial staff to convince photographers of what they wanted:

> We had a lot of trouble with our photographers until they got the idea. They could use all their lights and techniques, they could shoot from the floor or the chandeliers, and they could do all the tricks and stunts in the business—we wanted them all—but they had to tell stories. (Peters 1941, 115)[6]

As with discourse about photography as a medium of record, here too the editorial staffs of the picture magazines produced discourse that took exception to the predominant tone of devaluation. Interestingly, references to the disembodied photographer seemed to suggest that the camera was a more loyal or accurate recorder than was the photographer. The photograph and camera became an index of all reportorial practice, rather than a tool to be used by either photographers or reporters. Disembodiment in this case occurred as a way of inflating the image's authority rather than constraining it. But anywhere other than among *Life* personnel, such comments were unusual in the 1930s, before the events of the war forced a greater number of photographers to think along such lines.

The disembodied photographer eventually gave way to the undisputed presence of photographers in daily news. Particularly as the events of the war pushed photographers directly into the role of documenting the events of "real" life, reporters were left with little alternative but to relent and embrace the entry of photographers into the journalistic community. Their initial attempts to downplay the authority of the image by disembodying the photographer would unravel largely through the events of the war, when photography as a tool of documentation was pushed beyond the boundaries initially accorded it by journalists. By that time, picture journalists were being called into service to document the inadequacies of print journalism.

The entry of the United States into World War II changed both the expectations and the role of the American photographer. The war raged on five continents and a dozen different fronts, presenting a logistic nightmare to those needing to document its events.[7] Photographers readily adopted a wartime persona, being called upon to document the war in many ways—as professionals, as advanced amateurs with some photographic training, and as full amateurs with no training at all. Not only were they attached to the various military divisions, the Signal Corps, and various relief organizations, such as the Surgeon General's Office and the American Field Service, they also simply took snapshots with their private cameras. As one soldier later claimed, "The photographs I shot are dim, for I was not a photographer" (Young 1982). A wartime photographic pool was formed to facilitate wide distribution of the images they produced. Photographic documentation was so extensive that it came to be seen as one of the outstanding achievements of the wartime experience.

This situation considerably enhanced the status of photojournalists, simultaneously consolidating their thrust toward professionalization and forcing print journalists to take them more seriously. The war effort permeated the existing photographic forums. By 1942, nearly every issue of the ranking photographic journals featured articles on wartime photography, discussing such issues as military credentials, censorship, and photographic wartime pools. Advertisements began to define good photographic equipment as equipment that could produce good photographs of the war.[8] Fundamental tasks were altered, as exemplified by one article that explained how to wash camera equipment and materials in seawater (Eaton and Crabtree 1943).

Civilian news organizations began training photographers for a stint in the military (Moeller 1989, 184).

Through it all, the triumph of news photography was tied up with the photographer's ability to record, reference, and report reality, rather than interpret it. As discourse about photographs in news became more frequent, its resonance depended on the degree to which the photograph was seen as upholding its denotative function. This may have had direct repercussions in practice, in that news organizations appear to have formulated insufficiently a repertoire of practices related to the incorporation of photographs in news, including captions, credit lines, and other routines for bringing images and texts together.[9] This different view of the authority of the image became even more pronounced as the image was co-opted as part of the war effort, which in itself suggested a wholehearted adoption of the tenets of photographic realism. One view suggests that the awareness of history is an interpretation of the past that has succumbed to a faith in history as that of accurate representation. In playing down the photographer's role as interpreter in order to stress that of the documenter, the photograph and the photographer were thus codified somewhat propagandistically in a way that would help secure military victory. This made it even more difficult to open up discourse concerning the image's interpretive role.

By the end of World War II, neither the value of photography nor its natural place within the ranks of journalism constituted a topic of discourse. The move to professionalize photographic journalists in the United States took on distinct momentum in 1942, when the dean of the Journalism School at the University of Missouri, Frank Mott, coined the term *photojournalism* for his school's sequence of academic training. Training sequences in photojournalism were set up in journalism schools across the country, and journalism schools held special seminars that taught the rudiments of good photography in news (Kany 1947; Walker 1947b). In 1946, the first national organization for newspaper photographers—the National Press Photographers' Association (NPPA)—was established, and the press duly labeled it an organization of "reporters with cameras" (*Newsweek* 1946). Shortly thereafter, the NPPA began to publish its own official organ, the *News Photographer.*

Thus, news photography was seen as a legitimate field of journalism by the late 1940s. Oddly enough, it appeared to have been born of disparate beginnings, in that many of the wartime photographers were not photojournalists. Yet, by the time the war ended, and in the years immediately following, journalists were expected to develop "a new news sense . . . an eye for story-telling pictures" (Johnson 1949, 12). Journalism educators, looking ahead to the era of television, hailed a "new field of news, told in word and picture" (Spencer 1949, 49). Claims that had long characterized discourse about the image underwent subtle alterations. The long-standing comparison between word and image began to work in favor of the image. One participant in a 1947 seminar on press photography recounted how news pictures of FDR in the months before he died "showed the true condition of the president's health more effectively than did published news reports based on statements of the chief executive's personal physician" (cited in Kany 1947, 8). Claims that "pictures can be more informative than type" proliferated, and photographs came to be seen as instrumental, not voluntary, to newswork (8). One editor proclaimed that "the assignment and presentation of news and pictures cannot be segregated; they must be treated together as a unit for most effective use" (8); news photography deserved "a status equal to that of any reporter" (10). Most important, disembodiment had given way to the presence of the photographer. Numerous articles recounted the number of photographers being added to news staff (Spencer 1949). The *Quill* ran an article subtitled "Photographer as Reporter," in contrast to earlier articles that had insisted on reporters' taking on the role of photographer (Kany 1947). The difference was telling. To quote photojournalist Margaret Bourke-White, the "responsibility of the photographer is greater now than it has ever been. The little black box with a hole in it . . . has become the chief recorder of history" (quoted in Rhode and McCall 1961, 29). Photojournalism had become a legitimate domain of journalistic practice.

This is not to say that all tension disappeared. As late as 1947, photo-journalists still argued that newsroom editors paid "lip service to the use of pictures, treating them as fillers and story illustrations but not as a principal method of telling the news" (Kany 1947, 10; see also Walker 1947a). Other news photographers admitted that they continued to "await the day when newspapers will fully realize the impact of pictorial journalism" (Spencer 1949, 49); even today, some thirty-five years later, similar tensions persist. Yet photographs and photographers had come a long way, and that advancement later generated claims of a fundamental linkage between wartime and the legitimation of photographic journalism. World War II emerged as a critical incident in the professionalization of photojournalism. If there "is a dominant trend in the post World War II period," said one such review, then "it must be reportorial photography" (Rhode and McCall 1961, 28). The Second World War helped develop photographers into "an experienced, highly organized body of recognized status" (Lewinski 1978, 136). Although people before the war "had never heard of the word 'photojournalism,'" they "handsomely recompensed any publication that carried the new reportage" by the time of World War II (Moeller 1989, 200). Photographing the war thus came to be seen as an undisputed marker of professional photojournalism.

However, neither pictures nor words constituted the primary medium through which people experienced the war. Sound assumed that role, and the primacy of radio in shaping the experience of World War II remained supreme. Yet, the picture and the word competed for their own space as tools of documentation through a shared medium of communication—the press. It was within that medium that their competition over technology and professional status was staged.

It is telling that the thrust toward professionalization came on the back of considerable ambivalence on the part of journalists. Conflicted about the rising presence and importance of images, journalists were prompted to shift the boundaries of what constituted appropriate behavior in news. Their ambivalence generated an initial codification of photojournalism as a primarily denotative set of practices that set it up as a medium of record produced, ironically, by disembodied photographers. Such a view proliferated despite the fact that circumstances suggested a far "larger" view of the craft. This was because the "small" view of photojournalism secured the threatened turf of reporters. Only when the events of World War II changed that turf entirely did newsworkers relent and finally admit photographic reporters into their midst.

The accommodation of journalists to the burgeoning presence of the photograph in news raises fundamental questions about the ability of professionals to reconstitute themselves around new and changing pictorial technologies. Today, new modes of news gathering and news presentation suggest that the patterns of technological adaptation witnessed during the 1930s and early 1940s may have set the stage for later patterns of adaptation among American journalists in regard to the visual image. Although the image and the image maker became integral parts of journalism through later events, such as the Korean War and Vietnam, World War II consolidated photography's port of entry into daily news. Yet the reluctance of journalists to anticipate and accommodate the ascent of photojournalists at that time may serve as a marker of contemporary patterns of professional adaptation surrounding the pictorial technologies of news, whether they be cable-driven images, newsreels, or computer graphics. This suggests a need for closer examination of the intraprofessional negotiation by which professional communities adapt to changing technologies, for such negotiation is instrumental in shaping the collective authority of these communities and makes the consideration of changing technologies during an earlier era an even more valuable tool for understanding the contemporary practices of media workers.

## Notes

1. The link between photographs and realism has accompanied the photograph in various forms over the past 150 years. It was so great in the late 1800s that magazines and tracts having nothing to do with photography took on names like *Daguerreotypes* and *Sunday School Photographs* just to associate themselves with photography. See Goldberg (1991, 10).

2. There are both traditional and critical overviews of the history of the photograph. Whereas the traditional view holds that pictures in general have moved increasingly toward providing an accurate reflection of the world, the critical view argues against both the notions that pictures reproduce reality and that painting and photography generate unconnected modes of representation. Critics argue instead that photographs use artificial conventions, often borrowing from painting, that have been labeled natural by society. For lucid discussion of these competing narratives, see Barnhurst (1994) and Szarkowski (1973).

3. Raymond Willliams (1961) argues that changes in attitudes toward the press helped prepare the ground for incorporating images into news. These included the growth of advertising, concentrated ownership, and circulation.

4. In fact, "readability" was a critical notion for many news organizations of the time, who sought to maximize their readership by enhancing what they called "readability." In 1947, for instance, the Associated Press started its own "Readability Campaign" to help "make the news report easier and more interesting to read." Experts and consultants were brought in to discuss relevant dimensions of newswriting, such as sentence length and word choice ("Readability" 1949, 138).

5. This can be contrasted with developments ten years later, when the newly formed National Press Photographers' Association would label the very issue of picture taking in courts a crucial turning point for photographers. At that point, the NPPA demanded equal status to that accorded print journalists, "who are permitted to gather word information in courts" (cited in Kany 1947, 10). This view was not prevalent ten years earlier, however.

6. This persona—of the bumbling news photographer—has certainly persisted in the collective imagination, exemplified in both the Jimmy Olson character in the Superman series and the "Animal" persona in the *Lou Grant* television show. I thank Kevin Barnhurst for his comments on this point and others.

7. Complaining that the war was not "conveniently concentrated," one photographer said that it "wasn't a war which a resourceful cameraman could cover on a bicycle. . . . It posed entirely new problems of manpower, expense, transport, and communication" (Turner 1943, 77).

8. "Great Pictures of the War . . . Made with Fairchild Cameras," read one such advertisement, as it boasted an official U.S. Navy photograph of the bombing of Pearl Harbor (*American Photography* 1944). Also see the advertisement "Graflex Sees the War" (*American Photography* 1943).

9. For instance, through the late 1940s, news organizations struggled to develop standards for writing captions that would capture a news editor's eye. A "photograph can be sold to a newspaper editor only if it carries his kind of caption," one that "should have all the pertinent facts" and should never be faked, "for you can almost be hanged for it" (MacPherson 1946). At its 1948 convention, the Associated Press's Managing Editors' Association lamented that its guidelines for writing captions, set out the previous year, were not being followed.

# References

*American Photography.* "Graflex Sees the War" (advertisement). Oct. 1943, 34-35.

————. "Great Pictures of the War" (advertisement). July 1944, 3.

American Society of Newspaper Editors, Committee on Schools of Journalism. "Report of Committee on Schools of Journalism." In *Problems of Journalism,* American Society of Newspaper Editors, 41-46. Washington, D.C.: American Society of Newspaper Editors, 1928.

Arnheim, Rudolf. "The Images of Pictures and Words." *Word and Image* 2, no. 4 (1986): 306-10.

Associated Press. *The Associated Press Thirty-eighth Annual Report of the Board of Directors.* New York: Associated Press, 1938.

Barnhurst, Kevin G. *Seeing the Newspaper.* New York: St. Martin's, 1994.

Barthes, Roland. "The Photographic Message." In *Image, Music, Text.* New York: Hill & Wang, 1977a.

————. "The Rhetoric of the Image." In *Image, Music, Text.* New York: Hill & Wang, 1977b.

Bent, Silas. "Lindbergh and the Press." *Outlook,* Apr. 1932, 214-40.

Bingay, Malcolm. "The News and Pictures: Cameras and Reporters." In *Problems of Journalism,* American Society of Newspaper Editors, 49-53. Washington, D.C.: American Society of Newspaper Editors, 1935.

Blanchard, L. R. "The News and Pictures: Cameras and Reporters." In *Problems of Journalism,* American Society of Newspaper Editors, 53-59. Washington, D.C.: American Society of Newspaper Editors, 1935.

Brandenburg, George. "Huge Gain in Use of Pictures Shown in Survey of Dailies." *Editor & Publisher,* Feb. 8, 1938.

Brucker, Herbert. "The Glut of Occurrences." In *Interpretations of Journalism,* ed. Frank Luther Mott and Ralph D. Casey, 219-44. New York: F. S. Crofts, 1937. Revised from essay in *Atlantic Monthly,* Aug. 1935.

*Camera.* Editorial. Feb. 1942, 4-5.

————. "War Photography: Past and Present." Mar. 1943, 37-41.

Cooke, David D. "News Pictures." *Photo-Era Magazine,* June 1931, 313-17.

Cooper, Kent. "Report of the General Manager." In *The Associated Press Thirty-first Annual Report of the Board of Directors,* Associated Press, 6-10. New York: Associated Press, 1931.

————. "Report of the General Manager." In *The Associated Press Thirty-second Annual Report of the Board of Directors,* Associated Press, 6-9. New York: Associated Press, 1932.

————. "Report of the General Manager." In *The Associated Press Thirty-third Annual Report of the Board of Directors,* Associated Press, 7-11. New York: Associated Press, 1933.

————. "Report of the General Manager." In *The Associated Press Thirty-fifth Annual Report of the Board of Directors,* Associated Press, 7-9. New York: Associated Press, 1935.

————. "Report of the General Manager." In *The Associated Press Thirty-seventh Annual Report of the Board of Directors,* Associated Press, 7-9. New York: Associated Press, 1937.

————. *Kent Cooper and the Associated Press.* New York: Random House, 1959.

Drummond, Roscoe. "Keeping Pace with the Picture Parade." *Quill,* June 1937, 10-11, 20.

Eaton, G. T., and J. I. Crabtree. "Washing Films and Papers in Sea Water." *American Photography,* June 1943, 12-15.

*Editor & Publisher.* "Gannett Reporters Will Carry Cameras." June 11, 1932, 18.

————. "People Are Picture Nuts." Apr. 24, 1937, 86.

————. "Photo of Hindenburg Disaster Wins News Picture Contest." Feb. 19, 1938, 3.

Fulton, Marianne. "Bearing Witness: The 1930s to the 1950s." In *Eyes of Time: Photojournalism in America,* ed. Marianne Fulton, 105-71. New York: New York Graphic Society, 1988.

Gannett, Frank R. "Sensational Newspapers Near End of Vogue Here and Abroad." *Editor & Publisher,* Apr. 1931, 30.

Gidal, Tim. *Modern Photojournalism: Origin and Evolution, 1910-1933.* New York: Macmillan, 1972.

Goldberg, Vicki. *The Power of Photography.* New York: Abbeville, 1991.

Grier, Albert O. H. "Report of Committee on Cooperation between the Press, Radio, and the Bar." In *Problems of Journalism,* American Society of Newspaper Editors, 129-33. Washington, D.C.: American Society of Newspaper Editors, 1939.

Hall, Stuart. "The Determinations of News Photographs." In *The Manufacture of News,* ed. Stanley Cohen and Jock Young. London: Sage, 1973.

Hammesfahr, A. C. G. "Roto Takes on a New Role." *Quill,* Oct. 1936, 3-4, 15.

Hardt, Hanno, and Karin B. Ohrn. "The Eyes of the Proletariat: The Worker-Photography Movement in Weimar Germany." *Studies in Visual Communication* 7, no. 3 (1981): 47-57.

Johnson, Ed H. "T-V Wants News Sense plus Pictorial Eye." *Quill,* June 1949, 12, 21.

Jussim, Estelle. *The Eternal Moment: Essays on the Photographic Image.* New York: Aperture, 1989.

Kany, Howard L. "Experts Eye Pictures: Photographer as Reporter." *Quill,* Apr. 1947, 8, 10.

Keating, Isabelle. "Reporters Become of Age." *Harper's,* Apr. 1935, 601-12.

Lewinski, Jorge. *The Camera at War.* New York: Simon & Schuster, 1978.

*Life.* "Camera as Essayist." Apr. 26, 1937, 62-63.

———. "A Giant Grows Up" (advertisement). May 15, 1939, 80-81.

———. "Three Americans." (editorial). Sept. 20, 1943, 34.

———. "War Photographers' Stories." June 26, 1944, 13-14.

Lippmann, Walter. "Two Revolutions in the American Press." *Yale Review,* Mar. 1931, 433-41.

MacPherson, M.W. "Newspaper Picture Captions." *American Photography,* Sept. 1946, 46.

Mahoney, Tom. "Let's Have a Look at *Look.*" *Quill,* July 1938, 8-9, 17.

Marzolf, Marion Tuttle. *Civilizing Voices: American Press Criticism, 1880-1950.* New York: Longman, 1991.

Meyers, Alexander M. "The Camera: A Silent Witness." *American Photography,* June 1943, 20-22.

Moeller, Susan D. *Shooting War.* New York: Basic Books, 1989.

Newhall, Beaumont. *The History of Photography.* New York: Museum of Modern Art, 1982.

"The News and Pictures: Cameras and Reporters" (general discussion). In *Problems of Journalism,* American Society of Newspaper Editors, 62-70. Washington, D.C.: American Society of Newspaper Editors, 1935.

*Newsweek.* "News Photos, Their Price Runs Well in Thousands." May 13, 1932, 28-29.

———. "Reporters with Cameras." July 1, 1946, 56.

Olson, Kenneth E. "The Press in Times of Social Change." *Journalism Quarterly* 12, no. 1 (1935): 9-19.

Peters, Ralph L. "No More Dutch Windmills." In *Problems of Journalism,* American Society of Newspaper Editors, 112-18. Washington, D.C.: American Society of Newspaper Editors, 1941.

Pew, Marlin E. "Newspaper Loyalties." In *Problems of Journalism,* American Society of Newspaper Editors, 29-39. Washington, D.C.: American Society of Newspaper Editors, 1930.

Pollard, James E. "Who's a Journalist? Writers No Longer Have Sole Claim to Title Many Have Scorned in the Past." *Quill,* Nov. 1937, 9, 20.

Price, Jack. "Eyes of the Press." *Editor & Publisher,* Aug. 24, 1935, 22.

————. "Journalism Schools Lack Photo Equipment." *Editor & Publisher*, Jan. 4, 1941, 26.

*Quill*. Editorial. June 1937, 10.

————. "This Is the *Life* Story." May 1938a, 10-11, 19.

————. "Candid Camera Close-ups of Ideas" (advertisement). Nov. 1938b, back cover.

"Readability." In *Reports and Discussions of the Continuing Study Committees of the Associated Press Managing Editors Association, 1948*, Associated Press. New York: Associated Press, 1949.

Rhode, Robert B., and Floyd McCall. *Press Photography*. New York: Macmillan, 1961.

Ritchin, Fred. *In Our Own Image*. New York: Aperture, 1990.

*Saturday Review of Literature*. "Report on Photography." Jan. 15, 1938, 8.

Sekula, Allan. "On the Invention of Photographic Meaning." In *Photography against the Grain*, 3-21. Halifax: Press of the Nova Scotia College of Art and Design, 1984.

Smith, Henry Ladd. "What Should the Schools Do about Pictorial Journalism?" *Quill*, Feb. 1938a, 5, 20.

————. "The News Camera on Trial." *Forum*, Nov. 1938b, 267.

Spencer, Otha C. "Photographers Seek Story of a Town in Pictures." *Quill*, Aug. 1949, 49-50.

Stanley, Edward. "This Pictorial Journalism." *Quill*, Nov. 1937, 5, 14.

Stapp, William. "Subjects of Strange . . . and of Fearful Interest: Photojournalism from Its Beginnings in 1839." In *Eyes of Time: Photojournalism in America*, ed. Marianne Fulton, 1-35. New York: New York Graphic Society, 1988.

Stott, William. *Documentary Expression and Thirties America*. Chicago: University of Chicago Press, 1973.

Stouffer, W. C. "The APME: A History." In *Reports and Discussions of the Continuing Study Committees of the Associated Press Managing Editors Association, 1948*, Associated Press, xi-xxii. New York: Associated Press, 1949.

Szarkowski, John, ed. *From the Picture Press*. New York: Museum of Modern Art, 1973.

*Time*. "Death Pictures." Oct. 28, 1935a, 46-47.

————. "Prize Shot." Dec. 23, 1935b, 35-36.

————. "Prize Pictures." May 17, 1937, 67-70.

Turner, Ralph H. "Photographers in Uniform." In *Journalism in Wartime*, ed. Frank Luther Mott. Washington, D.C.: American Council on Public Affairs, 1943.

Walker, Jerry. "A Lot of Lip Service Is Paid to Pictures." *Editor & Publisher*, Nov. 9, 1947a, 26.

————. "Day Is Coming When Photography Will Have B.A." *Editor & Publisher*, Dec. 7, 1947b, 64.

Watson, Elmo Scott. "The Return to Personal Journalism." In *Interpretations of Journalism*, ed. Frank Luther Mott and Ralph D. Casey. New York: F. S. Crofts, 1937.

Williams, Raymond. *The Long Revolution*. New York: Columbia University Press, 1961.

Worth, Sol. *Studying Visual Communication*. Philadelphia: University of Pennsylvania Press, 1981.

Young, Raymond J. "Letter to John B. Coulston." From file "Jews in the American Army Liberation of Ohrdruf," document B/60; K/15/82. Yad Vashem Archive, Jerusalem, 1982.

Zelizer, Barbie. *Covering the Body: The Kennedy Assassination, the Media, and the Shaping of Collective Memory*. Chicago: University of Chicago Press, 1992.

————. "Journalists as Interpretive Communities." *Critical Studies in Mass Communication* 10, no. 3 (1993): 219-37.

————. "Journalism's 'Last' Stand: Wirephoto and the Discourse of Resistance." *Journal of Communication* (forthcoming).

# 7 / Alternative Visions

## *The Intellectual Heritage of Nonconformist Journalists in Canada*

David R. Spencer

In 1853 in Toronto, Ontario, Canada, members of the Society of Journeymen Printers withdrew their services from George Brown's newspaper the *Globe,* complaining about working conditions and wages. In many respects, the job action differed little from those that were to follow as Canada, in league with its North American and European counterparts, began the long and torturous march on the road to large-scale industrialization. Yet the position taken by the printers extended beyond the purely economic considerations they presented. The cleavages that distinguish the ruler from the ruled ascended to the surface. In their memorial issued on the eve of the strike, the printers condemned not only Brown's attitude toward them as his employees but his feelings about working people in general. Although the printers viewed themselves as an elite within the working class, arguing that they fanned "the flame of civilization and intelligence and trimmed the lamp of liberty," they also noted in a statement directed to Brown that "he who is illiberal to one portion of the working classes is illiberal to all" (*To the Working Classes* 1853, 6).

The birth of dissident journalism in Canada and the now-forgotten newsworkers who founded and nurtured it is the story of class conflict. Although the names of Thomas Phillips Thompson, Alexander W. Wright, George Wrigley, R. Parmeter Pettipiece, William U. Cotton, Joseph Marks, and a host of others have been to a large degree consigned to the dustbin of history, these individuals left an indelible mark on the social landscape of contemporary Canada. They were the intellectual and literary spirits behind a series of journals that rose and fell in the late nineteenth and early twentieth centuries sponsored by trades unions, agrarian reform movements, anarchists, and virtually every stripe of socialist from evolutionary to revolutionary. More often than not, these newspapers survived because they became the reflections of the persons who edited them. The editorial offices seldom employed more than two or three persons, with the result that the majority of these journals used reprints from larger and mainly U. S. newspapers complemented by editorials and some local news written by overworked journalists who were editors, reporters, typesetters, and commentators all wrapped up in one. Although their professional lives were, to a large degree, disrupted by one journalistic disaster after another, the ideas that appeared in their presses offered a kaleidoscope of ideological alternatives to the dominant business and industrial culture. It was through this journalistic effort and only in this journalism that they were able to reveal their critiques of and solutions for what they regarded as the horrors of industrial urban society.

In most respects, the Canadian experience differed little from that of the United States, with the exception of the outcome. Canada established long-lasting social democratic parties, whereas the United States did not. Yet much of the inspiration for dissident journalism in Canada came from American rebels of the ilk of John Swinton, Julius Augustus Wayland, and Gaylord Wilshire, to name a few. In the closing years of the nineteenth century, these dissidents and their Canadian counterparts provided the only class-based alternative to daily newspapers "and the opinions they expressed [that] were conditioned by a demanding commercial environment and by the consolidating institutions of the Victorian political party" (Beavan 1983, 317-19). The late-nineteenth-century dissidents were not the first journalists to defy established authority, however. They had the legacy of social outcasts such as William Lyon MacKenzie and Étienne Parent upon which to build.

Legends emerging from the careers of MacKenzie and Parent are well known to history students in both English and French Canada. MacKenzie, a mercurial Scots immigrant, and Parent, the descendant of French-speaking "habitants" stranded by the conquest of Canada by Great Britain in 1759, both sought to temper the rigidity of ruling authority in the colonial Canadas of the early nineteenth century. MacKenzie, through his *Colonial Advocate,* and Parent, in *Le Canadien,* were hardly class-based rebels. Their fiery invectives, directed at a Tory, antiegalitarian, and antirepublican establishment in what is now Ontario and Quebec, sought to bring democratic government to the colonies. Their writings inspired the ill-fated rebellions of 1837 and 1838. For their efforts, both felt the steely hand of the law. MacKenzie narrowly escaped the hangman by seeking political asylum in New York State. Although Parent did not participate directly in the rebellions, he was convicted of conspiracy and, in 1838, spent some time in jail. Both were eventually forgiven their transgressions and returned to public life.

The ideological perspectives brought to Canadians by MacKenzie and Parent provide an interesting contrast. Parent, deeply steeped in the protectionist attitudes of the French-speaking Roman Catholic Church in Quebec, sought to use his journalism to protect the fragile existence of French culture in North America. His newspaper carried the motto "Nos Institutions, Nos Langue et Nos Lois" (Fetherling 1990, 24), which means "Our Institutions, Our Language and Our Laws." Quebec had been allowed to retain the civil Napoleonic code following the British victory at Quebec City in 1759, in return for allegiance to the British Crown. Until the Quiet Revolution, which began in 1960, French-speaking nationalism remained as Parent and others had constructed it, primarily protectionist, with a mission to ensure the survival of eight million Francophones in sea of 250 million English-speaking North Americans.

MacKenzie, on the other hand, was deeply influenced by British intellectuals, in particular William Cobbett. MacKenzie was the first Canadian dissident journalist to look beyond Canada's borders for inspiration. It was a tradition that he was to leave to the rabble-rousers who rose to prominence later in the century. MacKenzie had been privileged to have dined with Cobbett in a country house in Kensington, England, in July 1832. He left the meeting describing Cobbett as "evidently a man of an ardent temperament, of strong and powerful passions, and I believe his object is to increase the comforts and lessen the misery of the great body of people; but it is evident he is not very scrupulous as to the means of bringing about this great good" (Fetherling 1990, 11). His meeting with Cobbett only reinforced the vision of the world that he had developed after meeting Andrew Jackson at the White House in Washington in 1829. MacKenzie eagerly conformed with Jackson's populism, especially his deep suspicion of banks and paper money. It was a social vision that the president also shared with Cobbett. In the final analysis, MacKenzie's view of the world was more of that of Jeremy Bentham and Aaron Burr than that of Robert Owen. For Mackenzie, social reformation began with political transformation, in particular the adoption of universal democracy. It was not a position that would be adopted completely by his successors.

With the failure of the 1837-38 rebellions, dissident journalists retreated to the safety of a Rip Van Winkle existence. The country had settled into a deep but somewhat troubled sleep in which the dreams of most Canadians revolved around solving the nation's constitutional difficulties. London had sent John Lambton, Earl of Durham, to the colonies to investigate the causes behind the disturbances. Durham returned to England with a vision of a second North American state stretching from sea to sea, a nation founded on solidly conservative but democratic values. It was to avoid the rugged individualism and frontier psychology attributed to the first new nation that was so aptly documented by the French aristocrat Alexis de Tocqueville in the previous decade. At Durham's insistence, the old colonial masters, known as the Family Compact in Ontario and Le Chateau Clique in Quebec, surrendered their right to rule arbitrarily, and responsible government came to the colonies. Pending the development of a plan for national expansion, Ontario and Quebec were joined in 1841 to form the Province of Canada (Stevenson 1989, 21). The business of the state was to encourage immigration and to build canals and railways as the infrastructure for a new commercial and industrial economy. This it did, and in 1854, with the Reciprocity Treaty, the Province of Canada signed its first free trade deal with the United States (Innis 1973, 161).

Although some nonconformist newspapers, sponsored in the main by the embryonic trades union movement, began publishing in the industrial corridor that was emerging along the north shore of the Great Lakes before Canadian confederation in 1867, most were only temporary blips on the journalistic horizon. It is probable that the majority were one-issue endeavors published in the spirit of the printers' memorial, focusing on a strike or some persistent grievance that remained unresolved. In 1863, a working-class journal appeared in Hamilton, Ontario, a city destined to become one of the nation's major steel-producing centers in the twentieth century. Little is known about the *Working Man's Journal*. No copies survived. The personalities who would later become the driving forces behind nonconformist journalism were not associated with this paper. In 1867, a printer named Eugene Connolly launched the *Union Advocate* in Newcastle, New Brunswick, in a region dependent on natural resources such as coal and timber. It too was short-lived (Hann et al. 1973).

In 1869 the *People's Journal,* a weekly broadsheet, began publishing in Hamilton. The newspaper moved to the Ontario provincial capital at Toronto in October 1870 and vanished in the summer of 1871. Its editorial objectives were to expose the "evils" of free trade and to promote a national tariff to both protect and encourage the development of Canadian-owned industry.

Its owner and editor, John MacLean, used the newspaper to attempt to forge a coalition of industrialists and laborers against free trade. Although MacLean was hardly a member of the class he sought to reach, his Saturday editions frequently addressed a wide array of the most dominant working-class issues of the mid-nineteenth century, such as working conditions and wages.

MacLean's journal was funded by a prominent Hamilton industrialist, Isaac Buchanan. Buchanan was also a trusted confidant of Canada's first prime minister, Sir John A. Macdonald. Buchanan was convinced that working-class Canadians had a vested interest in a national industrial tariff. He also knew that industrial peace and cross-class solidarity would enhance his war against free traders. The journal noted:

> The labouring classes generally, in the manufacturing districts of this country, and especially in the iron and coal districts, are very little aware of the extent to which they are often indebted for their being employed at all to the immense losses which their employers voluntarily incur in bad times, in order to destroy foreign competition and to gain and keep admission of foreign markets. (Hamilton, Ontario, *People's Journal,* Feb. 19, 1870)

As well as financing MacLean's newspaper, Buchanan was known to solicit political support by generously donating free intoxicants and sums of money to the various clubs and guilds that were by now part of the Hamilton working-class culture. Despite his loftier class status, he claimed that "he would never lose sight of the essential integrity of the working people" (Palmer 1979, 102). As a consequence, many budding dissident journalists, among them Thomas Phillips Thompson and Alexander W. Wright, became frequent contributors to his weekly, in particular after its move to Toronto.

Buchanan's influence was not limited to Hamilton, Ontario, or, for that matter, the newly born Canadian state. He was well known as an activist among American protectionists who had allied themselves with the National Labor Union and the Greenback Party. When Buchanan and MacLean decided to close the *People's Journal,* the industrialist rewarded his journalistic protégé with an appointment to the Ontario Industrial Association, the leading anti-free trade lobby in the province.

Buchanan and MacLean had a decided influence on Sir John A. Macdonald, although it is foolish to pretend that they alone shaped the prime minister's industrial strategy. Macdonald rewarded his supporters with the National Policy of 1879, a legislative package that imposed a series of punitive tariffs on American-made products attempting to access both the Canadian and British Empire markets. American industrialists reacted by establishing branch plants in the Ontario-Quebec industrial corridor in order to obtain the necessary "Canadian citizenship" to trade freely with Great Britain and its dominions and colonies. Nonetheless, the National Policy remained as the cornerstone document of Canadian economic policy until it was replaced by the 1988 Canada-U.S. free trade agreement. The ghostly hands of Buchanan, MacLean, and their fellow travelers extended well into the twentieth century. It is not an exaggeration to claim that a significant amount of the support these people received came from the communications they transmitted through organs such as the *People's Journal*. In comparison with the decidedly working-class journals that were to arise a short time later, the *People's Journal* was one of the few examples in Canadian nonconformist journalism where a collusion of class and interest made for common "bedfellows."

Ironically, it was George Brown's second confrontation with the Toronto Typographers' Union that gave birth to a more permanent working-class nonconformist journalism. In the spring of 1872, his printers went on strike, demanding a nine-hour workday. In Brown, a father of confederation, a founder of the Canadian Liberal Party, and a devout Scots Presbyterian, they had a formidable foe. Brown, and his political cohorts, harbored a great deal of sentiment for social Darwinist political and economic philosophies, which he did not hesitate to disseminate in his newspaper, the *Globe*. With his devotion to Manchester liberalism, Brown had developed

> an intellectually consistent set of doctrines regarding economic freedom and natural laws that he ardently believed were right and almost divinely revealed. Second, his swift, authoritative nature was no more happy to accept conditions of direction imposed by others in his business affairs than in his politics, and least of all in his newspaper office, his first love outside of his family. (Careless 1963, 290)

For Brown, a job action by employees amounted to treason. He retaliated by leveling criminal charges of unlawful assembly against the strike leaders, an action that led directly to the birth of the *Ontario Workman*.

Brown suspected that his old political rival, Canada's prime minister Sir John A. Macdonald, would attempt to benefit from the turmoil in Toronto. Macdonald had successfully institutionalized industrial discontent within the rules dictated by the dominant culture. Macdonald, sensing a growing agitational stance by working-class Canadians, founded and funded the English-speaking Workingmen's Liberal-Conservative Associations and their French-language counterparts, Les Cercles Fontaines. By the dawn of the 1870s,

virtually all true trades unionists in Canada were either members of the
Liberal-Conservative Party or adherents to its policies.[1]

Supported by a secret donation of five hundred dollars from Macdonald,
James S. Williams founded the Toronto Cooperative Printing Association, and
the *Ontario Workman* was born to challenge Brown's economic and political
views. In the first issue, it published a letter signed by a Hamilton reader who
referred to himself as "Humanitas." Although the letter was undoubtedly solicited by the editors, the communication nonetheless provided readers with
the mandate of the new journal:

> Your paper by honestly giving expression to the wants and desires of
> the workingmen, and cultivating their minds aright upon questions
> of broad national policy, will be the means of hastening the good
> time coming, when inequalities before the law shall be abolished,
> and the artificial distinctions of society be remembered among the
> things that were. (Toronto, Ontario, *Ontario Workman,* Apr. 25, 1872)

The letter was one of many references to the class cleavages separating
working people from their industrial masters that appeared in the *Ontario
Workman* during the three years it published in Toronto. However, it would
be an exaggeration to claim that class issues drove the editorial perspective of
the journal. It was first and foremost an appendage of the federal Liberal-
Conservative political apparatus. Williams, David Sleeth Jr., and Joseph C.
MacMillan, who joined the management team in September 1872, were all
well-known Macdonald loyalists as well as professional journalists. They bore
little resemblance to the gang of intellectual radicals who were to attach
themselves to the Knights of Labor publications in Toronto and Hamilton a
decade later. The *Ontario Workman* occupied the offices of and published on
the presses of the Liberal-Conservative *Toronto Daily Telegraph*. When the
newspaper ceased publication sometime in 1874, Williams, Sleeth, and
MacMillan founded a new journal, the *Societies Recorder and Canadian Workman,* as the voice for the numerous fraternal and benefit societies emerging at
the time. Macdonald, who was probably no more sympathetic to trades
unions than was Brown, rewarded his labor allies by legalizing the organizations in 1872. Brown continued to resist the organization of his newspapers
and was eventually assassinated by a disgruntled employee in 1880. (Fetherling 1990, 60, 99). However, following the strike at the *Globe,* the country
sank into a deep depression that directed the few surviving unions away from
class-based journalism. Working Canadians were savaged by catastrophically
dropping wages, massive unemployment, and collapse of their unions, clubs,

and guilds. Movement cultures that were emerging before confederation in 1867 were severely impeded in any desire they may have had to form a single, working-class culture. Among others, they lacked effective channels of communication, in particular a press of their own.

Although the *Ontario Workman* was the first class-based journal to survive more than a few isolated issues, it would be a mistake to clothe it in any form of radical garb. It sought to find solutions to working-class grievances within the framework of an existing political culture. Even by mid-Victorian standards, it was editorially quite conservative. Although it was born in the midst of a vicious and prolonged labor dispute, Williams, Sleeth, and MacMillan opposed strike action and fought for compulsory arbitration. It had no objection to capitalism per se, but abhorred the formation of oligarchies and monopolies. Yet it reserved some of its harshest words for its own constituency:

> We stand aghast at the enormous mass of ignorance and apparently non-progressive elements composing the producing classes, that lays before us, and we feel half inclined to exclaim, can those degraded menials ever occupy a more elevated position? Poor fellows, apparently dead to all but the lowest animal sensations, eat, drink, sleep and toil. (Toronto, Ontario, *Ontario Workman,* May 16, 1872)

The journal condemned women who were not attentive to their husbands, and the editors urged young men to learn to rely on themselves to make their own way in the world and not to depend on organizations and government to take care of them. Williams and his colleagues urged working people to explore the possibility of becoming capitalists in their own right. They argued that if labor were able to increase the wealth of the owning class, it should be able to create some of that wealth for itself.

Wealth was clearly an issue as the depression dragged on toward the dawn of the 1880s. Macdonald had been defeated at the polls in 1873, having been found guilty of padding the pockets of too many political allies in his obsessive desire to build a railway from Montreal to Vancouver. However, memories associated with the "Pacific scandal" were dim and distant when the leader of the Liberal-Conservative Party approached Canadian voters again in 1878. The majority were willing to forgive and forget and returned the old warrior to office with yet one more government. However, the five years spent on the opposition benches had been costly for Macdonald. His carefully crafted coalition of industrial elites and unionized labor began to unravel from the extreme pressures exerted on working people by the voracious appetite of industrial capitalism. Working Canadians were about to abandon Macdonald and his grand design for the construction of North America's second new nation.

The 1880s and 1890s were significantly different from the 1870s. The dreams of national conciliation and class peace envisioned by Williams, Sleeth, and MacMillan were ruthlessly thrust from the national agenda as the depression waned and prosperity returned to the country. Workers began to reestablish their unions and societies, in particular under the sponsorship of the Philadelphia-based Noble and Holy Order of the Knights of Labor. They were determined to regain all they had lost in the previous eight years.

Workers did not act in isolation. Established values were under assault on all sides. Other social and political actors entered the public arena, seeking a new social contract between ruler and ruled. Science and social science, and in particular Darwinism, began to undermine long-held traditional religious values. It was a significant development, because adherence to various Christian traditions was one of the few avenues of social intercourse shared by both the dominant and working-class cultures. The ideas of John Stuart Mill, Karl Marx, Friedrich Engels, Henry George, Edward Bellamy, and Prince Kropotkin were debated in both elite and working-class circles. As working-class Canadians sought security in trades unions and fraternal societies, they realized along with their rulers that old ways of doing business were rapidly being relegated to a past that would never return. Only in French Canada did established institutions seem able to weather the storm. Even there, it was to prove a temporary phenomenon.

Until Charles Darwin questioned the divine origins of the species, religion, history, and science were integrated as companion ideologies in the Canadian Victorian intellectual climate. Naturalists, historians, and theologians generally shared a belief that the laws of nature operated within a preconceived design inspired by a "transcendent guiding intelligence" (Berger 1983, 32). After Darwin published his theories, the triumvirate fragmented. Some clerics and scientists suggested that God had designed evolution, thus making it socially and theologically acceptable. However, many Canadians lost their faith because they recognized that Darwin was arguing a materialist, scientific model. In 1884, a leading Canadian intellectual and educator, William Dawson LeSueur, wrote: "Men do not believe what they once did. They cannot believe as they once did; though they may religiously utter old formulas and close their eyes harder and harder against the growing light" (quoted in Cook 1985, 41). LeSueur committed the ultimate heresy, suggesting that it was only a matter of time before science would supersede theology in the quest for the perfection of both the spiritual and material human being.

LeSueur's rejection of Victorian orthodoxy was supported by the Pioneer Free Thought Club, founded in Montreal in the early 1880s by Robert Chambliss Adams, an American immigrant and a disciple of the English intellectual Charles Bradlaugh. Drawing LeSueur to his side, Adams spread his message across the country and eventually to the Toronto-Hamilton area, where it was eagerly adopted by a group of dissident journalists who had flocked to the Knights of Labor movement. Adams sought to free humanity from Christian theological superstitions. He rejected Original Sin and the belief that people were basically evil in nature. He could not accept the prospect of eternal damnation for the unfaithful. His argument that social imperfection was directly attributable to a lack of material resources found a sympathetic audience among trades union intellectuals. Adams argued that advancing technology would not only be able to supply basic human wants and needs but would supply them in abundance if only the owners of the means of production would be willing to recognize and reward the contributions of the lower classes—in particular, their laborers. Adams was convinced that a new social contract between owner and producer was capable of building a new national morality, which in turn would destroy outdated ideas on class divisions. He believed that advancing technology required a rational material human mind with an accompanying secular code for human conduct (Cook 1985, 61).

Although not robed in the fine tapestry of intellectual debate governed by LeSueur and Chambliss, the issue of class conflict was foremost on the mind of Alexander W. Wright when he founded the Toronto working-class journal the *Commonwealth* on July 22, 1880. At the time, Wright was an obscure journalist from the mid-Ontario town of Guelph, where he had eked out a living as a reporter. He was also an activist in Macdonald's Workingmen's Liberal-Conservative Union. Wright had broken with Macdonald after the prime minister turned over millions of acres of government-owned land in the undeveloped west to speculators, who in turn attempted to sell it at inflated prices to settlers anxious to move from the urban centers in Ontario and Quebec. The collusion of government and land companies had been one of the grievances that led to the uprisings of 1837-38. Wright interpreted the government's actions as an affront to working Canadians. It was an injustice he was determined to reverse. He convinced the Workingmen's Liberal-Conservative Union to break from the federal party and endorse him, in Toronto, as an independent candidate in the 1880 federal election. The *Commonwealth* would be the organ of his newly independent political organization (Toronto, Ontario, *Commonwealth*, July 29, 1880).

The journal, which folded shortly after Wright's unsuccessful parliamentary bid, was a mix of seemingly paradoxical nonconformist ideas that were just beginning to find favor in the Canada of the 1880s. Primarily, it appealed to the class interests of working Canadians and attempted to influence voting during the 1880 election:

> A fitting time has arrived for a concerted and united action on the part of the working classes throughout the length and breadth of our Dominion so as to procure from our rulers in Parliament, recognition of our just rights and reasonable demands. Our interests as workingmen are identical. . . . We have been too long kept asunder by the arts and wiles of cunning politicians whose professions of sympathy and pledges of support on the eve of elections (made to deceive) have kept us divided and widely separated. . . . The makers of members of Parliament are today without one representative on the floor of the House of Commons to assert their rights, advocate their interests, or champion their cause. Capital alone is represented while labor is entirely ignored. (Toronto, Ontario, *Commonwealth,* July 29, 1880)

Wright's appeal to the working people of Toronto West was hardly revolutionary. However, while the editor was imploring voters to become involved in the existing political process, he was simultaneously condemning those who opposed theories advocating its destruction, namely, communism and socialism. Wright observed that "communism merely aims at the abolition of the present system which enables a class of idlers and non-producers to filch from industry the fruits of its labors." He believed that "socialism is the rising giant reformer of the age. All the wrongs and abuses that have cursed men for centuries will go down before its triumphal progress" (Toronto, Ontario, *Commonwealth,* July 29, 1880).

During the last two decades of the nineteenth century, ideological conflicts of this nature were not uncommon in nonconformist circles. Dissidents of all creeds were held together by the common belief that it was legitimate to question and oppose the established authority. Although each of the myriad of groups could outline on request a specific agenda for reform, most were content to leave their ideas aside until they had succeeded in destroying ruling elites. In this respect, Wright's journal was typical and became a model for those that were to follow. His successors saw no conflict in publishing single taxers, nationalists, Marxists, Fabians, liberals, agrarian rebels, and monetary reformers side by side while arguing the legitimacy of each. It was a social critique that was primarily critical and, in many ways, it mattered little who was arguing for it.

As a short-lived journal, Wright's newspaper made one significant contribution. The aspiring independent politician managed to collect around
him virtually every dissident journalist at work in Toronto at the time. As well
as J. R. Cameron, a colleague on the *Guelph Herald*, Wright solicited the support of E. E. Sheppard, who three years later was to become one of the city's
most influential journalists and editors; Louis Kribs, well-known to *Globe*
readers as a satirical columnist who wrote under the pen name Pica; and
Phillips Thompson, a reluctant lawyer and sometime poet, and grandfather of
the modern popular Canadian historian Pierre Berton. In contemporary par-
lance, Thompson, who could be found in virtually every dissident organization available in Toronto, could only be described as a causal person. It was
Thompson who would set the tone and character for nonconformist journalism for the next decade.

Born in Newcastle-on-Tyne in Great Britain in 1843, Thomas Phillips
Thompson came to Canada at age fourteen. As a young man, he became interested in law and eventually obtained a degree in the discipline. However,
Thompson had become jaded by the experience, as his later writings would
show, and he decided to become a journalist. He launched his career as a police reporter in 1867, working for the city's most notorious tory, John Ross
Robertson. While on Robertson's *Telegraph,* he turned his hand to humor,
amusing readers as the mythical columnist Jimuel Briggs, D.B. of Coboconk
U—the D.B. stood for Dead Beat. Tiring of his association with Robertson
and chafing under the ideological straitjacket designed by the *Telegraph's*
boss, Thompson decided to launch his own journals. By the mid-1870s, he
had tried and failed to keep two newspapers, the *Daily City Press* and the
*National,* alive. In 1876, he attempted to escape the Canadian depression and
Robertson by moving to Boston, where he became literary editor of the
*Evening Traveller.* He returned to Toronto in 1879 and in quick succession
held positions at the Liberal-Conservative newspaper, the *Mail,* and the Liberal Party organ, George Brown's *Globe* (Hann 1976, 39). He was in Brown's
employ when he wrote the words to the "Rights of Labor" for Wright's
*Commonwealth:*

In the crowded scenes of toil,
In the workshop and the mine,
There are those who sigh the weary hours away,
With no single ray of hope on their wretched lot to shine
Or the promise of a brighter, fairer day.
CHORUS

March, march, march, the ranks are forming,
Cheer up, friends, the day has come
When the toilers of our land will begin to understand
Their just rights to comfort, liberty and home. (Aug. 26, 1880)

Thompson realized that many of his constituents had only limited reading and writing skills. Education, compulsory in the province of Ontario
only since 1871, had a minimal impact on working-class culture (Legislative
Assembly 1891, 5). Throughout his long career as the leading intellectual in
numerous nonconformist movements, Thompson regularly combined his
flowing prose with hundreds of rhymes. When he composed a series of
poems and songs as editor of the Knights of Labor's *Labor Reform Songster,* he
observed, "Songs will reach thousands to whom arguments would at first be
addressed in vain, and even veterans in the movement will listen to an argument in a better mood for having drank [*sic*] in some familiar truth in the setting of a well remembered air" (Foner 1975, xv).

Thompson was already deeply involved with the Knights of Labor as a
writer and traveling lecturer when he accepted an invitation, in 1883, to leave
the *Globe* and join E. E. Sheppard's *Toronto News* at a significantly reduced
salary. The rebellious Thompson and the erratic Sheppard made a powerful
editorial team until both left the journal in 1887. Sheppard was the son of a
clergyman in the Disciples Church who both preached and farmed in Elgin
County on the north shore of Lake Erie. During his childhood, he absorbed
enough religion to turn him permanently against any form of theology. In his
youth he worked at odd jobs, with the intent of saving enough money to enroll at Bethany College in West Virginia, where tuition fees were cheaper than
in Ontario. He succeeded, but left college before completing his degree. He
took up the life of a wanderer, later claiming to his friends that he had been a
cowboy and stagecoach driver in Texas. Sheppard returned to Canada in
1878, complete with a style of dress that resembled Buffalo Bill, an incurable
tobacco-chewing habit, a pattern of speech that made the roughest of individuals turn in shame, and some journalistic experience. He worked in and
around his native territory in southwestern Ontario before joining Toronto's
*Mail* in 1882 (Hann 1976, 40-41). It was during this phase of his career that
he came in contact with Phillips Thompson, the person who shifted
Sheppard's journalistic attention to working-class issues and the Knights of
Labor specifically.

Thompson assumed the position of assistant editor and chief editorial
writer at the *Toronto News.* At the same time, he was writing for the Hamilton,

Ontario, Knights of Labor weekly the *Palladium of Labor*, which began publishing on March 24, 1883. The journal was the successor to a previous Knights newspaper in Hamilton published under the banner the *Labor Union*. During September, October, and November of that year, Thompson's views appeared in a column titled "Our Social Club." When the column was discontinued, he became a front-page editorialist and used the pseudonym Enjolras, after one of the leaders of the peasants' revolt in Victor Hugo's classic *Les Miserables*. More than anything else, the name provided clues to the constant state of the columnist's mind. The columns, both savage critiques of Victorian political and social life, also differed from many other social criticisms of the period by offering what Thompson believed were workable solutions for the amelioration of increasing class tensions (Hann 1976, 40–41). After the *Palladium of Labor* folded in 1887 following an unsuccessful attempt to become a daily, Thompson collected his thoughts in his only book, *The Politics of Labor*, published simultaneously in the United States and Canada.

His association with the *Palladium of Labor* was to prove the most productive period in his journalistic life. Although he was basically at home with Sheppard and the *Toronto News*, the editor was never really comfortable with Thompson's theories on social reform. Sheppard believed, as did Toronto's most prominent unionist, Daniel O'Donoghue, that Thompson was a "radical" who was "peculiar in many ways" (Hann 1976, 41). William H. Rowe, publisher of the *Palladium of Labor*, possessed no such reservation. He gave Thompson free reign to express himself in his weekly Enjolras column. Like Thompson, who had met Henry George while covering the Irish Land League agitation in 1881 for the *Globe*, Rowe was a decided disciple of George's land reform policies. In concert with Rowe, and in contrast with Sheppard, Thompson became aware of the enormous cultural impact that radical journalism could have on shaping dissident and movement cultures. For the rest of his long and active life, Thomas Phillips Thompson could not separate reporting the news from making it.

Just what were the ideas that Thompson communicated to his constantly suffering constituency? Having survived the cataclysm that was the late 1870s depression, Thompson became a bitter foe of industrial capitalism. Musing as Enjolras, Thompson asked:

> Why should any man willing to work be compelled to starve or steal when there is food for all—and suffer from cold when clothing is so super abundant, that the mills are closed up on account of "over production"? Why, if there must be reductions of pay should

not the principle be carried out fairly all round including bank
managers, cabinet ministers, railroad presidents and all the rest? Why,
if money is scarce and dear, should not the government remedy that
part of the evil and checkmate the schemes of the usurers who fat-
ten like carrion birds on the prostrate bodies of decaying industry
and commerce by supplying the deficiency? And finally why should
the people who are robbed and spoiled every turn by capitalists and
monopolists of every sort, continue to submit to these wrongs by
voting into office the tools and creatures of the money power?
(Hamilton, Ontario, *Palladium of Labor,* Dec. 15,1883)

Although he shared some of the European thinker's leveling views, unlike Marx, Thompson was not convinced that a revolution from below could
succeed. He advised his readers that rebellion based solely on the principles
of setting right old wrongs was doomed to failure. Revolutions, he argued,
were the product of many years of forging a dissident and activist culture that
not only had the power to relieve itself of its oppressors, but set into motion
the mechanisms to create a new society. Like the Lenin to follow, Thompson
argued that this objective could be achieved only through education, and that
only an advanced, intellectual vanguard could accomplish such a result:

The intellectual side of the labour reform movement should be
more prominently kept in view. Men who understand these questions should spread the light so far as their opportunities permit by
speaking and writing upon them. Those who have read books likely
to awaken interest in the subject should lend them to others. A
Labour Paper containing a telling article should be passed around
from hand to hand. The leading principles of the movement should
be made a frequent subject of conversation among friends. Ideas
should be exchanged, ideas compared, and the later phases and developments of the agitators considered. . . . The political struggles
should not absorb so much of the attentions of our friends that they
are obliged to neglect what is a really more important duty of acquiring and diffusing sound views on which to base future action.
(Hamilton, Ontario, *Palladium of Labor,* Jan. 5, 1884)

In stepping away from Marx and Engels, Thompson laid one of the essential foundations for the movement cultures that eventually coalesced to bring
social democracy to the Canadian political culture. By this time in his life, he
was well acquainted with the activities of the British artist and socialist
William Morris. There is little doubt that Morris's ideas had a strong influence
on Thompson's writings. Like Morris, Thompson never lost the opportunity

to decry, often in exaggerated prose, the miserable condition of the working classes in the world's industrial centers. And in concert with Morris, he argued for a "complete change of the system and the gradual substitution for it of constructive socialism, with commerce not, as at present, as a competitive, but as an associative basis" (Hamilton, Ontario, *Palladium of Labor,* Jan. 12, 1884).

It would be a disservice to Thompson to define him as merely one more critic of late Victorian capitalism. Thompson's restless mind surveyed the entire landscape of the Canada of his day. As much as he despised the economic organization of the nation in which he lived and worked, he never lost faith in the people who populated its towns, cities, and farms. These were the people for whom the struggle for meaningful reform became a valued enterprise. He rejected with vehemence the suggestion by industrial and political elites that the coarseness of working-class culture was an inevitable fact of life. He wrote:

A very common argument in the mouths of those who oppose social and political progress is that "you cannot change human nature." It is an argument which is advanced against the enfranchisement of women, democratic institutions, prohibitory liquor laws and industrial reorganization indiscriminately. It is assumed that existing institutions are based upon certain inherent instincts of the human race which are ineradicable, and must in the long run triumph over any system founded in defence of them. This opposed instructive selfishness, meanness, and general depravity of human nature has done duty so long as to reason why mankind should travel along complacently in the ruts of conventionalism that it is time to examine the premises upon which it is based. The truth is that "human nature," instead of being fixed and unchangeable, is a most variable thing. What was contrary to Roman or Greek human nature is found to be quite in accordance with that of modern civilization. Ideas which were always repulsive to the general sense of society in the Middle Ages are now universally accepted as principles of Government and social organization. (Hamilton, Ontario, *Palladium of Labor,* Feb. 23, 1884)

During his development as one of the leading dissident journalists, Thompson rejected the Christian church and became a member of the secular movement. Not only had Thompson discovered the "truth" in Henry George, he started to read the writings of the British intellectual and political rebel Charles Bradlaugh in the secular journal, the *National Reformer.* In reality, Thompson had few axes to grind with the basic humanitarian teachings in

Christian theology, but he did have plenty to say about the class alliances between industrial and political elites and the church hierarchy:

> Everywhere in Europe the masses of the people are in revolt against clericalism—not so much because they object to the abstract doctrines taught by the church—but because they see that practically religion has become part of the intellectual and political machinery on which the upper class depends for keeping the lower in subjection. And this feeling is rapidly extending to this continent. (Hamilton, Ontario, *Palladium of Labor,* Dec. 20, 1884)

With his critique, Thompson placed himself squarely on an ideological tightrope. In his heart, he knew that Canadian workers were not about to abandon their religious beliefs for some form of materialist alternative. Although many working people were prepared to divorce themselves from the organized church, most maintained some form of token religious affiliation. Churches, concerned about growing materialist and secular views, reacted by offering both social and economic programs to relieve the plight of the poor. This made competition more difficult for secular institutions, in particular trades unions, socialist clubs, and fraternal societies, which were forced to confront the more affluent religious groups that could provide higher-quality social services. As a result, Thompson (n.d.) cautioned against wasting enthusiasm, money, and labor in propagating what he called "anti-theological views." He argued that no God could have created a world in which the vast majority of human beings were subject to deprivation and defeat. Such a view, he wrote, was inconsistent with basic logic, both secular and Christian. "It is not possible to conceive of any more shocking or heinous blasphemy than is embodied in such a conception of the universal Father" (Hamilton, Ontario, *Palladium of Labor,* Feb. 3, 1884).

In spite of his acquiescence, Thompson never suggested that the more humanitarian aspects of the Old and New Testaments be incorporated into the reform agenda he was advocating. That was to be the mission of a devoutly religious reformer and radical journalist, the eccentric Anglican George Wrigley, whom Thompson met in Toronto in 1894. The year 1887 proved ominous for Thompson. E. E. Sheppard lost control of the *Toronto News.* The Knights of Labor District Assembly 61 of Hamilton, Ontario, bled by continual losses and a failure to convert its journal to a daily, closed the *Palladium of Labor.* A distraught and discouraged Thompson decided to return to the land of his birth to work with Charles Bradlaugh and his brilliant disciple, Annie Besant. His exile lasted nearly three years. When he returned to Canada in

1890, Thompson declared his allegiance to both socialism and Theosophy, the fruits of his relationship with Bradlaugh and Besant. He was determined to re-enter the field of nonconformist journalism. Because Toronto was devoid of any such publication, Thompson founded his *Labor Advocate* in December 1890.

Although lacking none of the contempt that he felt for late Victorian industrial society, Thompson's new journalistic effort demonstrated a maturity in both his perception of the world around him and the manner in which he expressed it. His rage had been tempered, having been replaced by a keen and penetrating intellectual approach to social problems. In every respect, the eleven-month life of the *Labor Advocate* gave insight to both the complexity and humanity of Thompson's thought. The editor was enjoying, perhaps for the first time in his life, an allegiance to an idea set that filled a void neither Christianity nor secularism could answer.

For Thompson, Theosophy allowed him to enjoy the benefits of all of the world's religions while rejecting none of them. It protected him from what he felt was the insularity of Christian dogma. Not only did Theosophy freely extract the elements of humanity in a global sense, it attempted to bridge the gulf between religion and science by applying the evolutionary concepts of human development that had been articulated by Darwin. In Theosophy, there was no distinction between the secular and the sacred worlds (Cook 1985, 167). As Thompson often argued in the pages of the *Labor Advocate,* Theosophy was the natural intellectual companion to Edward Bellamy's concept of materialist socialism, which he had anointed "nationalism."

In this respect, Thompson did not veer far from the path he had trod in his days as Enjolras at the *Palladium of Labor.* He believed that Theosophy and nationalism shared a faith in the essential goodness of humanity, a concept that, he was quick to point out, had its origins in the New Testament. It was a far more potent doctrine with which to treat the ills of industrial society than secularism, which Thompson came to believe was inhibited by its one-dimensional attack on Christianity. In the pages of the *Labor Advocate,* Thompson presented the belief that a coalition of materialist socialists and Theosophists could conduct human affairs with a sense of fairness, equality, and justice, both materially and spiritually (Cook 1985, 168). It was a formula for human emancipation that transcended both Marx and Engels. In the first issue of the Toronto, Ontario, *Labor Advocate* (Dec. 5, 1890), Thompson outlined his agenda:

> The labor question will be presented as a much wider question than that between employer and employee as regards wages or

hours. It ought, at this stage, to be generally understood that no permanent or satisfactory solution is possible, which does not change the underlying conditions of industrial servitude, by an entire re-organization of the system of distribution. Realizing that the monopoly of land, capital and the means of exchange and transportation is the cause of the poverty of the masses, the *Labor Advocate* will keep steadfastly in view the need of abolishing monopoly in all its forms, asserting the right of the workers to control for their own benefit all the opportunities and requisites for production. At the same time it will strenuously urge such temporary and partial reforms as are likely in some degree to better the lot of the toiler and to lead up to more radical measures in the future.

By the early 1890s, Thompson's ideas on class and class action had moved from the predominantly defensive stance of the 1880s to an aggressive, interventionist set of arguments. He argued vociferously for the abolishment of capital punishment and military training, a compulsory part of elementary and secondary school curriculum. Surprisingly, in an article decrying the state of the unemployed, he suggested that economic decisions should be made within the confines of a planned economy, but this planned economy should never be identified as socialist. "The term Nationalism should be used, but never Socialism, which is susceptible to a variety of meanings and liable to be misunderstood" (Toronto, Ontario, *Labor Advocate,* Dec. 12, 1890).

Contemporary critics may have little patience with his views on women's issues, but it should be remembered that Thompson was as much a product of late Victorian romanticism as his English mentors, such as Bradlaugh, Besant, and Morris. He wrote little on the subject of gender equality, choosing instead to express himself through extracts from other nonconformist journals. From these articles, it is possible to determine that he was distressed by the treatment of women in the workplace, although he did see clear gender-based work roles. Nonetheless, he was an early supporter of female suffrage, which he believed would increase the political clout of working-class voters. For Thompson, extension of the franchise was a class issue rather than a gender issue. He applauded women activists who sought to improve life in the shops and factories for the millions of women who were becoming critical cogs in the social and economic machinery of industrial society. In one of his own writings on the subject, he urged male workers to support their laboring sisters: "Instead of attempting to fight the women workers, most of the unions recognize their right to work, where they can, and endeavor to help them, at the same time protecting their own interests by demanding equal pay for work of equal value. In that way lies the only solution to the question" (*Labor Advocate,* Feb. 27, 1891).

The *Labor Advocate* published its last issue on September 25, 1891. For Thompson, it was a bitter pill to swallow. At its peak, the journal never reached more than 750 issues per week. As the editor noted in the final issue:

> The result has been a lamentable failure, so far as getting a paying constituency among them [workers] was concerned. The more active and progressive men of the labor movement have given us their support and used their best endeavors to increase our subscription list, but the great mass of organized workingmen have been utterly apathetic and indifferent. Our subscribers are only numbered by hundreds, where judging from the assurances given us at the outset, we had a right to expect thousands; and of these, probably fully half have been obtained outside the ranks of organized labor.

The last line of Thompson's lament reveals more than the editor probably intended. The decade between his Hamilton days and the *Labor Advocate* had refined Thompson into a first-class intellectual. Unwittingly, he had slowly removed himself from the constituency that he had dedicated his life to serve. He no longer spoke the language of the working class. (The divide between brain worker and hand worker is a curse that continues to haunt Canadian social democracy.) Instead, he buried himself in the philosophical and abstract tracts that were becoming the cornerstone of European dissent. Tolstoi, Bernstein, Hardie, and to some degree Marx and Engels meant more to the editor than the vernacular ramblings that had dotted the pages of the *Palladium of Labor.* His attempts to make the transition to a North American climate had been a failure. Although he would never again edit a nonconformist journal, Phillips Thompson was far from a spent force.

With the collapse of his journal, Thompson pursued two courses of activity. He continued to write and lecture, and he also became an organizational activist. He had come to believe that the definition of the working class had to be extended beyond unionized, urban laborers. In the summer of 1894, he participated in a speaking tour of the province of Ontario. His mission was to work with agrarian reformers and nonorganized workers to convince them of the wisdom of unified class agitation against the purveyors of power. On this trip, he worked with his new ally, fellow socialist and nonconformist journalist George Wrigley. Together, they founded the Unity Association, a group of radicals dedicated to forging a rural-urban alliance (Cook 1984, 5, 17-18). The new coalition also included Alexander W. Wright, who by this time had given up on nonconformist journalism. Although the project never realized its full potential, for a time the agrarian protest group, the Patrons of Industry, and the Toronto-based Trades and Labor Council participated in joint deliberations. However, the grand alliance envisioned by Thompson, Wrigley, and Wright would come together in yet another time and place, in 1932 in Calgary, Alberta, long after nonconformism had ceased to be associated with their names and their works.

Whereas most Victorian nonconformist journalists actively discussed Marx and Engels, Phillips Thompson and George Wrigley, although they wrote from very different and seemingly opposing perspectives, best represent the socialist legacy. Thompson sought ideological satisfaction in trendy secular ideologies and obscure religious philosophies; Wrigley became a devout adherent to the British-based Christian Socialist movement.

Ironically, Christian Socialism owed a considerable intellectual debt to two seemingly contradictory forces: the humanist reform movement that was increasing its influence in British Protestantism, and the materialist social arguments of Eleanor Marx Aveling (Karl Marx's daughter) and her husband, Edward Aveling. When chapters were established in both Canada and the United States, Christian Socialism found many sympathizers in Edward Bellamy's Nationalist movement, which, along with the Avelings, brashly predicted the end of capitalism in North America. For evidence, they pointed to the growth of groups advocating replacement of competition with cooperation and private ownership by social ownership. Many anticapitalist journalists regarded the founding of the Ruskin Cooperative in Tennessee, dedicated to the British radical and writer John Ruskin, as a significant event in the move toward economic cooperation and eventually socialism (McCormack 1978, 22).

In North America, the Society of Christian Socialists was founded in 1889 by a coalition of clerics and university-based intellectuals. Their leader was the Reverend William D. P. Bliss, who edited the society's magazine, the *Dawn*. Professors George D. Herron and Richard T. Ely acted as lecturers and writers for the movement. At their founding meeting, Bliss, Herron, and Ely declared that their purpose was to harmonize all political and industrial relationships with teachings in the Holy Bible (Foner 1955, 44). Near the turn of the century, Herron's major work on Christian Socialism, *Between Caesar and Jesus,* was serialized in most Canadian nonconformist newspapers. Herron told his readers that the accumulation of material wealth was as immoral as social violence. He wrote: "A rich Christian is a contradiction in terms. A man cannot be Christian without being practically communistic" (Victoria, British Columbia, *B.C. Workman,* July 15, 1899). In Canada, Herron's devotees could be found in the farm reform movement, the Patrons of Industry, where they exerted a permanent influence on a young George Wrigley. By the turn of the century, Christian Socialism and working-class emancipation were inseparable themes in Wrigley's journalistic mission.

Born on June 24, 1847, in the tiny farming community of Wrigley's Corners, Ontario, Wrigley entered the world with a first-class radical pedigree. His father, Sylvanus Wrigley, the township tax collector, supported Mackenzie's abortive 1837 rebellion. For his efforts, he was deprived of his liberty for a three-month period. In later years, Sylvanus Wrigley's grandson G. Weston Wrigley would continually point to the events of 1837 as a watershed in the rise of Canadian socialism. In 1903, before an American audience in Chicago, he claimed that "many of the descendants of the rebels of 1837 are taking an active part in socialist propaganda" (Penner 1977, 40).

Not unlike many of his contemporaries, George Wrigley took up farming after his graduation from elementary school. Displeased with the long and arduous days under the hot southwestern Ontario sun, he gravitated to the classroom, where he took up teaching. His restless soul interfered with his ability to achieve happiness in this profession, however, and he resigned, determined to become a journalist.

After writing for a number of rural newspapers and a series of tragic failures to become a magazine entrepreneur, in 1887 he purchased a St. Thomas, Ontario, working-class journal, the *Canada Labour Courier,* from Andy Ingram, a local railway brakeman who had been elected as a Liberal-Conservative member of the federal Parliament. Wrigley was aware of the growing Knights of Labor Assemblies in the Great Western railroad yards in St. Thomas, and he attempted to develop a clientele among them. Although he attracted a reasonable readership, his numerous appeals for official endorsement and financial support were ignored. After a bitter confrontation with the Knights' leadership and Ingram over the issue, he closed the newspaper and moved north to London (Cook 1984, 8). There is no evidence in the few surviving editions of the *Canada Labour Courier* that Wrigley was aware of the early days of the Christian Socialist movement in Britain, and his ideas on class and class conflict came directly from the Knights of Labor handbook. His journal contained many of the same social critiques as other Knights of Labor journals in the 1880s and early 1890s.

After a one-year stint as editor of the Liberal Party's local organ, the *London Advertiser,* in London in 1891, Wrigley launched the *Canada Farmers'*

*Sun*. In almost every way, the early years of the *Canada Farmers' Sun* resembled Wrigley's *Canada Labor Courier* and nearly all other nonconformist journals of the period. The pages were filled with transcripts published earlier in other journals, reflecting a broad range of nonconformist perspectives. The journal was born with the consent of John Cameron, owner of the *London Advertiser*, who saw an opportunity to advance Liberal Party issues directly to the farm community. The adventure also had the sympathy of one of Wrigley's newfound friends, Caleb Mallory, grand president of the agrarian reform movement, the Patrons of Industry. In concert, they used the *Canada Farmers' Sun* to advocate an alliance of rural and urban dissidents for the purpose of conducting class warfare against Canada's industrial power bases (Good 1958, 65, 121). By this time in his ideological development, it would be safe to restrict George Wrigley solely to the role of dissenter. He had yet to develop a clear agenda for his reformist zeal.

Wrigley's new ally, Caleb Mallory, added a decidedly partisan political flavor to the Patrons movement, which, previous to his election in 1892, had attempted to steer clear of party politics. By 1893, rural discontent had reached the boiling point in Ontario. Wrigley and Mallory actively conspired to convince the movement that it had no alternative but to enter the political arena. Acting on Wrigley's motion, passed in Toronto during the 1893 convention, the Patrons fielded candidates in nearly all of Ontario's rural ridings. On election night, the long-ruling provincial Liberal administration found itself facing seventeen Patrons in the Ontario Legislature. Had Wrigley and Mallory and their friends been able to shift an additional 3 percent of the vote in some twenty marginal ridings, the Patrons would have elected enough members to have formed a government (Cook 1984, 8). This marked the first time in Canadian history that a third-party movement had been able to elect more than a handful of followers. It was George Wrigley's first attempt to move political questions beyond the exclusive hold enjoyed by the two major parties, the Liberals and the Conservatives. It was not to be his last. The event also marked the end of his London, Ontario, tenure. Buoyed by their success, the Patrons insisted that Wrigley and his newspaper move to the provincial capital in Toronto. In 1894, he consented.

Following his electoral successes, Mallory noted: "The members of the labor organizations in the towns and cities did us good service in the provincial campaign and, by that course, have proven their willingness to cooperate with us for the relief of the masses. When such organizations exist in any part of the constituencies, I would advise that they be invited to participate by sending delegates to our conventions" (Cook 1984, 7-8). In spite of Mallory's appeal, a working relationship between the Patrons and labor never matured. By 1896, the Patrons of Industry had virtually disappeared from Canadian politics.

Wrigley founded another newspaper before he surrendered his interest in the *Canada Farmers' Sun* on April 29, 1896, to Toronto intellectual and social gadfly Goldwin Smith. The more philosophic and reflective journal the *Brotherhood Era* first appeared on October 16, 1895, as a supplement to the *Canada Farmers' Sun*. It is here that Wrigley the socialist emerges. In his first issue, the editor published a spirited defense of his new philosophy:

> Socialism does not propose to divide existing wealth, but to assume control of all monopolies and sources of natural wealth, and so utilize them as to place it beyond the power of any man to become a millionaire, and insists that every individual citizen shall have equal opportunities with every other citizen. Under socialism the shiftless and vicious would suffer most, and the poorest citizen who was industrious and moral could aspire to any position in the land. (Toronto, Ontario, *Brotherhood Era,* Oct. 16, 1895)

It is also in this journal that Wrigley's never-wavering devotion to his Christian roots also appears. In the centerfold, he began publishing a serialized version of the Sermon on the Mount. Extracts from the Bible were planned as a continuing feature in the *Brotherhood Era*. Learning from some of his earlier disasters, Wrigley also attempted to market the journal. He offered readers a discount if they would include the Hamilton, Ontario, temperance newspaper the *Templar* as part of a combined subscription. The incentive was a gift of a Bible made in England by the firm of Samuel Basger and Sons (Toronto, Ontario, *Brotherhood Era,* Oct. 16, 1895).

The short-lived *Brotherhood Era* became a gathering place for Toronto intellectual dissidents much in the way that previous journals such as the old Knights of Labor papers had some fifteen years previously. The guest commentator in the first issue was none other than Phillips Thompson, who composed a rousing condemnation of the state of the unemployed in Toronto. If Wrigley's dedication to evolutionary collectivist philosophies had ever been in doubt, the shadows were cast aside when he decided to publish the entire text of Robert Blatchford's *Merrie England,* three chapters at a time, starting with his second issue. He also acted as one of Blatchford's North American agents, selling the popular volume to subscribers for ten cents each.

Wrigley's pen touched upon those who were clearly left out of the increasing late-Victorian mania for profit and prosperity. They included

unionized and nonunionized workers, women, religious minorities, and
advocates of communal cooperatives whom he regarded as the core players
for a new rising class of socialist activists. He donated space to the local
Jewish community and invited its members to share their unique cultural
and religious life with his readers. He was a staunch supporter of gender
equality. He offered two continuing columns to Victorian feminists, "Gossip
by Portia" and "Women and Work," which also carried the subtitle "Sister-
hood as Sacred a Tie as Brotherhood." These two features were specifically
aimed at working women outside the trades union movement.

The *Brotherhood Era* ceased publication when Wrigley gave up the
*Canada Farmers' Sun* because Smith began to exercise more influence and
editorial control favoring a proindustrial and continentalist policy (*Brotherhood Era,* Nov. 20, 1895). Judging from its appearance and content, it is likely
that the *Brotherhood Era* was the forerunner of Wrigley's most important
journal, *Citizen and Country,* which he founded in 1898. Receiving an official endorsement from Toronto's Trades and Labor Council, *Citizen and
Country* published articles by dissident journalists who had been associated
with Wrigley in the past, in particular Phillips Thompson and Alexander W.
Wright (Cook 1984, 12). Along with its noticeable prounion stance, following the founding of *Citizen and Country,* Wrigley's journalism became
increasingly identified with Christian Socialism.

Throughout its three-year life span in Ontario's capital, *Citizen and
Country's* front page regularly carried Wrigley's weekly reflections on the
state of the world, neatly segmented into a combination of boldfaced, capital-
ized titles, incomplete phrases, and lengthy sentences, all of which exposed his
commitment to the principles of Christian Socialism. The editor never wa-
vered in his conviction that "modern civilization is crushing the soul out of
the people" (Toronto, Ontario, Mar. 11, 1899). Wrigley was convinced that
the contradictions in industrial society that produced obscene accumulations
of great wealth alongside persistent and debilitating poverty had to be incorporated in the study of what he defined as the new political economy. He argued that the Christian church, while supporting principles of good citizenship in both spiritual and earthly codes of conduct, must subject its theology
to the analytic scrutiny of sociology if it were to become a relevant force in
resolving the problems of industrial society. Not surprisingly, Wrigley called
for a permanent marriage of theology and socialism, which he believed
would elevate human beings to their most exalted state in both heaven and
earth. Wrigley, a lifelong practicing member of the Church of England, found
the doctrine appealing on two accounts: it argued for a collectivist moral and

spiritual critique of industrial society while simultaneously rejecting the atheism of materialist Marxism.

With the appearance of his journal, Wrigley, in cooperation with Phillips Thompson, founded the Canadian Socialist League. The new organization spread rapidly throughout Ontario. By 1900, it had sixty branches in the province and had formed an alliance with a like-named organization in British Columbia. Both groups adopted *Citizen and Country* as their official organ. The group was no Marxist mouthpiece. It was solidly entrenched in the beliefs expressed by Henry George, Edward Bellamy, Robert Blatchford, and Phillips Thompson. For the first time in his long journalistic career, Wrigley recognized the importance of Eugene V. Debs to American dissidents. Debs's writings were a regular feature in the pages of the Wrigley newspaper, and his ideas were openly debated in meetings of the Canadian Socialist League.

In 1901, the ever-restless Wrigley decided that Ontario did not provide a hospitable environment for socialist ideas and moved to Vancouver. He changed the name of his journal to the *Canadian Socialist*. By this time in his life, he was a spent man. He had moved to a province and a city fraught with infighting among socialist groups defining themselves across an ever-expanding continuum from evolutionists to revolutionists. Two years after moving to the west coast, he sold the journal to an Ontario-born printer, R. Parmeter Pettipiece. Wrigley's days as a journalist had come to a close. Shortly after the sale of the newspaper, he suffered a near-fatal stroke that left him partially incapacitated. He moved to his son Edward's home in Winnipeg, where he died from a second stroke in 1907.

Wrigley's arguments influenced a number of dissident journalists near the end of the Victorian period. In 1898 in Winnipeg, Manitoba, Arthur Puttee's labor newspaper the *Voice* (Feb. 11, 1898) claimed that "it [socialism] is the practical and logical outcome of the teaching of Christ. It is the same system as that instituted among His disciples [Acts IV: 31-35]." Christian Socialism was more successful in finding a sympathetic hearing than was Marxism in a basically Christian Canadian working-class culture. As a prominent Canadian Christian Socialist leader, the Reverend Charles H. Shortt, explained, "The phrase Christian Socialism therefore was used to show that atheism was really no part of Socialism and was repudiated by those Christians who were also socialists, as He was" (London, Ontario, *Canada Farmers' Sun,* Mar. 28, 1893).

It is difficult to define a clear line between Wrigley's Christianity and his socialism. He considered himself the harmonization of both. In his *Citizen and Country,* he published consistent condemnations of church practices while appealing directly to parishioners to help achieve working-class goals. His editorial admonitions did not spare the upper echelons of the Canadian clergy: "You undertake missionary work, home and foreign, but far nearer home than you imagine, there is work for you to do. There are men at your doors ready to receive a message of life from you—life in this world as well as life in the next" (London, Ontario, *Citizen and Country,* Oct. 21, 1899).

Wrigley never surrendered his membership in the Church of England, writing in 1899 that he "clung to it hoping to see it become as much sociological as theological" (London, Ontario, *Citizen and Country,* Oct. 21, 1899). Wrigley's theological and sociological ideas became the founding articles in the credo of the National Christian Citizenship League, a Canadian-based organization founded to promote the principles of Christian Socialism that he published in total in *Citizen and Country.* Wrigley claimed that only the teachings of Jesus Christ should be used to interpret human life, law, and civil relations. In secular economic relationships, he advocated replacing competition with cooperation and producing for use, not profit (Toronto, Ontario, *Citizen and Country,* Aug. 17, 1900). Wrigley and the Christian Socialists left their mark on Canadian history. They were influential with Fabians in the trades unions, assisting the social democratic movement in its numerous struggles with Marxists (Fox 1963, 81). Until the emergence of labor-based political parties, Christian Socialists shared the public platform with Marxists and liberal interventionists, all of whom offered the working class their specific indictments of industrial capitalism (McCormack 1978, 16).

Although it was hardly his intention, as one of the prominent dissident journalists, Wrigley helped to decrease the pervasive influence that Protestantism held in Victorian working-class culture. By the time of his death in 1907, theology was being reformed by sociology. His journals, including the *Canada Farmers' Sun,* the *Brotherhood Era, Citizen and Country,* and the *Canadian Socialist,* created a limited but influential public sympathy for Christian Socialism that Marxism never enjoyed. It is a legacy that remains today.

Critiques delivered by Christian Socialists that had roots in the beliefs of George Wrigley and Phillips Thompson eventually leapt from the labor movement to provide the ideological impetus for the social gospel. Eventually, Pettipiece's coeditor, the west coast Marxist Edward T. Kingsley, became a convert. In 1910 in Montreal, Kingsley declared publicly that he believed that there was little difference between Christianity and socialism (Allen 1968, 388-89). The social analysis that first appeared in the journals founded by people such as Thompson and Wrigley gave birth to the coalition of farmers, laborers, and clergy who gathered together to found the Co-operative Commonwealth Federation (CCF), which remains Canada's third political party under its new name, the New Democratic Party (NDP).

The activities of the dissident journalists outlined in this chapter by no means provide a complete picture of the influence of newsworkers on the political culture that began to emerge in late-nineteenth-century Canada. As Phillips Thompson and George Wrigley began to pass into history, they were replaced by others who inherited their mantles and their ideas. In London, Ontario, a young tinsmith named Joseph T. Marks founded the country's most successful nonconformist journal, the *Industrial Banner.* Marks's monthly survived for three decades, from 1892 until 1922. Marks used the newspaper to launch a successful entry into third-party politics. His Independent Labor Party, which failed to elect a single councillor in London in its first entry into the political arena in 1896, eventually became a coalition partner with the United Farmers' movement in the government of Ontario between 1919 and 1923. It was the first social democratic administration in Canada, but it was not the last. The Independent Labor Party was represented at the founding convention of the CCF in Calgary in 1932.

Another notable journalist was R. Parmeter Pettipiece. Pettipiece assumed ownership of Wrigley's *Canadian Socialist* after Wrigley suffered his first stroke. Eventually, he changed the name of the journal to the *Western Clarion,* in honor of Robert Blatchford's English newspaper the *Clarion.* Unlike the British journal, Pettipiece's publication was far from a moderate supporter of social democracy. Pettipiece, who was instrumental in the formation of the British Columbia locals of the Western Federation of Miners and the Trades and Labor Congress of Canada, became a dedicated Marxist. His newspaper continued until 1921 as the voice of the Socialist Party of Canada, descendants of the Canadian Socialist League of George Wrigley. The party sent two delegates to the founding convention of the CCF in 1932.

Finally, a small tribute should be paid to William U. Cotton of Cowansville, Quebec, founder of *Cotton's Weekly.* Although published in the scenic Eastern Townships of Quebec, the journal became the voice of the Canadian Socialist Federation, headquartered in Ontario. Cotton used his journal to promote the concept that Jesus Christ was the world's first Bolshevik and the world's first trades unionist. The fiery Cotton also devoted most of his center pages to the temperance cause, arguing that "beer soaked brains do not absorb socialism" (Cowansville, P. Q., *Cotton's Weekly,* Feb. 25, 1909). The journal lasted just eight years, ceasing publication in 1917 at the hands of the federal government, which, in response to the Bolshevik Revolution in the Soviet Union, declared Cotton's newspaper a threat to Canadian security.

All these dissident journalists shared a deep suspicion that the state system had been deliberately stacked against working people. They also held in common the perspective that working people were largely ignorant of the sources of their economic, political, and social subservience. They wanted to communicate a vision of a Canada that exposed the privilege enjoyed by members of the dominant culture—the politicians, the industrial and resource capitalists, the exploiters of women and children, members of the Canadian Manufacturers' Association, and elites such as Goldwin Smith.

Their pleas were heard. Although many of their journals lived on the precipice of disaster, it would be simplistic to dismiss their contributions as minor. Within the trades unions, the farm protest groups, and social reformation societies, the newsworkers became intellectual leaders. And, as E. P. Thompson (1963, 28) observes in his history of the rise of the English working class, dissident movements could not have survived without their journals. It is in these journals that the modern scholar can find the roots of contemporary social democratic thought. Modern Canadians who enjoy the benefits of this legacy, such as Medicare, senior citizens' pensions, trade union rights, and an activist, interventionist government philosophy that is still hanging on in this day of global competition, can point to those intellectuals and writers who set the pace for social reform more than a century ago.

## Note

1. In the Canada of the early 1870s, political parties had just started to form. Macdonald's party was known as the Liberal-Conservative Party, which eventually became the modern Progressive Conservative Party. Brown was the founder of the centrist Reform Party, which became the modern Liberal Party. Any contemporary similarities in names are purely coincidental.

## References

Allen, Richard. "The Social Gospel and the Reform Tradition in Canada 1890-1928." *Canadian Historical Review* 49, no. 4 (1968): 381-99.

Beavan, Brian P. N. "Partisanship, Patronage and the Press in Ontario, 1880-1914: Myths and Realities." *Canadian Historical Review* 64, no. 3 (1983): 317-53.

Berger, Carl. *Science, God and Nature in Victorian Canada.* Toronto: University of Toronto Press, 1983.

Careless, J. M. S. *Brown of the* Globe (Vol. 2), *1860-1880.* Toronto: Macmillan, 1963.

Cook, Ramsay. *Tillers and Toilers.* Canadian Historical Association Papers, 1984.

———. *The Regenerators: Social Criticism in Late Victorian English Canada.* Toronto: University of Toronto Press, 1985.

Fetherling, Douglas. *The Rise of the Canadian Newspaper.* Toronto: Oxford University Press, 1990.

Foner, Philip S. *History of the Labor Movement in the United States* (Vol. 2). New York: International Publishers, 1955.

———. *American Labor Songs of the Nineteenth Century.* Urbana: University of Illinois Press, 1975.

Fox, Paul. "Early Socialism in Canada." In *The Political Process in Canada*, ed. J. H. Aitchison, 79-98. Toronto: University of Toronto Press, 1963.

Good, W. C. *Farmer Citizen.* Toronto: Ryerson, 1958.

Hann, Russell. "Brainworkers and the Knights of Labor: E. E. Sheppard, Phillips Thompson and the Toronto News, 1883-1887." In *Essays in Canadian Working Class History,* ed. Gregory S. Kealey, 35-57. Toronto: University of Toronto Press, 1976.

Hann, Russell G., Gregory S. Kealey, Linda Kealey, and Peter Warrian. *Primary Sources in Canadian Working Class History.* Kitchener, Ont.: Dumont, 1973.

Innis, Harold. "Introduction to Canadian Economic Studies." In *Essays in Canadian Economic History,* ed. Mary Q. Innis, 56-175. Toronto: University of Toronto Press, 1973.

Legislative Assembly of Ontario. *Report on Compulsory Education in Canada, Great Britain, Germany and the United States.* Toronto: Legislative Assembly of Ontario, 1891.

McCormack, A. Ross. *Reformers, Rebels and Revolutionaries: The Western Canadian Radical Movement 1899-1919.* Toronto: University of Toronto Press, 1978.

Palmer, Bryan. *A Culture in Conflict: Skilled Workers and Industrial Capitalism in Hamilton, Ontario, 1860-1914.* Montreal: McGill-Queen's University Press, 1979.

Penner, Norman. *The Canadian Left: A Critical Analysis.* Scarborough, Ont.: Prentice Hall, 1977.

Stevenson, Garth. *Unfulfilled Union* (3rd ed.). Toronto: Gage Educational, 1989.

Thompson, Edward P. *The Making of the English Working Class.* Harmondsworth, Eng.: Penguin, 1963.

Thompson, Thomas Phillips. *Secularism.* Phillips Thompson Papers, Archives of Ontario, M.U. 2983, n.d.

*To the Working Classes by the Journeymen Printers of Toronto* (memorial). Ontario Archives, MFM B15, 1853.

# 8 / Newsboys

## *The Exploitation of "Little Merchants" by the Newspaper Industry*

### Jon Bekken

Distribution is at the nexus of the valorization of capital in the newspaper business, and newsboys have long been key to the distribution process. In 1933, the American Newspaper Publishers Association reported that 500,000 boys worked as newsboys, "far outnumbering all adults connected with the newspaper business" (*ANPA Bulletin* 1933). The Newspaper Association of America estimates that there are a total of 473,367 carriers for U.S. newspapers today, nearly 60 percent of them youths.[1] Yet, despite their central role, newsboys have been studied primarily as a social problem instead of for their role as newspaper workers. Such studies proliferated at the turn of the century; as reform movements faded and newsboy work moved from selling papers on the street to delivering them to subscribers' homes, newsboys ceased to be viewed as a social problem. Instead, the industry characterization of newsboys as "little merchants," a symbol of the capitalist system at work, is now generally accepted. Although the notion that newsboys are merchants in any real sense of that term is more than slightly bizarre, this essay argues that newsboys do indeed offer a potent symbol of the capitalist system at work.

The term *newsboys* is used here to describe not only children, but all persons employed in the sale and delivery of newspapers to individual readers—whether on the streets or to their homes. Such usage is not uncontroversial—past studies have drawn a sharp distinction between street sellers, termed newsboys, and carriers, and the organizer of a union of (adult) street vendors of the *San Diego Street Journal* in the early 1970s has indicated his objections to the term (Arthur J. Miller, personal communication, Nov. 1993).² Nonetheless, these workers have been generally known as newsboys, despite the fact that many—older men, young girls, women—have not in fact been boys. Unsatisfactory as the term may be, no substitute better captures the diversity of these workers and any such substitution would necessarily sacrifice the cultural resonances newsboys evoke. Moreover, the distinction between carriers and sellers has always been somewhat arbitrary. The penny press has been celebrated in the literature for its reliance on newsboys, but in 1835 Benjamin Day's *New York Sun* newsboys delivered eight copies to subscribers for every one sold on the street (Nerone 1992, 164). Although few newspaper carriers today sell individual copies on the side, the practice was still widespread in the 1930s.

Newsboys have long played a prominent role in American popular culture—one actively encouraged by the newspaper industry (Tebbel 1971). In 1895, a statue was erected in Great Barrington, Massachusetts, to honor newsboys. A Newspaperboys' Hall of Fame (sponsored by the International Circulation Managers Association, now merged into the Newspaper Association of America) boasts portraits of businessmen and others willing to agree that their success was facilitated by their work as newsboys (Marks and Emley 1953; *New York Times* 1967). A three-cent postage stamp was issued in 1952 honoring newsboys, bearing the legend "Busy boys—better boys" (*New York Times* 1952a).³ And a recent Disney movie musical, *Newsies* (1992), draws heavily upon popular mythology in its portrayal of the New York City newsboys strike of 1899 (Maslin 1992).

The mythical newsboy is a rugged individualist, plucky, competitive, successful, but also docile and industrious. As early as 1844, a short-story writer praised newsboys as "an incarnation of the [commercial] spirit of the day." Newsboy work not only embodied American values, but "if genius is ever latent, the life of the newsboy must bring it forth" (Neal 1844; quoted in Whisnant 1971, 276-77). As David Whisnant (1971) notes, "The newsboy, however indicative he may be of our broadly shared national values, is a cherished cultural image partly because he has proved so useful to special interests" (271-72). The myth suffuses the entire culture—even the *Black Panther* once ran an advertisement recruiting newsboys by promising that they could earn enough to buy a new bike in only three weeks. Forced to confront the reality that most newsboys were poverty-stricken, ill fed, and ragged, apologists developed the rags-to-riches narrative. By mid-century, newsboys became a staple of popular fiction, perhaps best exemplified by Horatio Alger's five newsboy novels.

Other, more critical, observers lambasted the notion that newsboys were capitalists in the making:

> I sell papers. Don't blame me
> For the lies they print and the news they see.
> Getcha paper! Sports and Finance.
> Atom bomb found in statesman's pants!
>
> Do I make much money selling these things?
> Yes, lady, I hope to retire at Palm Springs. . . .
> The patch in my pants, and this dirty old suit?
> Why, lady, I wear it because it looks cute. . . .
> Sure newspaper publishers are a generous pack
> They'd never allow me to earn my beans . . .
>
> They'd never allow me to earn my beans
> If these papers would fit into slot machines.
> Economists say future dark,
> Severed head found in park. (Quinn 1960)

The origins of the newsboy appear to lie in the apprenticeship system. By the 1760s, newspapers were commonly distributed to city subscribers by apprentices who also helped to print the papers. As newspaper circulations soared in the mid-1800s, the apprentice force became inadequate to handle newspaper sales, necessitating the hiring of a large sales force to handle distribution. These distribution workers were ill paid from the start, and frequently came into conflict with their employers. As early as 1799, a fired newspaper carrier arranged with a publisher from an adjacent town to distribute that paper to his route instead (Fuller et al. 1799; Green 1799). As boys could be hired more cheaply than grown men, they were quickly impressed into service where rural routes or great distances did not require adults on horseback. More recently, newsboys played a key role in crippling the *Wilkes-Barre* (Pennsylvania) *Times-Leader* when virtually the entire carrier force decided to distribute the union-published strike daily to their routes rather than carry newspapers printed by strikebreakers. The newsboys stuck with the production unions and their *Citizens' Voice* even after management offered a pay raise and threatened to fire any carrier who did not return (Keil 1988, 156-57).

Historically, newsboy work has paid very poorly. A 1917 study of Cincinnati newsboys found that weekly earnings averaged just $1.22; nearly two-thirds of the newsboys earned $1.20 or less each week. A Baltimore study found average earnings of $1.35, and a New York City study found most newsboys earned between $1.50 and $2.00 a week. But such averages conceal a dramatic range in incomes. The Cincinnati study found newsboys earning as little as 6 cents a week and as much as $9.00; the mode was 60 cents, the median 90 cents (Hexter 1919, 125-26). In Des Moines, Iowa, earnings for street sellers ranged from 5 cents daily up to $1.10, though most earned between 30 and 40 cents; in Davenport, Iowa, carriers received between $6.00 and $10.00 a month for their labors (Brown 1922).

Earnings varied from city to city, depending upon the level of competition, commission rates, and the way the work was organized. In Dallas, a 1920 study reported average weekly earnings of about $3.15, but cautioned that the data were self-reported and probably exaggerated (Civic Federation of Dallas 1921). More typical was a Buffalo, New York study that found half of the newsboys earned less than $2.00, not even enough to pay for their own food, and contributed the bulk of their earnings to their families' budgets (Juvenile Protective Department 1925, 32-33). A 1927 Labor Department study found that newsboys' reported median earnings fell between $3.00 and $5.00 weekly in four of seven cities studied. In the other three cities, newspaper carriers worked fewer hours but earned only $1.00 to $2.00 weekly (McGill 1928, 28, 38). And in the 1930s, newsboys writing to the National Recovery Administration reported wages as low as $1.50 per week, and often urged the NRA to adopt a minimum wage. One newsboy calculated that he received one-fourth of a cent per paper he delivered, "and that isn't very much when you figure I have to do all the collecting too" (quoted in Postol 1989, 15). A Portland newsboy pleaded, "I wonder if something cannot be done . . . to help the News Boys of Portland, Ore. These boys, a great many of them past sixty years of age, . . . working from 10 to 16 hours a day, and the majority make less than 6 cents per hour" (15). Others asked for a minimum wage, the right to determine how many papers they would take (rather than being forced to "eat" extra copies), and protections against retaliation when they organized for better conditions. One newsboy explained their plight in a letter to the President:

> Now that industry of all kinds is raising wages, I think newspaper companies should be asked to raise the wages of newsboys.
>
> A great many of us newsboys are going hungry. . . . I make about 6.50 a week. By the time I'm through paying rent, laundry and eating, I haven't much left. . . . If I did buy a pair of socks, shoes, or a shirt, I'd have to go hungry for days after. (quoted in Postol 1989, 15)

Wages were so low for some classes of work, particularly magazine selling, that publishers relied on prizes and contests to lure workers.[4] Although
street sellers typically worked on speculation (carriers were originally paid a
fixed rate per subscriber), this was not always the case. In Hoboken, New
Jersey, a fourteen-year-old girl was paid a flat rate of a dollar a week for working five and a half hours a day at a newsstand (Bremer 1912, 3-4). Even today,
some newspapers pay a flat rate per subscriber for delivery, and a few promise
to make good any uncollectible accounts. And some 29,000 carriers (a negligible proportion of the total) are recognized as employees by the newspapers
that hire them.

For decades newspapers were notoriously unscrupulous in their efforts
to control newsboys:

> I'm going to sell The New Majority if they put me in jail. The daily
> papers and the police have tried to make slaves out of the newsboys
> for the last ten years. . . . During the strike of 1912 . . . Capt.
> Paddy Lavin and Lieut. Larkin, with guns drawn[,] . . . told us to
> "go back to work or you'll never get out of this hall." The boys
> went back up stairs and climbed out of the fire escapes. That's a
> sample of how the police work hand in hand with the daily news-
> papers. (*New Majority* 1919)[5]

Even apologists acknowledge that newsboys were subjected to abuse in the
past. For example, "Horace Greeley backed his carriers to the limit. Each day
he would write a strong editorial about this brutal and unfair competition."
It is, of course, much easier to wage such a heroic struggle from the safety of
one's office (Marks and Emley 1953, 87).

Publisher-inspired intimidation and violence against newsboys continued into this century. In Cincinnati the morning papers compelled newsboys
to sell both competitors on an equal basis, even though the margin on the
*Enquirer* was twice that on the *Commercial*. The afternoon market was more
competitive. In the summer of 1917 the two evening papers, the *Times-Star*
and the *Post,* each trumpeted accusations that the other had hired "criminals,
thugs and prize fighters" to bully newsboys into selling its paper exclusively, a
battle reminiscent of circulation wars at the turn of the century, when
Cincinnati publishers encouraged their newsboys to drive newsboys working
for competing papers off the streets by force. Cincinnati publishers hired circulation men who would not shrink from violence to get the job done—of
twenty-three street men hired by the *Times-Star* and the *Post* to distribute

papers to newsboys, thirteen had criminal records, ranging from gambling to loitering to attempted murder (Hexter 1919, 142–46).

In Chicago, upstart papers delighted in reporting on their more established rivals' efforts to intimidate newsboys into increasing orders or giving more prominent display to their papers. Max Annenberg hired a "staff of thugs proficient with brass knuckles" to build sales for Hearst's *Chicago American*, and the *Tribune* hired him back several years later for $20,000 a year to rebuild its circulation with the aid of sluggers and revolvers (Forbes 1991). After the *Tribune* had employees of the rival Hearst and Lawson papers arrested, the *Chicago Daily Socialist* (1907a) concluded: "During the trial the public learned that all the big editors hired sluggers, bribe one another's newsboys, lie and steal, just like common thieves."[6] In 1909, a Hearst slugger attacked Willie Baker, throwing his stand and papers into the street, as part of the *American's* efforts to ensure that the *Daily News* was not given preference (*Chicago Daily Socialist* 1909a).[7] Another newsboy was slashed across the neck with a razor by an *American* employee when he refused orders to improve the paper's display. At least twenty-seven newsboys had been killed during circulation wars by the end of the newsboys' 1912 strike against most Chicago dailies in solidarity with locked-out members of the pressmen's union (*American Pressman,* Nov. 1912, 489–90; *Chicago Daily Socialist* 1909c; *Who Is Back of the Gun-Men* 1912).[8]

In Milwaukee, newsboys handling the fledgling *Leader* were regularly attacked by thugs who sought to force them off street corners (*Milwaukee Leader* 1911a, 1911b). When Moe Annenberg was working for Hearst's fledgling *New York Daily Mirror,* he hired mobster Lucky Luciano to ensure the paper's presence on the streets. "Luciano soon had goon squads assaulting newsboys and delivery drivers, overturning delivery trucks, dousing newsstands with kerosene and setting them afire, and intimidating tobacco shop owners who sold rival papers" (Berkeley 1992, 20).[9]

Although publishers did not hesitate to play newsboys off against one another, or to use them as cannon fodder in circulation wars, they willingly cooperated when their mutual interests were at stake. Publishers entered into agreements with each other to prevent newsboys from playing them against each other to win better wages or more advantageous terms. Chicago evening papers, for example, agreed to a common rate of 60 cents per hundred, outlawed returns or exchanges for later editions, and barred "rebates, prizes or bonuses to newsdealers, carriers or newsboys."[10] Except during periods when their circulation wars heated up, publishers demanded that newsboys and dealers handle all newspapers equally: "You must sell *all* the newspapers in this association . . . or you cannot sell any of them" (Victor Lawson Papers 1898).[11]

In the early years of this century, newsboys were often forced to bribe supply men to hold lucrative corners or to ensure timely delivery of their papers. In Cincinnati one newsboy reportedly paid $7.50 a week to hold a particularly attractive corner, and payments of 5 to 25 cents weekly were common (Hexter 1919, 147). Although bribery is doubtless a relic of the past, newsboys continue to receive very low wages. Indeed, the share of newspapers' sales price going to newsboys has dropped sharply in the past century as a result of constant chiseling at newsboys' margins. Whereas 50/50 splits were common in the 1890s, and most newsboys received 40 percent in the early decades of this century,[12] *Presstime* estimates that youth carriers today receive between 20 and 30 percent of the retail price of a newspaper (Rykken 1991).

Some adult carriers now get as much as 40 percent, but must provide their own cars and pay for their own fuel. More typical is the *Santa Rosa* (California) *Press Democrat,* which pays its adult carriers $2.35 a month per subscriber (29 percent of the subscription rate) and estimates that its carriers deliver an average 225-paper route in two hours, which would require folding, wrapping, and delivering 1.8 papers a minute to suburban and rural homes (not counting time spent picking the papers up and getting to the route). In 1971, a survey found that newsboys in Utah's Salt Lake Valley averaged 84 cents an hour ($45.26 a month) at a time when the federal minimum wage was $1.60—not surprisingly, 81 percent of newsboys' parents and newsboys themselves termed the pay "low" or "very low" (Tebbel 1971, 57). Also in the 1970s, a National Labor Relations Board administrative law judge found that newspaper carriers earned about $2.00 a day. In 1991, an executive at a 12,000-circulation daily newspaper estimated that it would add $132,000 a year in wages alone if his paper were to be required to pay its 100 adult carriers minimum wage. Of course, Social Security taxes, unemployment and workers' compensation insurance, and so on would cost newspapers tens of thousands of additional dollars if newsboys were to be granted employee status (Goltz 1991, 18).

In most states, newspaper sellers and carriers are not covered by the social programs that many workers take for granted. Newspapers have invested substantial resources in battles to persuade legislators and judges that newsboys are not their employees, but rather independent merchants over whom publishers have no control and for whom they have no responsibility (Linder 1990, 839–49; *New York Times* 1937; U.S. Congress, House 1946). The legal issue has often arisen in regard to compensation claims in behalf of newsboys who had been maimed or seriously injured on the job, and judges have often, but by no means always, been persuaded by publishers' arguments.[13] In 1937 it was estimated that granting newsboys employee status would add some $4 million in payroll taxes to annual operating costs (Rohleder 1937, 62).[14] New York State newsboys are covered by workers' compensation, though not by other employee benefits, because then-Governor Dewey vetoed legislation regulating newsboys and defining them as independent contractors excluded from workers' compensation (*New York Times* 1952b, 1953). But publishers' efforts to exempt newsboys from coverage continues. At the behest of newspaper executives, Montana excluded newspaper carriers and freelance reporters from unemployment insurance in 1990; they had been excluded from workers' compensation three years earlier. Also in 1990, Washington State passed a law defining carriers as independent contractors for purposes of workers' compensation, and required carriers to buy their own liability insurance to cover any injuries to third parties. The American Newspaper Publishers Association (now the Newspaper Association of America) established its Independent Contractors Working Group in 1990 to assist publishers in avoiding the costs of treating newsboys as employees, issues "including, but not limited to, workers' and unemployment compensation, Social Security, income taxes, unionization and whether an 'employer' [*sic*] is liable for acts committed by independent contractors [*sic*]" (Goltz 1991, 17).

Newsboys were one of the earliest groups to attract the attention of urban social reformers. The first annual report (1854) of the New York Children's Aid Society announced the opening of the Newsboys Lodging House in the *Sun* building for homeless newsboys. By 1864 the Lodging House had nearly 150 beds and was at the center of Charles Loring Brace's reform program to transform corrupted children into respectable, devout citizens (Whisnant 1971, 286-87). Children's aid societies in other cities established similar lodging houses, and social reformers and newspapers alike developed newsboy programs. Investigations in scores of cities documented the appalling conditions in which newsboys lived and worked.

But social reformers were less interested in documenting earnings and working conditions than in demonstrating that city streets were an unfit place for children. Thus, several studies have examined the percentages of boys in reformatories who had sold newspapers, and the extent to which newsboys were behind in school (Trattner 1970, 262 n. 42). As part of their effort to establish that newsboys' income was not necessary, social workers carefully compared the names of newsboys' parents to charity and welfare rolls to determine how many newsboys came from destitute families or were orphans (Brown 1922; Clopper 1910). They documented instances of under-aged boys, while often ignoring newsboys over the age of ten or twelve (e.g., Bremer 1912, 14). And many were wholly unsympathetic to the newsboys' aspirations: in Camden, New Jersey, one social worker cited a newsboy who had bought a violin and was paying for music lessons as proof for her contention that most newsboys were feebleminded. This condescending attitude carried over to the U.S. Labor Department's Children's Bureau as well; its studies simply ignore newsboys age sixteen and over (McGill 1928).[15] Typically, reformers were more interested in forcing newsboys (at least the younger newsboys) off the streets than in helping them to improve their conditions. Their objection to the work was not so much the low wages or harsh working conditions, though they often pointed to these, as the fact that newsboys were working on the street, which they saw as a domain of bars, prostitutes, and corruption. Thus, reformers willingly acceded to newsboy legislation that exempted small cities and towns, where the corrupting influence of the street was presumably less (as was average pay), and argued that lower-paying carrier work was less of a problem, pointing to the "better class" of children so employed (Felt 1965, 159-68).

Indeed, even reformers often succumbed to the argument that newsboys were "self-employed . . . independent contractors," "rugged individuals starting on the road toward success." The problems identified with newsboy work, in this view, arose, not from the work itself, or from the terms imposed upon the newsboys, but rather from the lack of adult supervision and the moral temptations to which the boys might be exposed (Trattner 1970, 110-11).

Yet, although most newsboy work, particularly that sponsored by the newspapers, was paternalistic, some reformers pursued self-help policies that by the turn of the century produced newsboys' associations such as the Newsboy Association of Toledo (Ashby 1984). These associations often combined rescue work with a limited arena for newsboys' self-organization in civics and other uplift programs. The Toledo association was not founded by newsboys, but by John Gunckel, its president and a social reformer who tried to solve the "newsboy problem" through a combination of welfare and moral uplift programs. Gunckel's association displaced the Toledo Bootblacks' and Newsboys' Union, a newsboy-controlled organization that sought to improve working conditions (Ashby 1984, 108). It sponsored dinners, encouraged newsboys to attend Sunday school, maintained a gymnasium and library, and operated a self-government scheme in which Toledo newsboys elected representatives and operated a court to try newsboys charged with misconduct. The court also worked with juvenile court officials to warn youths away from saloons and poolrooms and to discourage swearing. Unlike most social reformers, who favored strict regulations on newsboy work, Gunckel believed that the newsboy problem lay within the newsboys themselves, and could best be addressed through the development of their moral character. His approach spread to other cities. In 1904, Gunckel founded the National Newsboys' Association, which by 1913 claimed 28,000 members (membership was free upon a declaration of one's bad habits and a pledge to stop them) in 200 branches (Ashby 1984, 126-27). But when Gunckel appealed to newspaper publishers to organize branches in their areas, he first had to reassure them that the organization was not a union (Associated Ohio Dailies 1905, 52). The Toledo Newsboys' Association continued until the 1930s, when it was reorganized as the Boys' Club of Toledo.

In Boston and a few other cities, newsboy courts were placed in charge of enforcing regulations against underaged newsboys, night selling, and dangerous practices. In others, newsboys' associations were formed in which newsboys had a substantial voice in determining the recreational and social programs offered. More frequently, reformers or school officials exercised tight control over the newsboys' associations. Yet, as historian David Whisnant (1971) explains:

> whatever their conception . . . lodging houses and self-help associations by their very existence acknowledged one incontrovertible fact: unconscionable social abuses were invariably associated with the lives of newsboys. . . . However, the newsboys' lodging houses and associations unfortunately tended to treat only their symptoms—malnutrition, homelessness, illiteracy—rather than their cause. (288-89)

Despite the efforts of gunmen, social reformers, and circulation departments, newsboys generally held to their own ethical code. Once a newsboy had established a corner, other newsboys respected it as his so long as he continued to sell papers there—if someone tried to horn in or to dispossess the legitimate "owner," other newsboys would join in defense of their fellow worker's rights. But the situation might well look different to a new newsboy; a Portland newsie recalled that it wasn't safe for younger boys to sell downtown: "The boys were very jealous of the corners on which they sold and interlopers were made unwelcome. Competition was very heavy; it sometimes resulted in fights, black eyes and bloody noses" (Toll 1982, 62).

Social reformers did not show much interest in improving the conditions of work—their emphasis was on securing the passage of legislation barring newsboys from working until they reached a specified age (early laws sought a minimum age of ten; by the 1930s the goal was sixteen). Where such laws were violated, the penalties fell not on the newspaper but on newsboys and their parents. These laws hit young women particularly hard. A bill introduced in the Illinois General Assembly in 1911, for example, barred boys under age ten and girls under sixteen from selling newspapers in cities of 100,000 or more, and required boys ten to sixteen to obtain permits from the Board of Education (Jane Addams Papers, reel 38, frames 0424-433).

Newspapers cheered child labor laws in general but vigorously resisted efforts to regulate newsboys (Bromley 1935; Trattner 1970, 193). The American Newspaper Publishers Association denied that "the delivery and sale of newspapers" was child labor; rather, it was "a fine preliminary training which is just as essential a part of the boy's education as work done in school" (Stodghill 1933, 638). The New York State Publishers Association urged the State Legislature to reject the Child Labor Amendment in "behalf of the boys and girls of America." Heywood Broun (1934) questioned this mandate: "The Publishers' Association is desirous of availing itself of cheap labor wherever possible. . . . Does anybody sitting in a pleasant place 25 stories from the street ever hear the cry of children who are oppressed and exploited?" *Editor & Publisher* (n.d.) noted "the undoubted fact that the circulation department can hire little kids cheaper than big ones," but argued that newspapers could easily live with a law barring the employment of children younger than fourteen.

In 1933, the American Newspaper Publishers Association reported that the country's half million newsboys, "the brightest, most ambitious, most worthwhile boys in this country," earned approximately $100 million a year and worked less than an hour and a half a day. If these figures are accurate, newsboys earned about 38 cents a week, or 3.6 cents an hour. The ANPA added, "The work of delivering newspapers is essentially boy's work, not suitable for adults," who were presumably reluctant to work for what the ANPA conceded was a "small income" (*ANPA Bulletin* 1933, 637-38). However, although the ANPA estimates of employees' average earnings are in line with other figures, independent studies found that newsboys worked longer hours—sometimes substantially longer—than the ANPA estimated.

A 1927 study of newsboys in several cities found they averaged 16 hours a week, though some worked as many as 46.5 hours on a regular basis; more than 40 percent of newsboys in Atlanta and Omaha reported working 24 or more hours per week, and nearly a third reported such hours in Columbus and Washington, D.C. Carriers typically worked shorter hours, usually less than 12 hours a week except when they were required to sell new subscriptions or to collect from subscribers. Such data, however, can be difficult to gather, as few newsboys keep detailed financial or time records. A 1941 study based on a national survey of circulation managers and a cluster survey of 706 newsboys in fifteen cities found that newsboys estimated it took 14.43 hours a week to deliver their routes, whereas circulation managers estimated that it took just 1.11 hours a day. And whereas thirty-three newsboys reported earning only fifty cents a week, circulation managers estimated that no newsboys earned that little (thirty-nine newsboys also reported earning more than the highest rate reported by the managers, though most were among sixty who worked two routes). Newsboys reported delivering an average of 92.87 papers daily, whereas circulation managers reported 64.37. The vast majority of circulation managers considered newsboys independent merchants and required them to sign contracts, though a few employed newsboys were on straight salary (McDaniel 1941, 56-64).

Although newsboys' work hours fall far short of full-time work, it should be noted that most newsboys combined work and school. A 1926 study of New York newsboys found that they were generally healthy; two-thirds of the 1,078 newsboys examined were behind in school—the examiners attributed this to their long working hours, though the *New York Times* (1926a) argued that most would be behind in school whether or not they sold papers. Virtually every study of newsboys found that they were behind in their schoolwork, although newspaper publishers vigorously contested the findings with statements from sympathetic school officials (Brown 1922, 142-45; Diamond 1922; Minor 1924, 8).

In addition to long hours, newsboys suffered from other poor working conditions. Newspapers can be quite heavy; a 1921 study found that fifty Toledo papers weighed more than 21 pounds—a fairly substantial weight for young newsboys to carry. Yet newsboys often serviced routes of seventy-five to one hundred papers (Minor 1924). By 1940, a study found that the average newsboys' paper load weighed 36.73 pounds (McDaniel 1941, 66).

Newsboy work can also be quite dangerous. The National Child Labor Committee records are filled with examples of newsboys killed or maimed on the job (Hall 1937; *Knickerbocker Press* 1934). To this day, newsboys are regularly struck by cars and buses while selling or delivering papers (*Editor & Publisher* 1994; *Johnson v. Workmen's Compensation Appeal Board* 1993; *Swartz v. Eberly* 1962). In 1934, for example, newsboys suffered four deaths and seventy reported accidents on the job. A tabulation of New York State injuries to newsboys under age eighteen found fifty-seven compensated accidents between 1935 and 1937—most entailed broken bones, but one fourteen-year-old newsboy was struck by a car and killed (Compensated Accident Cases n.d.; Compensated Industrial Accidents n.d.). In Los Angeles alone, seventeen newsboys were killed and 283 injured in the 1940s while selling papers (*Time* 1950). These dangers led to intense struggles over whether newsboys would be covered by workers' compensation and disability insurance. Newsboys were excluded by statute from Social Security (after the Social Security Administration determined that many newsboys were in fact covered under the original law), the Fair Labor Standards Act, and many other protective laws (*New York Times* 1937).

The courts have struggled with the question of whether newsboys are covered. The Michigan Supreme Court ruled that a substitute newsboy and his assistants were independent contractors, and thus, a five-year-old boy hit by a car and rendered a paraplegic while assisting in delivering newspapers was not eligible for compensation (*Higgins v. Monroe Evening News* 1978). The Commonwealth Court of Pennsylvania reached a similar decision, over a vigorous dissent, in the case of a seriously injured thirteen-year-old newsboy (*Johnson v. Workmen's Compensation Appeal Board* 1993); a twelve-year-old newsgirl left in a permanent vegetative state after being hit by a car while delivering the *Fremont Tribune* was ruled ineligible by the Nebraska Workers' Compensation Appeals Board (*Editor & Publisher* 1994). However, the Arkansas Supreme Court has ruled that whether or not newsboys are employees is irrelevant—that publishers are responsible when they place newsboys in dangerous situations (*Clark v. Arkansas Democrat* 1967).[16]

Newsboys are also easy prey for criminals (Rambo 1984). An eleven-year-old newsboy was strangled to death in Keyport, New Jersey, during a robbery (*New York Times,* Jan. 27, 1971, 24); a fourteen-year-old was stabbed to death while delivering *Newsday* in Long Island in March 1983 (*Presstime* 1983a); a thirteen-year-old was stabbed to death while delivering the *Omaha World-Herald* in September 1983 (*Presstime* 1983b); a fourteen-year old in Rockville Centre, New York, was robbed, raped and fatally stabbed in 1984 (*New York Times,* May 25, 1984, sec. 2, p. 2); a twelve-year-old Binghamton, New York, newsgirl was raped and strangled in March 1984 by a subscriber who had previously delivered the route (*Presstime* 1984a); and a thirteen-year-old newsgirl was murdered in Tempe, Arizona, while collecting subscriptions in May 1984 (Ruth 1984). A thirty-two-year-old carrier for the Spokane *Spokesman-Review* was beaten to death while delivering papers in February 1987; a twenty-year-old carrier was robbed of $60 and had his throat slit while making collections in Niagara Falls (*Presstime* 1987a); and a thirteen-year-old carrier for the Pinola, California, *West County Times* was killed in February 1989 (*Presstime* 1989a). The Sioux Falls, South Dakota, *Argus Leader* settled a lawsuit with a man whose eleven-year-old daughter was murdered while delivering the paper in 1991. Mike Clarey said the paper had received reports that the murderer had harassed other carriers months before his daughter was killed (*Editor & Publisher* 1993).

As newspapers moved from street selling to home delivery, many developed elaborate contracts for their newsboys. These contracts are strikingly different from those newsboys negotiated for themselves, in the rare situations where they were powerful enough to enforce collective bargaining. The *Daily Argus* (Mount Vernon, New York), for example, in March 1939 required newsboys to sign a contract in which the paper reserved the right to change the newspaper's price on forty-eight hours' notice, while requiring newsboys to sell at the paper's established price and to deposit a bond to ensure that all newspapers were paid for on a weekly basis. Returns were not permitted, newsboys were required to give two weeks' notice before quitting, and the paper was not liable for any failure to deliver the newspaper on a timely basis. "It is agreed that the relationship of the Distributor to the Company shall be that of an independent merchant purchasing newspapers from the Company and selling them, and that the Distributor . . . [works] at his own risk and expense." Both the newsboy and his or her parents were required to sign the contract (Contract between the Westchester Newspapers 1939).[17]

Contracts did not alleviate all questions, however. Many states found that contractual language or newspaper policy did not determine whether a newsboy was an employee or a merchant, but rather the actual relationship between the newspaper and the newsboy. Where the newspaper exercised substantial control, which was and remains the case in nearly every instance, newsboys might well be covered by workers' compensation, unemployment insurance, and other programs (Committee on Social Security 1937). State courts in Illinois, New York, and Oregon have ruled that newsboys are employees covered by state unemployment laws; publishers in Montana and Washington have persuaded state legislatures to exempt them by statute (*Gannett v. Miller* 1942; Goltz 1991; *Journal v. State Unemployment Compensation Commission* 1945).[18] Indeed, the question of whether publishers are required to treat newsboys as employees, and pay payroll taxes on them, has resurfaced as growing numbers of adults have been hired to deliver far-flung routes that can be handled only by car (Fram 1983; Goltz 1991; *Presstime* 1984c).

The *Daily Argus* contract is typical of the contracts newspapers still insist their newsboys sign. These contracts generally place all the obligations and risks on the newsboys, and reserve control and benefits for the publisher:

> There are those who maintain that former abuses have disappeared. Nevertheless, a newsboy . . . signs a contract which specifies that the "publisher shall not be . . . liable for any . . . injuries to [the] Carrier." . . . So that the last possibility of loss by the publisher may be covered, the young merchant's parents are required to post a security deposit before he may take his first step up the ladder of success. Some, after all, have been known to falter before reaching the top. . . . his contract specifies that "said route, the good will thereof [and] all subscription lists . . . shall remain the exclusive property of the publisher." (Whisnant 1971, 298-99)

However, when newsboys were in a position to actually bargain over contracts, the resulting agreements looked very different. A 1939 contract between Philadelphia Newspaper Carriers Union Local 20442 (AFL) and the Philadelphia *Bulletin, Inquirer, Public Ledger,* and *Record* guaranteed that newsboys would receive one-third of the cover price for newspapers, granted preferential treatment in filling vacancies for union members, and guaranteed bonus payments to newsboys who kept their stands open late at night to sell the "bulldog" editions of the morning papers (Memorandum of Agreement 1939). The more detailed contracts of the News Vendors Union of San Francisco's AFL Local 20769 specified that newsboys were not employees, outlined the ratio of adult to children newsboys (5 to 3) in the downtown district (the contract defined newsboys over age eighteen as news vendors, and those under eighteen as newsboys), granted preference to union members in filling vacancies, established a 40 percent margin on daily newspapers (25 percent on Sunday) with all papers fully returnable, established a maximum forty-six-hour week, protected vendors from being replaced by coin racks, prohibited political discrimination against union members, required publishers to preassemble newspapers, and guaranteed a minimum wage of $17.50 per week for those working a full forty-six-hour week (Union Agreement 1939). In 1938 the San Francisco union demanded recognition as employees so "that we may be eligible for workmen's compensation, social security and other benefits due every other employee, which we have been denied in the past," but were unable to win this demand at the bargaining table (American Federation of Labor Records, reel 32, frames 1027-37). A few years later, after the Social Security Administration began assessing payroll taxes against San Francisco publishers, newspaper publishers went to Congress to secure legislation exempting them from all payroll taxes (newsboys under eighteen were already exempted) and testified that vendors had always considered themselves "independent businessmen" and did not wish to be covered by the unemployment and Social Security systems. The chairman of the House Ways and Means Committee repeatedly interrupted Social Security administrators to ridicule the notion that newsboys were employees, and no newsboys were heard before these protections were stripped away (U.S. Congress, House 1946).[19]

At one point, newspapers reinforced the idea that newsboys were independent merchants by requiring them to buy routes and corners from their predecessors. This tradition apparently originated with street sellers who established small newsstands on the streets and considered them—and the corners they occupied—their property. These "corner men" often claimed the exclusive right to sell papers in their territories (though they might allow others to work on commission), and would back this right up by force if necessary.[20] A particularly good Chicago corner might sell for as much as $1,500 in the early 1900s (Hard 1908, 28). Such a tradition was well established among publishers and newsboys alike by the turn of the century, and in many cities it was carried over to the emerging home-distribution systems. The industry-sponsored Newspaper Boys of America (1932), for example, advised that "in most cities, the only way a boy can get a newspaper route is to buy one from a carrier who . . . wishes to sell his list of customers" (35). It did suggest, however, that circulation managers intervene to control prices and ensure that "unsuitable" boys not be sold routes. Under this system, newsboys might well feel that they owned their routes, raising issues of their rights not only to distribute other publications, but to set their own prices. As late as 1948 many newspapers did not maintain route books, giving carriers (who were required to turn over route books upon leaving their posts) at least the potential of completely cutting off circulation if they should organize (Texas Circulation Managers Association 1948, 115).

Given the low wages and the general disrepute in which newsboy work was held, publishers resorted to a wide range "of what might be called welfare work, were it not for the fact that their beneficence does not as a rule benefit the individuals involved" (Hexter 1919, 148-49). Publishers sought both to attract and retain newsboys[21] and to demonstrate their philanthropic impulses to the broader public. In Cincinnati, publishers spent as much as $4,000 a year on watermelon-eating contests, baseball leagues, wrestling matches, and free admission to theater matinees. In Grand Rapids, Michigan, the *Evening Press* established a brass band, dancing classes, bathhouse, library, athletic contests, lunch counter, and annual picnic/excursion for its one thousand newsboys. The paper also operated a one-room school for twenty to thirty newsboys kept out of school by their newspaper-selling duties (Forbush 1907; Ihlder 1907). Although such programs have declined in recent years, many newspapers continue to offer Christmas gifts, college scholarships, and prizes for good service records or sales of new subscriptions as part of their efforts to hold newsboys (Dyar 1942, 81–85; Rykken 1991; Terrell 1988).

In New York City, the Newsboys' Home Club operated sports and recreational facilities. Founded in 1907, its Board of Directors included such friends of the newsboy as William Randolph Hearst, Joseph Pulitzer, and Ogden Reid. In 1915, an observer described its hall as "inexpressibly dirty, dingy, grimy," and with little evidence of use (though she visited during the day, when newsboys would have been on the street). Facilities for many of the programs touted in its publicity brochure simply did not exist (Dwight 1915). By then, the Newsboys' Lodging House, organized in 1872, no longer served newsboys—its tenants were homeless factory workers—though newsboys did participate in some of its projects, such as an annual Washington's Birthday dinner (*New York Times* 1930b). Established by the Children's Aid Society, the Lodging House replaced a dormitory in the *New York Sun* building; it closed in 1943 and the seven-story building was turned over to the Coast Guard (*New York Times* 1943).

Social welfare programs were often strictly managed and controlled. When the *Syracuse Herald* announced a Christmas Eve feast for its four hundred newsboys, it published detailed instructions for them, including the order of the procession to the site and their required behavior at the hall. Newsboys were promised "appropriate and handsome presents" such as skates, banjos, drums, cornets, and sleds, but were emphatically prohibited from entering the stage, where the decorations and a two hundred-piece orchestra were placed (*Evening Herald* 1894).

Many organizations purported to organize newsboys or to work in their interests. The News Boys Protective Association of Cincinnati, for example, was ostensibly headed by a judge; but when Jane Addams sought information on how a new city ordinance was affecting newspaper sales, the *Cincinnati Post*'s circulation manager answered in its behalf (Jane Addams Papers, reel 34, frame 0434). The Newspaper Boys of America Incorporated, which operated in the 1930s, avoided mention of its sponsors, but its publications made it clear that local NBA chapters were run not by newsboys but by circulation departments. The NBA's "Ten-Fold Purpose" was "to promote the general welfare and business training of all newspaper boys *employed by its members*—the leading newspaper publishers." Specific objectives included providing circulation managers with a program for training and managing newsboys, developing better, "more profitable" distribution methods, and "informing" the public of the "vital public service" performed by newsboys and of publishers' efforts to promote their best interests (Newspaper Boys of America 1932, 5-6; emphasis added). Despite the name, the NBA was an association not of newsboys but of newspapers. The circulation manager of the *Evening News Leader* (Richmond, Virginia), for example, described his newspaper as the NBA's "Richmond member," pointing to its merit system of promotion for carriers as one of the scheme's strong points. Promotion carried not higher pay, but merit badges, certificates, and the opportunity to compete for a national scholarship (Stodghill 1933, 644-45).

The Burroughs Newsboys Foundation of Boston was primarily a social welfare organization, but operated as a membership organization with an elected Administrative Council. The Administrative Council addressed a wide range of issues, including efforts by newspapers to dislodge newsboys who had built up their own corners. When the "mayor" of "Newsboyville" complained of a proposed price increase and asked what action the foundation would take to defend newsboys' interests, Burroughs ruled out any action and emphasized the importance of cooperating with the newspapers. Although the council had the theoretical right to overrule Burroughs' decisions, he would then go to "the older boys" to seek their approval to do as he wished (Burroughs 1944, 279-88, 51). Much of the foundation's funding came from newspaper publishers:

> As newsboys sometimes have complaints against newspaper offices, I have felt it advisable not to have publishers on the board of trustees. On certain occasions, notably when there have been questions of legislation affecting newsboys, I have been glad of this policy. (34-35)

The Newsboys' Republic, in Milwaukee, was perhaps the most elaborate of these welfare programs. Sponsored by the Milwaukee public schools, the Republic sought to keep newsboys in schools, to enforce local regulations, and to shape their character through an elaborate structure of representational government, a monthly newspaper, an annual banquet, debate teams, and so on (National Child Labor Committee Papers, box 59). Newspapers also mobilized their newsboys against child labor and similar legislation that might adversely affect publishers. The Hornell, New York, *Evening Tribune-Times,* for example, presented its carriers with a preprinted letter for subscribers, asking them to write the governor to oppose ratification of the proposed Child Labor Amendment. Newsboys collected the letters while collecting subscription fees, and provided them to the publisher (New York Child Labor Committee Papers, box 34, folder 7).

Sometimes the reformers' "newsboys' associations" could take on lives of their own. The Portland Newsboys Association had its own clubhouse, which had been donated by a local philanthropist as part of social reformers' work with newsboys. When the reformers proposed to merge the "poorly supervised" clubhouse with a nearby facility, the newsboys refused. And when circulation departments forced newsboys to take more papers than they could sell, the newsboys met among themselves to develop a solution. As newsboy Manly Labby later recalled, they decided to take on the Portland newspapers one at a time:

> We took a strike vote and every one of us agreed that we were not going to let a newspaper out of the [*Oregonian*] building, whether it was by mail—many of the papers were mailed to subscribers— whether by truck or by street circulation. We wouldn't let the trucks back up; the trucks brought the papers out to various areas away from downtown, where the circulators distributed them to the route boys. When newspapers came out of the basement in bundles, we immediately shredded them to pieces. . . .
>
> The strike lasted for two days. No papers were going into circulation and people were clamoring for the news. . . . Finally the employers at the four papers agreed to meet with us. It was decided that the circulators would take back any newspapers that were unsold by 6 p.m., and would give us back the money we had paid for those papers. We had won our case. (quoted in Lowenstein 1987, 131-33)

Newsboys have not passively accepted their lot, despite the difficulties intrinsic to organizing such a disparate and dispersed workforce. In addition to the individual resistance endemic to such work, newsboys have organized unions in cities across the country for at least the past hundred years. Documented newsboy strikes have taken place in Boston (1901, 1908), Chicago (1912), Cleveland (1934), Des Moines (1922), Kansas City (1947), Lexington, Kentucky (1899), Minneapolis (1918), Mobile (1942), New York City (1893, 1899, 1918, 1922, 1941, 1948), Oakland (1928), Portland (1914), Saint Louis (1945), and Seattle (1917).[22]

These strikes typically followed publishers' unilateral decisions to undermine newsboys' established working conditions. During the Spanish-American War of 1898, Pulitzer's *Evening World* and Hearst's *Morning Journal* took advantage of the heightened demand for newspapers to cut the commission on newspapers from fifty cents per hundred to forty cents. However, newsboys struck on July 20 when the papers refused to restore the old price. "Cries of 'Scab! scab!' followed the few who dared to handle the forbidden papers, and before long few of them were to be found on the streets" (*New York Times,* 1899a). The strike was also joined by Jersey City newsboys, who decided at a mass meeting not to sell the papers (Nasaw 1985b; *New York Times* 1899a).[23] A delegation approached the Knights of Labor for organization. Groups of a hundred of more strikers were reported destroying copies of the struck papers at newsstands. Some two thousand newsboys packed the New Irving Hall on July 24 for a mass meeting called by the nascent Newsboys' Union, while another three thousand clustered outside. Representatives of the Newsdealers' Association and several local politicians attended to express their support, while a union committee reported on the unsuccessful deliberations. One speaker reminded the newsboys of their victory over the newspapers in 1893. Although the *Times* (1899b) report was generally sympathetic, it was immediately followed by another headlined "Violent Scenes during Day"—a report of how hundreds of newsboys had blocked efforts to hire a force of seven hundred men to break the strike and had forced the struck papers off the street throughout the city (*New York Times* 1899c). Although the newsboys did not win the old price, the newspapers did concede a right to return unsold papers—a right that was still in force thirteen years later (Riis 1912, 250).

Unionization efforts were generally short-lived responses to changes in newspaper terms. When Chicago dailies determined that they would no longer accept returns of unsold papers—a right that newsboys had won just a few years before, when Hearst's entry into the market gave them the edge over the Publishers Association—newsboys in Chicago and Marion, Indiana (who handled out-of-town papers from Chicago and Indianapolis) decided to unionize (*Chicago Daily Socialist* 1907b, 1907c). Newsboys struck the *Boston American* in January 1908 when the paper cut their margin by ten cents a hundred and refused to continue taking returns. Hearst circulation sluggers quickly swung into action, attacking newsboys who were not selling their paper (typically, striking newsboys refused to handle the paper[s] against which they had a grievance, but would handle competing papers—thereby increasing the pressure on their target). Their battle ran several months before the newsboys were finally defeated (*Chicago Daily Socialist* 1908a, 1908b, 1908c, 1908d, 1908e).

Minneapolis newsboys struck twice in 1918, after local dailies cut their margin on papers from 50 to 30 percent and raised the price from one to two cents. The *Tribune* was the first to make the change, after three hundred news-boys elected a committee and declared that they would refuse to handle the paper unless it returned to the original terms; a compromise of 37.5 percent was struck pending further negotiations after the publisher's return from abroad (*Minneapolis Labor Review* 1918b). After six months, the newsboys struck the *Tribune, Journal,* and *Daily News,* demanding a return to the full 50 percent and the right to return unsold papers (*Minneapolis Labor Review* 1918c). Publishers refused to meet with the Newsboys' Union despite a re-quest from the typographical union, and so hundreds of newsboys launched a strike. They marched behind a banner asking readers, "Will You Help the Newspapers Starve the Newsboys?" After a few days of sharply reduced sales, local advertisers prevailed upon the publishers to compromise at 45 percent nonreturnable for evening papers and establish a grievance procedure (*Minneapolis Labor Review* 1918f). Far from assisting the newsboys in their ef-fort to improve conditions, social reformers seized upon the dispute as proof that "the effects of street life upon growing boys are such as imperil their de-velopment into future good citizens" (Waite et al. 1918).

Although newsboy unions generally sought affiliation with the Ameri-can Federation of Labor in hopes that solidarity with other newspaper unions and the broader labor movement would help them win their de-mands, such support was not necessarily forthcoming. In Boston, newsboys bitterly protested the typographers' union's refusal to support their strike, noting that they had always refused to carry newspapers struck by the ITU (*Chicago Daily Socialist* 1908f). Newsboys occupied an ambiguous position in relation to the publishers, and many in the labor movement shared the publishers' contention that they were more akin to small merchants than to workers.

Thus, when AFL Federal Labor Union Local 22371 called a strike against eight New York City newspapers in 1941, the American Newspaper Publish-ers Association appealed to AFL vice president and Teamsters president Dan Tobin to ensure that no solidarity would be forthcoming from other news-paper unions. Tobin replied that he "owe[d] nothing to the news publishers of New York, who have maintained an independent union of drivers," but nonetheless requested an investigation. ITU officials agreed that the news vendors were merchants, suggesting that the union was a cloak for racketeer-ing. The local had been organized a year previously and represented operators of small newsstands. When the local continued its selective strike, the AFL's representative wrote AFL president George Meany: "We would recommend the cancellation of this charter, excepting it would make a hero out of this present president, and time will eliminate the Union entirely. Our recommendation is that no more per capita tax be accepted" (American Federation of Labor Records, reel 46, frames 00129-151). Although the Newspaper Guild of New York and the CIO Greater New York Industrial Union Council stood by the AFL newsdealers, officials of the AFL Allied Printing Trades Council denounced them in the press (*New York Times* 1941a).[24]

Many of the union's demands had a familiar sound; others spoke to deteriorating conditions in the industry: full credit on returns of unsold papers, the right to determine how many papers they would take, 40 cents on the dollar margin, elimination of delivery charges, an end to coercion by circulation departments, and interest on newsdealers' bonds (*New York Times* 1941b). Some 1,700 newsdealers joined the strike, which began as a selective strike against the *World Telegram* October 11, and quickly spread as other papers refused to make deliveries to dealers who joined the strike (*New York Times* 1941c). The strike was suspended from October 22 through November 19, when Mayor La Guardia intervened, but resumed when publishers refused to modify their pay scales (*New York Times* 1941d, 1941e, 1941f, 1941g). Publishers then secured an injunction against the strike under state antitrust laws after the judge hearing the case ruled that the newsdealers were not employees. The newsboys were forced to capitulate, though publishers did announce several concessions (*New York Times* 1941h, 1941i, 1941j, 1941k, 1941l, 1941m).[25]

Later the union became embroiled in a jurisdiction dispute with the New York Newsboys Union (AFL Local 471) over which had the right to represent newsstand operators in negotiations with New York publishers; the court ruled that they were merchants, not employees, and therefore refused to allow the State Labor Relations Board to hear the dispute (*New York Post v. Kelley* 1946, 1947; *New York Times* 1947a). New York Newsboys Union 471 had no greater success with the courts than did its rival; when the union began picketing newsstands that did business with the Manhattan News Company to protest its imposition of new fees, the company quickly obtained an injunction against the union (*New York Times* 1949a).

In the 1940s, the International Printing Pressmen and Assistants Union attempted to organize newsboys across the country and vigorously protested the invasion of its jurisdiction when other AFL unions—notably, the International Alliance of Bill Posters, Billers and Distributors—sought to organize newsboys under their own auspices (Fink 1977; IPPAU 1940). IPPAU-affiliated newsboy unions waged several strikes, often with the support of union pressmen. In Kansas City, pressmen honored a newsboy picket line for sixteen days after the *Kansas City Star* refused to recognize their union. The strike ended when the *Star* granted a pay increase to the pressmen and agreed to "study" whether the newsboys were employees or independent contractors (*New York Times* 1947b, 1947c). In St. Louis, pressmen honored a picket line after local newspapers refused to bargain with their NLRB-certified newsboy union. The publishers insisted the newsboys were merchants, and pointed out that they had bought their routes, sometimes for thousands of dollars (*New York Times* 1945b).[26]

Publishers have exploited newsboys' ambiguous position to suit their interests—arguing that they are independent contractors outside the newspapers' control when it comes to workers' compensation and other protective legislation or to recognizing newsboys' unions (*Drukker Communications v. NLRB* 1983; Linder 1990; *NLRB v. A.S. Abell* 1964; *New York Times* 1948a; *Presstime* 1992a, 1992b),[27] but steadfastly maintaining that they are employees when the question arises before the National Labor Relations Board of whether newspaper deliverymen and other circulation workers are supervisors of newsboys, and hence managerial staff not subject to union representation (Newsom 1980). Courts have often proved sympathetic to both lines of reasoning, granting publishers antistrike injunctions on the theory that newsboy strikes are not labor disputes but rather unlawful restraints of trade (*New York Times* 1941l, 1947c).[28] A quite contradictory line of cases holds that newspapers can control the prices their "independent contractors" charge for the sale of newspapers, can prohibit them from selling or carrying other publications, can regulate delivery times and service standards, and can discharge newsboys whose work is unsatisfactory (*New York Times* 1922b, 1959b; *Sapienza v. New York News* 1979).

Given the difficulty of organizing the younger newsboys, and particularly the carrier force, many newsboy unions either defined younger workers outside of the bargaining unit or tried to eliminate them from the industry altogether. Los Angeles Newsboys Local Industrial Union 75 (CIO), for example, far from being an industrial union, was not even a trade union. Its bargaining unit was carefully defined to include only those long-term, full-time adults selling newspapers at established street locations (*Hearst Publications v. NLRB* 1943; Wood 1944). The San Francisco contract cited above specifically excluded young newsboys from the contract's coverage and limited their opportunities for employment, and the Philadelphia contract applied only to "corner men," who were to be protected from competition from "floaters, rovers and bootjacks." The Seattle Newsboys' Union was similarly established by corner men, in part as a mechanism to establish their rights to the corners on which they sold papers. The union only intermittently reached out to the younger newsboys without established corners who made up the bulk of the sales force, most notably from 1917 through 1919, and Seattle's Central Labor Council unsuccessfully demanded that the Newsboys' Union charter be revoked "on the ground that it is an organization controlled by corner owners who exploit small boys" (Simpson 1992).

In part, this stems from the fact that adult and child newsboys often have diverging interests, stemming from the former's need for full-time work at a living wage. (Younger newsboys, too, have often struggled for better wages, but where newspapers establish full-time newsboy positions children are forced off the job by the need to attend school.) Publishers have used younger newsboys to drive down wages in areas where they had existing agreements with adult carriers. In New Jersey, for example, the *Newark Evening News* introduced child carriers into areas where it had contracted with nineteen adult carriers, members of the Allied Newspaper Carriers of New Jersey, for home delivery. When the paper refused to withdraw the children, the ANC struck and its members distributed notices to subscribers accusing the paper of trying to drive them out of business and seeking men's work at boys' wages (*Evening News v. Allied Newspaper Carriers* 1959).

Despite low wages and hazardous working conditions, publishers have persuaded many people that newsboy work is rewarding. A survey by the Gallup organization (1942) found that 90 percent of respondents had no objection to letting "a son" of theirs deliver newspapers. "It is clear," Gallup concluded, "that the old-fashioned American philosophy of hard work and individual enterprise in order to get ahead is still very widely accepted. To many the newsboy is the living symbol of that philosophy." Yet newsboy work has undergone important changes in this century. Four decades ago, the *New York Times* (1954) predicted its passage:

> Carrier boy[s] . . . deliver 50,000,000 papers daily. . . . About the future, though, there may be some question. Technological unemployment may hit the newsboy [with] the new trend toward vending-machine distribution. . . . And then there is the competition from baby-sitting. . . . The pay is better, and . . . the hours are better too.[29]

Today many newspapers are indeed moving away from child newsboys. The *Pittsburgh Press,* for example, eliminated 4,500 young carriers and replaced them with adults as part of its effort to streamline its distribution operation (*New York Times* 1958; United Press International 1992). Slightly more than 40 percent of the national carrier force is now made up of adults, and because most adult routes are larger, adults probably deliver more papers (Newspaper Association of America 1993). Newspapers are turning to adult carriers to handle dispersed rural routes or inner-city routes where fears of crime discourage predawn deliveries, to reduce carrier turnover and the need for supervision, to evade legal restrictions on child labor, and because of the growing size of newspapers, which often are too heavy to be carried on a bicycle (Duscha 1991; Goltz 1987; Perry 1980; *Presstime* 1984b, 1988a, 1991b; Rykken 1991).[30]

Yet, although economic conditions may make it possible for newspapers to hire adults to do work at wages once only children would tolerate, newspapers remain dependent upon their increasingly adult newsboy force. Fully three-fourths of all paid circulation is distributed by carriers directly to subscribers—most of whom now pay directly to the newspaper, which reduces newsboys' losses from uncollectible subscriptions and the time-consuming collection process, but also reduces the sizable share of newsboys' income historically earned from tips. Less than 1 percent of single-copy sales are sold by hawkers on the street; their place has been taken by machines (Newspaper Association of America 1993; Terrell 1988). Many newspapers are experiencing a shortage of carriers, forcing supervisors to cover "down" routes. Newspapers have responded by seeking legislation lowering the minimum age for newsboys (to as young as nine years of age in Massachusetts) or expanding the hours they can work, by increasing newsboy earnings in order to compete with the minimum wage, by offering contests and scholarship programs, and by installing pay-by-mail plans, as well as by turning to more expensive adult carriers (Favor 1988; *Presstime* 1981, 1987b, 1987c, 1989b, 1990a, 1991a, 1994).

Although newsboys' unions may seem a relic of the distant past, newsboys in Providence recently organized the Rhode Island Newscarriers Association after management asked them to sign a one-sided contract declaring themselves independent contractors. Carriers are required to buy delivery bags, collection books, rubber bands, and liability insurance, and must arrange for, and pay, substitutes when they take vacations. The newsboys have not seen a pay raise from the *Journal* in years (though pay went up 17 percent shortly after the union organized). They must now collect their papers from distribution centers as much as ten miles away, and are now required to deliver soap, hair spray, and other products as part of their routes (Bixpa-Vazâo 1991; *Presstime* 1990c; Whitaker and Zuckerman 1989).

Such unionization is increasingly rare, however. The American Federation of Labor abandoned its efforts in the face of adverse rulings from the

National Labor Relations Board and changing circulation patterns that make unionization more difficult. Indeed, AFL unions' efforts to hold their existing organizations among circulation workers have led them to adopt the position that newsboys are not employees in order to circumvent publishers' arguments that their members are supervisory workers excluded from labor law protections. But regardless of the attitudes of the established unions, it seems unlikely that an increasingly adult newsboy force will tolerate its increasing immiseration. As newsboy wages have fallen over the past century, newspapers have experienced growing difficulty in securing the necessary labor.

It is no longer uncommon for businesses to externalize their costs through casual labor. Part-time and temporary work is growing rapidly in all sectors, and employers have converted many employees into "independent contractors" in order to hold down labor costs. In publishing, reporting, design, and even copyediting are increasingly jobbed out to freelance workers or external service agencies. Newsboys represented the vanguard of this process. From the very outset, publishers realized that young children could be induced to work on speculation under wages and conditions that adult workers would generally refuse. Although working conditions may have improved somewhat over the intervening years as publishers moved toward home delivery, wages have remained low and publishers have used the fiction that their newsboys are "independent merchants" to justify their refusal to cover newsboys under their unemployment, workers' compensation, liability, and health insurance plans. Most newsboys continue to earn less than the minimum wage even in optimal conditions, and run the risk of having their meager earnings further reduced by nonpaying subscribers. As a result, publishers save tens of millions of dollars each year.

Media historians have waxed eloquent on the roles of the publishers and editors who built the great newspapers and newspaper empires of the modern age. They might do better to turn their attention to the newsboys, whose underpaid labor brought those newspapers to the public and provided publishers with the profits that fueled their enterprises.

## Notes

Research for this chapter was supported in part by a Professional Development-Quality of Work Life grant from United University Professions and the State University of New York. I am indebted to Lisa Beinhoff for research assistance, to Harry Stein and Todd Postol for providing materials on newsboys in Oregon and Ohio, respectively, and to Lisa Cody of the Newspaper Association of America for providing contemporary information.

1. These figures come from a table dated October 4, 1993, sent to me by Lisa Cody, manager of circulation and readership for the Newspaper Association of America.

2. Todd Postol (1989, 7-8, 12, 18 n. 4) attempts to draw clear distinctions among newsboys (street sellers), carriers, and newspaperboys, a term he uses to encompass both, but makes it clear that newspaperboys themselves, to use his terminology, often do not recognize such distinctions and many combined both forms of work. Postol also distinguishes a third category, newsdealers, "adults who sold papers at busy stands and corners." But again, this distinction, "never clear to begin with," is often not recognized by the workers involved, as evidenced by letters he quotes in which people ranging in age from eleven to "well past 60" refer to themselves as newsboys. Postol, too, adopts this terminology, though insisting that "nearly 99 percent of the carriers . . . and street sellers are boys," a conclusion that may well result from these definitions. This chapter does not deal with other categories of newspaper distribution workers, such as cigar stores, stationers, or the "news butchers" who peddled newspapers, magazines, paperback books, snacks, and tobacco on passenger trains (Holbrook 1947).

3. Release of the stamp was timed to coincide with the observance of National Newspaper Boy Day. For one newsboys's bitter reflections on how the work shaped his character, see Studs Terkel's (1972) interview with fourteen-year-old newsboy Terry Pickens.

4. See, for example, Johnny Wideawake, *My Book of Prizes, Liberty* magazine boy sales division prize catalog 8, n.d., National Child Labor Committee Papers, box 59, Street Trades Scrap Book, 1932. A boy could buy a nickel Baby Ruth candy bar by selling twenty-two magazines, or a football by selling 2,875.

5. The newsboys were objecting to police orders banning them from carrying magazines on street newsstands and attempting to ban sales of the Chicago Federation of Labor's *New Majority*. The Newsboys' Protective Union promised that the paper would be sold at every newsstand under its jurisdiction (*New Majority* 1920).

6. Publishers also protested to one another over these practices. See, for example, Victor Lawson (*News*) to Turner (*Journal*), March 29, 1900, claiming that *Journal* carriers "used every means including revolvers, knives, razors and bull clubs, to drive other boys who sold papers off the corners." Lawson denied responsibility for activities by a local gangster, Clarke, insisting that he was not on the *News* payroll, but merely bought papers like any other dealer. In any event, after the *Journal* discharged Clarke from their circulation department they replaced him with a Mr. Brown. "Brown has hired the Finn and Ryan crowd, who are, if anything, worse than Clarke" (Victor Lawson papers).

7. The next day, the *Chicago Daily Socialist* (1909b) reported on efforts to organize a union, quoting newsboy John Barry: "We must organize or Hearst will take back everything we have gained by our decided stand when his papers tried to take away the last of our profits."

8. Years later, Chicago unionists shed no tears when a *Chicago Daily News* circulation slugger/gunman was shot dead (*New Majority* 1923b).

9. Annenberg was no stranger to such tactics. He organized strong-arm squads for Chicago newspapers in the early years of the decade, and was paid at least $1,000 during the 1912 Chicago newsboys' strike for unspecified strike-related services (ANPA, Chicago Chapter 1912).

10. Agreement signed by *Chicago Evening Post, Journal, Dispatch,* and *Daily News,* July 27, 1898. In Victor Lawson Papers, Outgoing Letters, Regular Series. Just two years before, newsboys had been charged 50 cents per hundred on penny papers bought at the office (60 cents if delivered), and $1.25 per hundred on two-cent papers (Victor Lawson to R. W. Patterson [*Tribune*], Feb. 15, 1896; Lawson Papers). A later agreement between morning papers had similar terms, except that the papers charged $1.40 per hundred (morning papers sold for a uniform two cents) (undated six-page agreement among the *Tribune, Times-Herald, Chronicle,* and *Record;* Lawson Papers, Dec. 5, 1899-May 24, 1899).

11. W. H. Turner (president, Daily Newspaper Association), "To the Newsdealer Addressed" (Lawson Papers, Dec. 1898). Similarly, the City News Company, jointly owned by the morning papers, refused to provide papers to "any carrier, boy or dealer that discriminates against the papers of any of the parties, as shall member papers" (City News Co. Bylaws; Lawson Papers, Feb. 15, 1896).

12. Seattle Newsboys Union members still got 50 percent, fully returnable, through October 1935 (*New Majority* 1923a; Steinmetz 1935), but in the 1920s Chicago's unionized newsboys made only 27 to 30 percent (*New Majority* 1922). But not all newsboys received the full margin—often younger newsboys obtained their papers from "corner men" who kept half or more of the margin for themselves (Hard 1908, 28-29).

13. For court decisions finding that newsboys are employees, see *New York Times* (1959a), *Veit v. Courier Post* (1977), *Buchner v. Bergen Evening Record* (1963), *Pacific Employers Insurance Co. v. Industrial Accident Commission* (1935), *Clark v. Arkansas Democrat Co.* (1967). Newsboys have also been held to be employees for purposes of labor law (*National Labor Relations Board v. Hearst Publications* 1944). For decisions that newsboys are independent contractors or merchants, see *New York Indemnity Co. v. Industrial Accident Commission* (1931), *Gaul v. Detroit Journal* (1916), *Balinski v. Press Publishing Co.* (1935), *Oklahoma Pub. Co. v. Greenlee* (1931), *Taylor v. Industrial Accident Commission* (1963). For overviews of the issue, see Linder (1990) and Rohlder (1937). Much of the latter is devoted to summaries of cases from across the country, with advice as to how publishers can structure their arrangements with newsboys to maximize the chances that they will be held merchants, rather than employees.

14. Publishers were concerned over the costs of covering other newspaper workers as well. See, for example, *New York Times* (1936).

15. The Children's Bureau did, however, concede that newsboys' income was probably essential to family economies, as "many workmen do not earn enough to maintain their families at the level of bare subsistence unless their wives and children also work" (McGill 1928, 25).

16. A concurring opinion held that newsboys were employees. For a similar ruling from Pennsylvania, see *Swartz v. Eberly* (1962).

17. See also "Typical Carrier's Lease or Contract" (McDaniel 1941, 137-38), an "agreement" that required newsboys to do all in their power to build circulation, to maintain the circulation list as the newspaper's exclusive property, and to collect only after papers were delivered, and that barred newsboys from delivering any other newspaper. Other contracts are reprinted or summarized in *Journal Pub. Co. v. State Unemployment Compensation Commission* (1945) and *Buchner v. Bergen Evening Record* (1963). Publishers have long insisted that newsboys sell papers at the established price, even when market conditions were such that customers were prepared to pay more. When newsboys selling the *New York Daily News* and *American* began selling the first or bulldog edition of the morning papers at a two-cent premium, the papers quickly raised the price; the *News* charged newsboys $3.00 per hundred for the two-cent paper. Of course, the newsboys refused to handle the papers under those terms. Members of the deliverers' union did not hesitate to cross the newsboys' pickets to distribute the bulldog editions to the scabs imported to break the strike (*New York Times* 1922a).

18. Judge Lusk, writing the majority opinion in *Journal,* provides a thorough deconstruction of the argument that newspaper carriers are independent contractors or merchants. He also considers the publisher's contention that even if the carrier in question was an employee, he was paid so little (and sometimes in produce and firewood, rather than cash) as to be ineligible for unemployment benefits. The dissent suggests that the carrier may actually have lost money working for the *Journal,* and that he was in any case an independent merchant.

19. The report includes the text of the decision in *Hearst Publications v. United States* and *Chronicle Publishing Co. v. United States,* where publishers' efforts to overturn the payroll taxes judicially were rejected.

20. "Once a boy has established a profitable stand, it becomes his property and other newsboys recognize it as his. . . . Corners in Boston have sold for as high as five thousand dollars" (Burroughs 1944, 266-68). Stands sold for as little as $10 and as much as $1,100 in 1917 (Simpson 1992, 22-23). St. Louis publishers bought routes from carriers to settle a strike; their estimated aggregate value was $2,250,000 (*New York Times* 1945a).

21. The Newspaper Association of America (1993) reports that carrier turnover averaged 64 percent annually in 1992.

22. Certainly other strikes have taken place, recorded only in the local newspapers of the affected towns and, perhaps, in the columns of the trade press, that have yet to be documented by media historians. In addition to the cities named, newsboy unions also operated in San Francisco, Philadelphia, Atlanta, Houston, Baltimore, Los Angeles, Newark, San Diego, and Providence, Rhode Island, among other cities. These unions have operated from the 1890s to the present day. Most have been short-lived, but one lasted for seventy years.

23. This was the strike that inspired the Disney movie musical *Newsies*.

24. The newsdealers were predominantly veterans and disabled workers operating sidewalk newsstands throughout the city. William Collins explained that "the charter was issued originally to prevent the C.I.O. from organizing these people." (American Federation of Labor Records, reel 46, frames 00140-141).

25. The government complaint charged that the Newsdealers Union had held meetings and agreed to act to gain better terms from the newspapers. The newspapers testified that the strike, which they termed a boycott, had seriously damaged their sales and threatened "irreparable" damage.

26. The Labor Relations Board, however, found the newsboys to be employees in one of its last rulings in behalf of a newsboys' union (*New York Times* 1946).

27. Judge Scalia (*Drukker Communications v. NLRB* 1983, 736) noted the publisher's "ironic contention" that younger newsboys were employees, and therefore that district sales representatives were supervisors, and mentions (736-37) two cases where the NLRB rejected petitions by unions to represent newsboys who cover their routes by automobile. Judge Boreman (*NLRB v. A. S. Abell* 1964, 9-10) similarly mentions a 1963 case where motor carriers were held to be employees, and Lindsay Newspapers was ordered to reinstate two newsboys fired for union activities. The NLRB had similarly held Abell's and Hearst's Baltimore motor carriers to be employees, but the Fourth Circuit Court of Appeals overturned that decision.

28. Although several early cases found newsboys to be employees, and hence covered by the National Labor Relations Act (*New York Times* 1941o; Wood 1944), in the late 1940s the Board began finding newsboys to be independent contractors and thus not entitled to union representation (*New York Times* 1948b, 1949b). Ironically, it has reached the opposite conclusion in cases where publishers pointed to circulation and delivery workers' supervision of newsboys as proof that these were supervisory workers (and hence, by implication, that the newsboys were employees) and hence ineligible for coverage (*Presstime* 1985a, 1985b). The *Oakland Press* was permitted to hold newsboys to be independent contractors for tax and other purposes, but as employees under the National Labor Relations Act (Newsom 1980), whereas the *Wichita Eagle* and other papers won rulings that carriers were independent contractors and hence not covered by unemployment insurance (*Presstime* 1992a, 1992b). Thus, newspaper publishers may have their cake and eat it too.

29. The bulk of this editorial is devoted to the many prominent men who got their start as newsboys, ranging from Dwight D. Eisenhower to Walt Disney.

30. Some publishers are returning to children, however. The *Columbus Dispatch* is in the process of converting several densely populated suburban routes from adult to child carriers (*Presstime* 1989c).

# References

Adams, Myron. *Children in American Street Trades*. New York: National Child Labor Committee. Reprinted from *Annals of the American Academy of Political and Social Science* 25, no. 3 (1905).

*American Federation of Labor Records, Part I: Strikes and Agreement File, 1898-1953* (microfilm). University Publications of America. Consulted at Labor-Management Documentation Center, New York State School of Industrial & Labor Relations, Ithaca.

American Newspaper Publishers Association, Chicago Chapter. "Minutes, Oct. 24, 1912." In John Fitzpatrick papers, box 1, Chicago Historical Society.

American Newspaper Publishers Association, Committee on Social Security. "Abstract of Report" (typescript) (1937). In New York Child Labor Committee Papers, box 29, folder 38.

*American Newspaper Publishers Association Bulletin*. "Empty Pockets, Enforced Idleness Threaten Nation's Newspaper Boys," Nov. 14, 1933, 637-38. Copy in Alfred E. Smith Private Papers, folder 32, Child Labor Amendment, New York State Library Special Collections, Albany.

Ashby, LeRoy. *Saving the Waifs: Reformers and Dependent Children, 1890-1917*. Philadelphia: Temple University Press, 1984.

Associated Ohio Dailies. *Proceedings of the Twentieth Annual Meeting of the Associated Ohio Dailies*. Columbia: Associated Ohio Dailies, 1905.

*Balinski v. Press Publishing Co*. 1935. 118 Pa. Super. 89.

Berkeley, Bill. "Press Gang: The Mob and the Magazines." *New Republic*, Feb. 17, 1992, 20-21.

Bixpa-Vazâo, Aldina. "Newspaper Carriers Organize." *Progressive*, Feb. 1991, 16.

Bremer, Harry. "Street Trades Investigation" (typescript, dated Oct. 11, 1912). In National Child Labor Committee Papers, box 4, folder "New Jersey—Street Trades—1912."

———. "Report of Investigation" (typescript) (1913). In National Child Labor Committee Papers, box 4, folder "New York—Newsboys—1913."

Bremner, Robert, ed. *Children and Youth in America: A Documentary History* (Vol. 3), *1933-1973*. Cambridge: Harvard University Press, 1974.

Bromley, Dorothy Dunbart. "The Newspapers and Child Labor." *The Nation* (Jan. 30, 1935): 131-32.

Broun, Heywood. "Some Publishers at Placid." *New York World-Telegram*, Jan. 16, 1934. Clipping in New York Child Labor Committee Papers, box 34, folder 7.

*Brown, Bryan, et al. v. Commercial Dispatch Publishing Company*. 1987. 504 So. 2d 245.

Brown, Sara. "Juvenile Street Work in Iowa." *American Child* 4 (Aug. 1922): 130-49.

*Buchner, Russell, v. Bergen Evening Record*. 1963. 81 N.J. Super. 121.

Burroughs, Harry. *Boys in Men's Shoes: A World of Working Children*. New York: Macmillan, 1944.

*Chicago Daily Socialist*. "Newspaper Fight Is All Over." July 12, 1907a, 3.

———. "Dealers War on Chicago Papers." Dec. 3, 1907b, 1.

———. "Ind. Newsboys to Fight Trust." Dec. 3, 1907c, 3.

———. "'Newsies' Make War on Hearst." Jan. 16, 1908a, 1.

———. "Newsboy Strikers Banish Hearst Paper from Boston." Jan. 28, 1908b, 2.

———. "Hearst Thugs Slug Newsies." Feb. 21, 1908c, 1.

———. "Unions Boycott Hearst Paper." Feb. 28, 1908d, 1.

———. "Hearst Invokes Courts in His War on Newsies." Mar. 9, 1908e, 1.

———. "Boston Newsboys' Union Hits Printers for Aiding Hearst." Feb. 13, 1908f, 1.

———. "Hearst Rowdies Attack Newsies." Mar. 25, 1909a, 1.

———. "Ban Removed from Newsboys." Mar. 26, 1909b, 1.

———. "Hearst Slugger Stabs Newsboy." Sept. 25, 1909c, 1.

*Christian Century.* "Newspaper Blood Money." Feb. 6, 1935, 166–68.

Civic Federation of Dallas. *The Newsboys of Dallas.* Dallas: Civic Federation of Dallas, 1921.

*Clark, Marvin, Guardian of the Estate of Thomas Harvey Cage, v. Arkansas Democrat Co.* 1967. 413 S.W.2d 629.

Clopper, Edward. *Child Labor in Street Trades.* New York: National Child Labor Committee, 1910.

Compensated Accident Cases in New York State to Minors under 18 Years of Age (tabulation) (n.d.). In New York Child Labor Committee Papers, box 29, folder 38.

Compensated Industrial Accidents to Newsboys, 1935–37. (tabulation) (n.d.). In New York Child Labor Committee Papers, box 29, folder 38.

*Constitution and Bylaws of Newsboys and Bootblacks Protective Union #8607.* Cleveland: Pamphlets in American History, n.d.

Contract between the Westchester Newspapers, Inc., and Its Distributors (1939). In New York Child Labor Committee Papers, box 3, folder 7.

Diamond, H. M. "Connecticut Study of Street Trades." *American Child* 4 (Aug. 1922): 97–103.

*Drukker Communications Inc. v. National Labor Relations Board.* 1983. 700 F.2d 727.

Duscha, Julius. "Newspaper that Switched to Adults Calls It a Good Move." *Presstime,* Feb. 1991, 21.

Dwight, Helen. "The Newsboys' Home Club" (typescript) (1915). In National Child Labor Committee Papers, box 4.

Dyar, Ralph. *Newspaper Promotion and Research.* New York: Harper, 1942.

*Editor & Publisher.* "Federal Child Labor Amendment and the Newspapers" (clipping) (n.d.). In New York Child Labor Committee Papers, box 34, folder 21.

———. "Suit Stemming from Carrier's Death Settled." Dec. 18, 1993, 31.

———. "Judgment against Paper Overturned." Mar. 5, 1994, 19.

*Evening Herald* (Syracuse, N.Y.). "Jolly Newsboys." Dec. 24, 1894, 6.

*Evening News Publishing Co. v. Allied Newspaper Carriers of New Jersey, et al.* 1959. 263 F.2d 715.

Favor, Cyrus. "Turnover by Carriers Can Be Reduced by Paying Them More Money." *Presstime,* Aug. 1988, 39.

Felt, Jeremy. *Hostages of Fortune: Child Labor Reform in New York State.* Syracuse: Syracuse University Press, 1965.

Fink, Gary, ed. *Labor Unions.* Westport, Conn.: Greenwood, 1977.

Forbes, Thomas. "Mean Street Sales." *NewsInc.,* Feb. 1991, 48.

Forbush, William. "A Western Newspaper and Its Newsboys." *Charities and the Commons* 19 (1907): 798–802.

Fram, Marcia. "Newspapers Try to Decipher How Tax Laws Affect Carriers." *Presstime,* Dec. 1983, 39.

Fuller, Thomas, et al. *To the Public* (Microfilm 48867). Early American Imprints, American Antiquarian Society, Worcester, Mass., 1799.

Gallup, George. "Newsboys Retain Popular Appeal." *New York Times,* Dec. 25, 1942, 13.

*Gannett Co. v. Frieda S. Miller, Industrial Commissioner (Matter of Claim for Benefits by Warren Whitcher).* 1942. 263 A.D. 906.

*Gaul v. Detroit Journal.* 1916. 191 Mich. 405.

Goltz, Gene. "More Adults Join the Ranks of Carriers." *Presstime,* Feb. 1987, 20–27.

———. "Newspapers Tangle with Federal and State Governments over Independent Contractors." *Presstime,* Aug. 1991, 16–21.

Green, Samuel. *Appeal to the Public* (Microfilm 48863). Early American Imprints, American Antiquarian Society, Worcester, Mass., 1799.

*Hahn v. Times Dispatch Pub. Co.* 166 Va. 102.

Hall, George. "Memorandum Submitted by the NYCLC in re Awards of Referees in Certain Cases of Minors Granted Compensation during 1936" (Aug. 1937). In New York Child Labor Committee Papers, box 29, folder 36.

Hard, William. "De Kid Wot Works at Night." *Everybody's Magazine,* Jan. 1908, 25-37.

*Hearst Publications v. National Labor Relations Board.* 1943. 136 F.2d 608.

Hexter, Maurice. "The Newsboys of Cincinnati." *Studies from the Helen S. Trounstine Foundation* 1, no. 4 (1919): 120-49.

*Higgins, Daniel v. Monroe Evening News.* 1978. 404 Mich. 1.

Hine, Lewis. "Conditions in Vermont Street Trades" (typescript) (1916). In National Child Labor Committee Papers, box 4.

Holbrook, Stewart. "News Butchers." *American Mercury* 64 (Apr. 1947): 434-39.

Ihlder, John. "The Press and Its Newsboys." *World Today* 13 (1907): 737-39.

International Printing Pressmen and Assistants' Union. *Convention Proceedings.* Rogersville, Tenn.: IPPAU, 1940.

Jane Addams Papers. University Microfilms edition. Peace Library, Swarthmore College, Swarthmore, Penn.

*Johnson, Stephen v. Workmen's Compensation Appeal Board.* 1993. 631 A.2d 693.

*Journal Pub. Co. v. State Unemployment Compensation Commission et al.* 1945. 175 Ore. 627.

Juvenile Protective Department. *Street Trades of Buffalo, New York.* Buffalo: Foundation Forum, 1925.

Keil, Thomas. *On Strike! Capital Cities and the Wilkes-Barre Newspaper Unions.* Tuscaloosa: University of Alabama Press, 1988.

*Knickerbocker Press* (Albany). "Car Kills 2 Boys Peddling Papers" (clipping) (Dec. 5, 1934). In New York Child Labor Committee Papers, box 29, folder 36.

Lee, Alfred McClung. *The Daily Newspaper in America: The Evolution of a Social Instrument.* New York: Macmillan, 1937.

Linder, Marc. "From Street Urchins to Little Merchants: The Juridical Transvaluation of Child Newspaper Carriers." *Temple Law Review* 63 (Winter 1990): 829-64.

Lowenstein, Steve. *The Jews of Oregon, 1850-1950.* Portland: Jewish Historical Society of Oregon, 1987.

*Manhattan News Co. v. New York Newsboys Union Local #471, A.F.L.* 1949. 85 N.Y.S.2d 601.

Marks, Sid, and Alban Emley. *The Newspaperboys' Hall of Fame.* Hollywood, Calif.: House Warven, 1953.

Maslin, Janet. "They Sing, They Dance, They Go on Strike." *New York Times,* Apr. 8, 1992, C17.

McDaniel, Henry Bonner. *The American Newspaperboy: A Comparative Study of His Work and School Activities.* Los Angeles: Wetzel, 1941.

McGill, Nettie. *Child Workers on City Streets.* Washington, D.C.: U.S. Department of Labor, Children's Bureau, 1928.

"Memorandum of Agreement" (1939; in force February 2, 1939, through May 1942). In American Federation of Labor Records, reel 28, frames 1249-50.

*Milwaukee Leader.* "Leader Newsboys Are Driven from Streets by 'Huskies.'" Dec. 14, 1911a, 1.

———. "Brutality Is Used to Hit Leader." Dec. 14, 1911b, 1.

*Minneapolis Labor Review.* "What Did They Want?" July 12, 1918a, 3.

———. "Newsboys Ask Square Deal from Tribune." Jan. 11, 1918b, 1, 3.

———. "Daily Papers, Burnquist, Langum Fight Newsies." July 5, 1918c, 1, 3.

———. "Home Guard Uses Club on Newsie." July 5, 1918d, 1.

———. "People of Minneapolis." July 5, 1918e, 1.

———. "Glorious Victory Won by Newsboys and Fairminded People from Daily Combine." July 12, 1918f, 1-2.

————. "Attempt to Suppress Labor Review Is Dismal Fizzle." Mar. 7, 1919, 1-2.

Minor, Jeanie. "Children in Street Trades." Unpublished paper presented to Association of Governmental Labor Officials of the United States and Canada, Chicago, May 19-23, 1924. Copy in New York Child Labor Committee Papers.

*Monthly Labor Review*. "Employment of Children." May 1935, 1234-39.

Nasaw, David. *Children of the City: At Work and at Play*. Garden City, N.Y.: Anchor, 1985a.

————. "Dirty-Faced Davids and the Twin Goliaths." *American Heritage* 36, no. 3 (1985b): 42-47.

National Child Labor Committee Papers. Manuscript Division, Library of Congress, Washington, D.C.

*National Labor Relations Board v. A. S. Abell Co.* 1964. 327 F.2d 1.

*National Labor Relations Board v. Hearst Publications*. 1944. 322 U.S. 111.

*National Labor Relations Board v. Houston Chronicle Publ. Co.* 1954. 211 F.2d 848.

Neal, Joseph. *Peter Ploddy and Other Oddities*. Philadelphia: Carey & Hart, 1844.

Nerone, John. "The Mythology of the Penny Press." In *Media Voices: An Historical Perspective*, ed. Jean Folkerts, 157-82. New York: Macmillan, 1992.

*New Majority*. "Off Again—On Again!" Oct. 25, 1919, 15.

————. "Union Newsboys Boost the New Majority." Jan. 24, 1920, 1.

————. "Will Not Eat Papers." Mar. 18, 1922, 3.

————. "Seattle Newsboys' Union Grows." May 12, 1923a, 6.

————. "Daily News Gunman Shot." Apr. 28, 1923b, 4.

New York Child Labor Committee Papers. New York State Library, Albany.

*New York Indemnity Co. v. Industrial Accident Commission*. 1931. 213 Cal. 43.

*New York Post Corporation v. William J. Kelley et al.* 1946. 61 N.Y.S.2d 264.

*New York Post Corporation v. William J. Kelley et al.* 1947. 296 N.Y. 178.

*New York Times*. "Newsboys Go on Strike." July 21, 1899a, 2.

————. "Newsboys Act and Talk." July 25, 1899b, 3.

————. "Violent Scenes during Day." July 25, 1899c, 3.

————. "Newsboys Form a New Union." July 31, 1899d, 4.

————. "Newsboys Still Hold Out." July 28, 1899e, 4.

————. "The Strike of the Newsboys." July 22, 1899f, 4.

————. "News and American Newsboys Strike." Apr. 27, 1922a, 2.

————. "Chicago Tribune Wins." Oct. 4, 1922b, 25.

————. "Newsboys Healthy." Oct. 12, 1926a, 26.

————. "The Rough Newsboy of the 50s." Sept. 19, 1926b, sec. 5, p. 54.

————. "The Newsboy Problem." Apr. 7, 1929, sec. 3, p. 4.

————. "Selling Newspapers Proves of Benefit to Schoolboys." Nov. 23, 1930a, sec. 3, p. 7.

————. "Ex-Gov. Smith Gets Newsboys' Homage." Feb. 23, 1930b, 19.

————. "Press Fight Urged to Keep Radio Free." Apr. 24, 1936, 14.

————. "Newsboys Not on Pension List." Jan. 15, 1937, 7.

————. "Says Newsdealers Rebuffed Union Aid." Nov. 29, 1941a, 9.

————. "Newsdealer Strike against Eight Papers." Oct. 18, 1941b, 11.

————. "Newsstands in Dispute." Oct. 12, 1941c, 55.

————. "Peace Move Made to Newsdealers." Oct. 16, 1941d, 12.

————. "Newsstand Strike Studied by Mayor." Oct. 19, 1941e, 34.

————. "Sale of Newspapers Resumed by Stands." Oct. 22, 1941f, 25.

————. "Newsstands Again Threaten Boycott." Nov. 20, 1941g, 29.

————. "Newsdealers Fight Trade Curb Charge." Nov. 21, 1941h, 22.

————. "Court Writ Issued on News Boycott." Nov. 22, 1941i, 8.

————. "Newsdealers Win Delay on Hearing." Nov. 25, 1941j, 32.

———. "State Urges Ban on News Boycott." Nov. 26, 1941k, 18.

———. "Injunction Stops Boycott of Press." Dec. 4, 1941l, 27.

———. "Newsdealers Give Reply." Dec. 30, 1941m, 37.

———. "NLRB Rules on Newsboys." Jan. 11, 1941n, 15.

———. "Rules on Newspaperboys." Jan. 23, 1941o, 37.

———. "Newsboys Strike in Mobile." Mar. 3, 1942, 14.

———. "Coast Guard Gets Newsboys' House." Jan. 24, 1943, 21.

———. "St. Louis Strikes End and 3 Papers Resume." Sept. 7, 1945a, 11.

———. "Carrier Strike Halts 3 St. Louis Papers." Aug. 17, 1945b, 11.

———. "NLRB Denies Union Plea to Control Carriers Distributing for 2 Philadelphia
  Newspapers." Aug. 9, 1946, 10.

———. "Rule Denied to SLRB over Newsboys' Case." Jan. 18, 1947a, 6.

———. "Kansas City Strike Ends." Feb. 2, 1947b, 30.

———. "Newspaper Pickets Restrained by Court." Jan. 29, 1947c, 11.

———. "Newsboys Would Bargain." Jan. 8, 1948a, 14.

———. "Carriers Who Deliver Newspapers to Homes under Contract Barred to Unions by
  NLRB." Feb. 29, 1948b, 42.

———. "Newsboys Lose in Court." Jan. 7, 1949a, 30.

———. "Bargaining Denied to Newsboys Here." Apr. 26, 1949b, 22.

———. "Stamp Honors News Boys." Oct. 5, 1952a, 28.

———. "Dewey Puts State in Water Project." Apr. 16, 1952b, 17.

———. "Dewey Signs Bill for Court Study." Apr. 12, 1953, 48.

———. "Topics of the Times." Oct. 2, 1954, 16.

———. "A Texas Paper Sends Men to Do Boys' Work." Apr. 23, 1958, 36.

———. "Newsboy Is an Employe." June 14, 1959a, 31.

———. "Newspaper Wins Right to Fix Price." Aug. 30, 1959b, 70.

———. "Newspaperboy Hall of Fame Adds Chandler and General." Oct. 15, 1967, sec. 5, p. 14.

Newsom, Clark. "NLRB Reverses Decision on Carriers." *Presstime,* July 1980.

Newspaper Association of America. "1992 Circulation and Product Distribution Survey."
  Unpublished tabulation, 1993.

Newspaper Boys of America Inc. *The N.B.A. Handbook for Newspaper Boys* (2d ed.).
  Indianapolis: Newspaper Boys of America, 1932.

*Oklahoma Pub. Co. v. Greenlee.* 1931. 150 Okla. 69.

*Pacific Employers Insurance Company v. Industrial Accident Commission et al.* 1935. 3 Cal.2d 759.

Perry, Marna. "Newspapers Starting to Use More Adult Carriers." *Presstime,* July 1980, 40–41.

Postol, Todd. "Hearing the Voices of Working Children: The NRA Newspaperboy Letters."
  *Labor's Heritage* 1 (July 1989): 4–19.

*Presstime.* "Change in N.Y. Education Law Helps Papers." Oct. 1981, 15.

———. "Carrier Missing; Appeal Issued." Dec. 1982, 46.

———. "Reward Offered for Information on Carrier Slaying." Apr. 1983a, 55.

———. "Carrier in Omaha Abducted, Killed; Assailant at Large." Oct. 1983b, 19.

———. "Girl Carrier, 12, Found Slain in Third Incident in Year." May 1984a, 56.

———. "Youth Carriers Still Predominate." Aug. 1984b, 46.

———. "Carrier Tax Reporting Rule Still Unclear." May 1984c, 56.

———. "Supreme Court Leaves Intact Ruling on Circulation District Managers." Apr.
  1985a, 34.

———. "NLRB Rules Deliverers Are Not Employees." Feb. 1985b, 49.

———. "Motor Route Carriers Found to Be Employees." Aug. 1986, 49.

———. "Adult Carriers Slain on Job." Apr. 1987a, 55.

———. "Dukakis Considers Lower Minimum Carrier Age." Aug. 1987b, 46.

———. "Carrier Turnover among Youths Approaches 100%." Nov. 1987c, 57.

———. "Survey Affirms Trend to More Adult Carriers." Aug. 1988a, 53.

———. "15 Illinois Papers Face Tax If Carriers Ruled Employees." Sept. 1988b, 46.

———. "Spokane Man to Be Sentenced in Carrier Death." Apr. 1989a, 72.

———. "Carrier Shortage Eases." Jan. 1989b, 40.

———. "Youth Carriers Stage Comeback in Some Places." Mar. 1989c, 48.

———. "Minimum Wage's Impact Discounted." Jan. 1990a, 51.

———. "Adult Carrier Trend Carries on, ICMA Says." Sept. 1990b, 44.

———. "Youth Carrier Group in Providence Makes Demands." Jan. 1990c, 51.

———. "Pennsylvania Considers Lower Age for Carriers." Nov. 1991a, 44.

———. "Adults Now Compose One-Third of U.S. Carriers." Apr. 1991b, 48.

———. "Distributor Classified as an Independent Contractor." Mar. 1992a, 48.

———. "Wichita Eagle Carriers Ruled Independent Contractors." May 1992b, 56.

———. "Carriers College Deals Score High." July/Aug. 1994, 18.

Quinn, Mike. "Newsie." *Maverick* (Jan.-Feb. 1960): 7. Copy in Wilcox Collection, Spencer Research Library, University of Kansas.

Rambo, C. David. "Newspapers Seek New Ways to Increase Carriers' Safety." *Presstime*, Sept. 1984, 6-7.

Rider, Esther Lee. "Newsboys in Birmingham." *American Child*, Feb. 1922, 315-24.

Riis, Jacob. "The New York Newsboy." *Century Magazine*, Dec. 1912, 247-55.

Rohleder, Charles. *The Newspaper Boy: Merchant or Employee?* Indianapolis: Newspaper Boys of America, 1937.

Ruth, Marcia. "Murder of Another Youth Carrier Raises 14-Month Toll to 4." *Presstime*, June 1984, 64.

Rykken, Rolf. "Shift to Adult Carriers Continues Apace." *Presstime*, Feb. 1991, 23.

*Sapienza, Guido et al. v. New York News, Inc. et al.* 1979. 481 F.Supp. 671.

Simpson, Roger. "Seattle Newsboys: How Hustler Democracy Lost to the Power of Property." *Journalism History* 18 (1992): 18-25.

Smith, Lloyd. *Newspaper District Management Including the Hour-a-Day Plan of Training Newspaper Boys to Sell.* Kansas City: Lloyd Smith, 1933.

*State Compensation Insurance Fund v. Industrial Accident Commission and Auguste Marc.* 1932. 216 Cal. 351.

Steinmetz, Virgil. Letter to William Green (Dec. 10, 1935). In American Federation of Labor Records, reel 1, frames 00469-73.

Stodghill, H. W. "H. W. Stodghill Replies to Allegations Made in Opposition to Paragraph Three of Daily Newspaper Code." *American Newspaper Publishers Association Bulletin.* (Nov. 14, 1933): 638-61.

*Swartz, Virginia, Administratix of the Estate of Cordell Miller, Deceased v. H. M. Eberly et al.* 1962. 212 F.Supp. 32.

*Taylor, Joe v. Industrial Accident Commission.* 1963. 216 Cal. App. 2d 466.

Tebbel, John. "The Changing American Newsboy." *Saturday Review*, Feb. 13, 1971, 56-58.

Terkel, Studs. *Working: People Talk about What They Do All Day and How They Feel about It.* New York: Pantheon, 1972.

Terrell, Pamela. "Is Tipping Slipping?" *Presstime*, Dec. 1988, 14-16.

Texas Circulation Managers Association. *Newspaper Circulation: Principles and Development of Modern Newspaper Circulation Methods Written Especially for the Study and Training of the American Newspaper Boy.* Austin: Texas Circulation Managers Association, 1948.

*Time.* "Street Fight." June 12, 1950, 40.

Toll, William. *The Making of an Ethnic Middle Class: Portland Jewry over Four Generations.* Albany: State University of New York Press, 1982.

Trattner, Walter I. *Crusade for the Children: A History of the National Child Labor Committee and Child Labor Reform in America.* Chicago: Quadrangle, 1970.

Union Agreement. Signed Jan. 24, 1939, by union, San Francisco Newspaper Publishers Association, Chronicle Publishing Company, Hearst Publications, and Daily News Company. In American Federation of Labor Records, reel 32, frames 1043-60.

United Press International. "Strikebound Pittsburgh Press to resume publication." Lexis/Nexis, July 14, 1992.

U.S. Congress, House, Committee on Ways and Means. *Newspaper Vendors: Hearings before Committee on Ways and Means.* 80th Cong., 1st sess., June 12, 1946.

U.S. Department of Labor, Children's Bureau. *Children Engaged in Newspaper and Magazine Selling and Delivering.* Washington, D.C.: U.S. Government Printing Office.

*Veit, Anne, v. Courier Post.* 1977. 154 N.J. Super. 572.

Victor Lawson Papers. Newberry Library, Chicago.

Waite, Edward F., et al. Letter to the editor, *Minneapolis Journal,* July 11, 1918. In New York Child Labor Committee Papers, box 31, folder 15.

*Western Union Telegraph Co. v. Lenroot, Chief of Children's Bureau, U.S. Department of Labor.* 1945. 323 U.S. 490.

Whisnant, David. "Selling the Gospel News, or: The Strange Career of Jimmy Brown the Newsboy." *Journal of Social History* 5, no. 3 (1971): 269-309.

Whitaker, Leslie, and Laurence Zuckerman. "Labor and Delivery." *Chicago Journalism Review* (July/Aug. 1989): 10-12.

*Who Is Back of the Gun-Men in the Chicago Trust Newspaper Lockout?* Chicago: n.p., 1912.

Wood, Lewis. "Gives Newsboys Employe Status." *New York Times* (Apr. 25, 1944): 14.

# Contributors

**Jon Bekken** is currently a visiting professor at Suffolk University and editor of the *Industrial Worker*. He has taught at SUNY Cortland and the University of Central Arkansas, and has published widely on newspaper business practices and the labor press.

**Bonnie Brennen** is assistant professor of communication at SUNY Geneseo. Her interest in a cultural history of the media is based on her professional media work. She has published several articles and is currently involved in an oral history project that deals with former reporters in the Rochester, New York, area.

**Hanno Hardt** is the John Murray Professor of Journalism and Mass Communication at the University of Iowa. He is interested in the intellectual history of communication studies and the uses of history in media research. His most recent book, *Critical Communication Studies: Communication, History, and Theory in America*, was published in 1992.

**Elizabeth (Elli) Lester** is associate professor in the Department of Advertising and Public Relations of the Henry W. Grady College of Journalism and Mass Communication at the University of Georgia. Her research interests include critical cultural studies and international communication.

**Marianne Salcetti** is assistant professor of communications at John Carroll University in Ohio. She has worked as a reporter and editor and was co-owner of the *Weekly News* in Johnson County, Iowa.

**William Solomon** is associate professor of journalism and mass media at Rutgers University. He has worked as a newspaper editor and does research on journalism history and on the sociology of news. His most recent book, coedited with Robert McChesney, *Ruthless Criticism: New Perspectives in U.S. Communication History*, was published in 1993.

**David Spencer** is associate professor in the Graduate School of Journalism, University of Western Ontario, Canada. He has authored articles and book chapters on journalism history for publications in both Canada and the United States.

**Barbie Zelizer** is assistant professor of rhetoric and communication at Temple University in Pennsylvania. A former reporter, she has published widely on journalism as a cultural practice. Her most recent book, *Covering the Body: The Kennedy Assassination, the Media, and the Shaping of Collective Memory,* was published in 1992. She is now working on a project about photo-journalism and the Holocaust, for which she has been designated both a Guggenheim fellow and a research-fellow at the Freedom Forum Center for Media Studies at Columbia University during the 1994-95 academic year.

# Index

229